# THE *Simple Comforts*

## STEP-BY-STEP

# INSTANT POT®

### COOKBOOK

**ALSO BY
JEFFREY EISNER**

*The Step-by-Step
Instant Pot Cookbook*

*The Lighter Step-by-Step
Instant Pot Cookbook*

# THE *Simple Comforts*

## STEP-BY-STEP
## INSTANT POT®
### COOKBOOK

## Jeffrey Eisner

PHOTOGRAPHY BY ALEKSEY ZOZULYA

**VORACIOUS**

LITTLE, BROWN AND COMPANY

NEW YORK / BOSTON / LONDON

Voracious / Little, Brown and Company
Hachette Book Group
1290 Avenue of the Americas, New York, NY 10104
littlebrown.com

First Edition: April 2022

Voracious is an imprint of Little, Brown and Company, a division of Hachette Book Group, Inc. The Voracious name and logo are trademarks of Hachette Book Group, Inc.

INSTANT POT® and associated logos are owned by Instant Brands Inc. and are used under license.

The publisher is not responsible for websites (or their content) that are not owned by the publisher.

The Hachette Speakers Bureau provides a wide range of authors for speaking events. To find out more, go to hachettespeakersbureau.com or call (866) 376-6591.

Photographs by Aleksey Zozulya
Food styling by Carol J. Lee

ISBN 9780316337458
LCCN 2021919579

10 9 8 7 6 5 4 3 2 1

CW

Printed in the United States of America

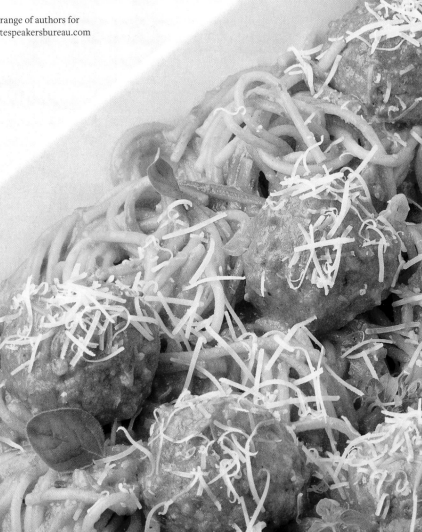

This book would not be here without you, my wonderful and loyal reader. Your stories inspire me to create, and this one's dedicated to you. May it bring comfort and stress-free deliciousness into your kitchen.

*I've heard it said you can only grow if you go outside of your comfort zone. I'm not saying that's untrue but sometimes we just want to wear sweatpants with a bowl of spaghetti in hand and give growth a vacation.*

—JEFFREY EISNER

# CONTENTS

♨ = AIR FRYER LID    DF = DAIRY-FREE

K = KETO    GF = GLUTEN-FREE

P = PALEO    V = VEGETARIAN

+ = COMPLIANT WITH MODIFICATIONS    VN = VEGAN

# INTRODUCTION

## SIMPLE COMFORTS

Food—and the stories that accompany it—provides
comfort and connection unlike anything else.

———

As far as I'm concerned, the only thing more enticing than a solid trilogy of books is one you can both read *and* eat through.

In my first book (the orange one), I made sure you and your Instant Pot became besties with simple, satisfying, step-by-step recipes that made you excited to cook magnificent meals like a pro. In my second book (the blue one), I took the same approach but gave you a trove of options with a lighter touch, highlighting key pointers on how to live a more conscientious lifestyle.

If something isn't broken, don't fix it. So this third book (the yellow one) will, once again, share top-notch, easy recipes with visual step-by-step breakdowns, along with suggestions to make these recipes fit into your lifestyle…but in this one, we're focusing on comfort food, done simply. And because I love a good, relatable, and comforting anecdote, I've added a special storytelling touch. More on that in a moment.

———

I've never been secretive about my background in cooking: I am a full-on amateur, have had no formal training, nick my fingers while slicing onions, and still can't pronounce certain ingredients properly ("Worcestershire," anyone?). Regardless of my culinary flaws, I love to cook. It is both my therapy and my happy place. The ultimate moment of satisfaction hits me when I take an empty pot or pan, fill it with flavorful ingredients, follow a few simple instructions, and then get to admire the tasty meal I've prepared. As simple as a dish is to make, there are few things that make me feel as accomplished a cook as preparing something such as my spaghetti and meatballs (page 95). The validation that comes when we serve something we've made and get to watch people's blissful reactions as they take the first bite? It just doesn't get any better.

When I was unhappy in my prior career of producing videos in the advertising world (filming a cowboy in Times Square singing about how toilet paper keeps his underwear clean might have been the tipping point), I would come home and cook new things as a comforting, creative outlet for myself. I have a love for gadgets and the latest and greatest household items, and so I had to get my hands on the Instant Pot in late 2016 when it was still pretty new. It would quickly become *the* top-selling countertop appliance, finding a home in millions of kitchens. But I soon realized that many who owned one were intimidated by it. I had a lightbulb moment, and saw an opportunity to get to know this mega-popular, yet slightly feared device like the back of my hand and then show other home cooks how friendly and game-changing it could be. I employed my producing (and performing) skills to film my own video on how to use the pot. It grew legs, *Pressure Luck* was born, it became my life, hundreds of recipes were written, and here we are.

## EVERY RECIPE HAS A STORY

As more people made my recipes, I began to receive more and more messages each day—many of which left and continue to leave my jaw on the floor. Never in a million years did I think I would receive thousands of stories from such lovely humans that would move me to tears, make me laugh, and help me realize how something as simple as a recipe I shared could make such a positive difference in one's life. These messages have taught me that every recipe has a story attached to it.

I'm often asked, "Jeffrey, how do you come up with your recipes?" It's an easy question to answer. A recipe doesn't exist without an ensemble of ingredients. And every cook, chef, or recipe developer needs ingredients of their own to be inspired and creative. For me, your special stories are the secret ingredients that make the gears in my mind spin. Your stories are the fuel for why and how I write my recipes to share with you. It's a beautiful relationship where we "feed" each other, so to speak.

We've all been through a lot in the last few years. When my first book was released in April of 2020, the very world as we knew it turned upside-down. I don't need to remind you of the maudlin details of the pandemic, but as a New Yorker living at the epicenter of all of it, and as my book entered hundreds

> My whole married life I made sure that my husband had lots of home-cooked meals. He came from a family of fourteen children and his mother was an absolutely wonderful cook. I was an only child so I really didn't have a whole lot of talent for cooking, but I did learn from my grandma because my mom worked. I had sixty-two years of good marriage and when my husband passed away in 2014 all of a sudden I didn't have anybody to cook for as my family lives far away. Then one day I discovered the Instant Pot, and then I discovered you, and from then on I have been eating healthy and am also able to share the extra food I make with my neighbors. Life is okay—I'm 84 and disabled and going blind, but I have not given up on life. The answer is to smile every day and act like it's your very last day on Earth.
>
> SANDY • **DES MOINES, IOWA**

of thousands of homes at the height of it, I quickly discovered that there's one thing we all crave: comfort. From the countless video calls with our nearest and dearest when we couldn't see them in person being the highlight of our days, to making meals (perhaps even over those video calls) to feed our souls, comfort has always helped us get through the tougher days. And the world could always use more of it.

Comfort: it's a word that even *sounds* comforting when said aloud, and it's also a word that everyone relates to differently. When it comes to food, some see it as warming up with a heaping bowl of Broccoli Cheddar Soup (page 64) on a cold winter's day or a generous plate of Mississippi Pot Roast (page 193) in the middle of July, but comfort goes so far beyond just the food itself. For many people, it's the idea of familiarity—an heirloom family recipe passed down through generations from a great-grandparent to a great-grandchild. For others, it's that sense of accomplishment one feels after preparing a meal for loved ones and watching their faces light up as they devour it. And for me, it's about discovering new ways of reinventing old classics in relevant and convenient ways—with the Instant Pot being a prime example.

Today, we cook in ways many of us wouldn't have dreamed of just ten years ago, giving us the option of a quick weeknight stew or pot roast that previously required all of Sunday to cook. Or a decadent pasta dish that's done in one pot with no colander required. The Instant Pot's arrival has changed the game and it has earned its spot on millions of countertops. For me, the idea of cooking epic, convenient, timely, and hassle-free meals in one pot is incredibly comforting, not to mention less intimidating than more traditional, messy, and time-consuming methods that may have turned people off cooking in the first place.

People often tell me that watching my videos and reading my books makes them feel like I'm an old friend right there in the kitchen with them, providing them with comfort and confidence as they cook. That is *exactly* my mission. Whether you're an Instant Pot pro or new to the kitchen, my keepin'-it-real approach and crystal-clear instructions will be sure to make you feel a newfound sense of simplicity and comfort in the kitchen.

———

Although my goal is to inspire you to cook something delicious, ultimately *you* inspire *me*. Peppered throughout this book you'll find *your* stories that you've so generously shared—because at the heart of every meal is a story just as delicious as the food itself. Some are relatable, some inspirational, and some hilarious—others may have you reaching for a box of tissues.

So welcome back, my friends. Read the stories, try the recipes, and, most importantly, find what comfort means to you.

> Simply put—cooking for and feeding someone is one of the most selfless acts that can be done. It is love in a pure form and disregards everything else.
>
> AMBER • **BRADENTON, FLORIDA**

## You Ask, Jeffrey Delivers

With your stories setting the stage, it's time to unleash a new trove of meals. I'm a firm believer in the saying, "Give 'em what they want." There were four key things people asked that I focus on in this book—and I promise to deliver.

### 1. Showcase recipes that have seven or less ingredients (including spices).

If you're as anxious as you are excited to break out that pot and get started, I suggest starting small and witnessing first-hand the magic this pot can conjure up. Check out my 7 Ingredients or Less chapter (page 32). From the most wonderful Cacio e Pepe (page 36) to Sweet & Sour Chicken (page 42), this chapter is perfect for newbies and skeptics alike, and just may turn you into a full-time wizard named Instant Potter (sorry, Harry).

### 2. Adjust recipes for households of one or two people.

Every recipe in this book is set up to feed a family of four to six (and in some cases up to eight). That said, you might either live by yourself or with one other person, and want meals for one or two with no leftovers. The way to modify my recipes to make less is incredibly simple:

**For soup, pasta, rice, and grain recipes,** halve everything in the recipe and keep the cook time the same.

**For chicken and seafood recipes,** halve the amount of the meat itself, but leave everything else in the recipe the same—including the cook time. The thing is, when pressure cooking, you need to have enough liquid in the pot to make it come to pressure. Therefore, you will have extra sauce—but you can freeze it for another day to serve over any future meat dishes, rice, pasta, or veggies!

**For meat recipes,** halve the meat itself and shave off about 7 minutes of cook time per pound of meat, *but only if the roast is kept whole* (like in my Mississippi Pot Roast, page 193, or my pastrami, page 208). If it's pre-cut into bite-size pieces, the cook time remains the same. As with chicken and seafood, you will also use the same amount of broth and spices, leaving you with some extra sauce or gravy, but it can be frozen and used for future meals.

**Desserts** should never be halved anyway because they're too delicious and there's no such thing as leftovers being an inconvenience there. 😊

### 3. Suggest lighter ingredients for more comforting recipes.

While all signs point to the recipes in this book being centered around comfort (which also happens to be my comfort zone when it comes to creating recipes), I've taken the best of both Volumes 1 and 2 and combined them into each recipe—so you have newly hatched comfort classics—along with suggestions on how to lighten each one up, or otherwise make it fit your mood or lifestyle. I call those Lighter Comforts and you'll see them within each recipe. I've also given you lifestyle-compliant icons to identify dishes that are or can be **K** (keto), **P** (paleo), **GF** (gluten-free), **DF** (dairy-free), **V** (vegetarian), or **VN** (vegan).

I decided not to include nutrition information in a book focused on comfort food. Since this book gives you free rein to use ingredients you prefer, along with providing options on how to lighten the recipes up, how one calculates nutrition info is all subjective. Every brand and product you choose for any given ingredient can vary greatly and lead to a wide range in the numbers. And I don't know about you, but when I go to the Cheesecake Factory, I really don't want to see the calorie count!

**Bottom line:** If you wish to know the nutrition info, use a reputable nutrition app or calculator and plug in the exact ingredient brands you've chosen. If you strictly follow a specific lifestyle, make sure you use compliant ingredients when making these meals. My lighter (blue) book's introduction covers all of this in great detail, although it's always best to consult a doctor or a nutritionist when making dietary decisions.

> Cooking is my creative outlet. I was a picky eater as a child but now I eat basically everything and anything. I love playing with different flavors and cuisines. I also enjoy sharing the food that I've made with love. I embrace my Jewish heritage and enjoy making dishes that my mother and aunt have made and taught me how to make.
>
> TRACY • **HIGH POINT, NORTH CAROLINA**

### 4. Include a broader range of familiar comforts inspired by food from around the globe.

Since travel has always been one of my biggest comforts and joys, this book is going to take us on a culinary adventure (one that requires no packing of bags or passports). As I wrote this during a pandemic, I was perpetually dreaming of taking a massive trip 'round the world while eating my way through it, *Very Hungry Caterpillar*–style. I'm talking about food inspired by the cooking of Japan, China, Italy, France, Eastern Europe, Thailand, Mexico, Spain, Canada, Korea, Britain, the Caribbean, and, of course, all regions of the United States. Each dish is tailored to be made in an Instant Pot, which led to ingredients or techniques that may differ from the classic dish that inspired it. As we know, there are countless ways to make many classic recipes, and I hope you enjoy my own personal spin on each.

## How to Instantly Use Your Instant Pot

Since we're on the subject of comfort, let's get you comfortable using your Instant Pot. At first it can be a bit intimidating with all those flashy buttons and sounds that remind you of R2-D2 (they actually made an Instant Pot model to resemble the beloved droid!). But once you take a few minutes to properly learn it, it's super-duper easy to use, and is thoroughly safe and trustworthy. For a complete introduction to the Instant Pot, check out my first book, *The Step-By-Step Instant Pot Cookbook*. If you don't have that one on hand, and want to get started right away, here's a crash course. There are a lot of different models, but all have the same key functions needed to make every recipe in this book.

If you're more a visual learner than a reader, this video covers everything you need to get started:

**1. PREP BEFORE YOU STEP.** One of the best tips I can give you is to make sure all of

your ingredients are out, chopped, and ready to go before cooking. This will prevent any frantic scramble for ingredients, especially once you've begun the sauté process. To make things extra easy, do what the French call *mise en place* and line them up in the order listed: that's the same order in which they'll be called for when you start cooking.

**2. PLOT THE POT.** If you're ready to cook and only see a

circular, gray heating element at the bottom of your pot, STOP! Always make sure the removable stainless steel liner pot is resting in the Instant Pot prior to cooking. If you pour ingredients into the Instant Pot without the liner pot in place, unplug it immediately. The ingredients will coat the heating element, seep out of the bottom and risk destroying the device. Also, *never* place your Instant Pot directly on a stovetop because if you accidentally turn it on or move it there while the stove was recently used, the plastic bottom is going to melt like the Wicked Witch of the West. Oh what a world, indeed.

**3. PLUG AND PLAY.** When the Instant Pot is first plugged

in (if the cord on your model is detachable, make sure it's firmly plugged into both the pot and the outlet), the display will read Off. So even though the screen is *on* and the device is now powered, the cooking element itself is *off*. Now that we've got the juice, it's time to let loose!

**4. SAUTÉ AWAY.** One of the most brilliant things about

the Instant Pot is that you can sauté directly in the pot before pressure cooking, treating it as if it's a pot or pan on the stove. If a recipe calls for it (and many do), hit the Sauté button, then Adjust the temperature to the More or High setting (which is what the recipes in this book call for most of the time). To adjust the temperature settings: If your model has an Adjust or arrow buttons, hit those; if it doesn't, hit the Sauté button again to adjust the temperature to either Less/Low, Normal/Medium, or More/High. If your model has only buttons, once you hit Sauté it will say On after a few moments and begin to heat up. If it has a knob or a Start button, hit that button to begin the process. Most models give you a max time of 30 minutes to sauté before it turns off. No recipe in this book will require you to sauté for longer than that, so you can leave the default as is. If the display reads Hot, that means the pot is as hot as it can get, but there's no need to wait until that point before you start sautéing, as you'll see in my recipe instructions (usually 3 minutes of heating will do).

**5. SWITCH GEARS.** When done sautéing, hit the Cancel or the Keep Warm/Cancel button, depending on your model. Think of this as the Home button on a smartphone. This will make sure your pot is back in the Off position so you can then select a different function.

**6. PUT A LID ON IT.** The gasket (the silicone ring under the lid) is the key to the Instant Pot sealing properly. Before pressure cooking, make sure the gasket is firmly in the metal grooves or it will not come to pressure and steam may escape from the sides. Once all is good, secure the lid by locking it into place. Make sure the valve is moved from the venting position to the sealing position. Some models automatically seal the pot for you once the lid is secured, but other models require you to do this manually.

**7. PRESSURE LUCK.** Depending on your model, hit either the Manual or Pressure Cook button (different from the Pressure button if your model has one). Then, to adjust the time, use the +/- buttons or knob (if yours has one) to go up or down in time. Hours are on the left of the colon and minutes are to the right, so 00:08 is 8 minutes (and 8:00 is 8 hours, which you'll never use except for yogurt if your pot has that function). On some older, original models it may just state the minutes. If that's the case, just 8 will be displayed, which means 8 minutes. If you wish to change the pressure level from High to Low, you can do so by either hitting the Pressure Level or arrow buttons, but all the recipes in this book call for everything to be cooked at high pressure. If the Less/Normal/More is lit up as well, always leave it on Normal when pressure

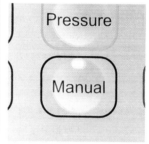 

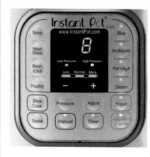 

cooking. If your Instant Pot model has only buttons, it will say On within a few moments of hitting the Manual or Pressure Cook button and begin to heat. If it has a knob or a Start button, you'll need to hit that button to begin the process. So when reading the instructions for each recipe, make sure you hit that Start button as well, should your model have one. Additionally, upon starting a pressure cooking cycle, check that the Keep Warm button is lit, as this means the pot will switch to keeping your food warm once the pressure cooking cycle is complete.

When the pot is On, that means it's building pressure. The higher the volume of ingredients in the pot, the longer it will take to come to pressure (I've specified the pressure building time for each recipe). Once there is enough steam built up inside the pot, the little metal pin in the lid will pop up, locking the lid. From there, a few moments (or minutes) later the display will shortly begin to count down from the pressure cook time you set it for. When finished, the pot will read 00:00 or L0:00 depending on your model, and then will begin to count up, showing how much time has elapsed since the pressure cooking cycle was completed. This comes in handy for measuring the time if a recipe calls for a natural release. Speaking of which…

**8. RELEASE WITH PEACE.** You've reached the final step in the pressure cooking process—releasing the steam! We use two ways to release the steam from the pot in this book:

***Quick release.*** Once the pressure cooking is complete, move the valve or press the button/slide the switch to the venting position and the steam will release. Just be careful not to have your hand directly over the valve while this happens or you could be in for a quick singe. When all the steam is released, the pin will drop, unlocking the lid for safe removal.

***Natural release.*** Once the pressure cooking cycle is complete, let the pot sit, undisturbed, for the specified amount of time so the steam dissipates on its own. For example, if the recipe calls for a 5-minute natural release, do nothing until the display reads L0:05 or 00:05, depending on your model. After that, finish with a quick release. If a recipe calls for a full natural release, it means you do nothing until the pin in the lid drops and the lid can be opened. This can take anywhere from 5 to 45 minutes depending on the volume of food in the pot.

**NOTE** While this is unlikely to happen with my recipes, if for whatever reason the valve begins to spit out some liquid while releasing due perhaps to altitude or another factor, either throw a dish towel over it or allow a full natural release. But make sure to never allow a full natural release for pasta or rice, as they will overcook.

**9. TRY AN AIR FRY.** One of the most genius things about the Instant Pot is that you can swap lids and transform it into an air fryer. A few recipes in this book call for that option and when it does, I provide clear instructions on just how to use it.

Whether you buy a stand-alone air fryer lid (currently for 6-quart only) or the Duo Crisp or Duo Pro models (6- or 8-quart), they all come with a resting disk to place the hot lid on once you're done cooking. When not using, flip the disk over and, once the air fryer lid is cooled, you can lock the open end of your lid with the bottom of the disk for easy storing and protection of the heating element.

Alternatively, if you don't have an air fryer lid, you can use your oven for a crispy finish; simply place the food in an oven-safe casserole dish and broil until the desired level of crispiness is reached.

Here's another video showing you how this works!

## The Evolution of Instant Pots and Their Buttons

In the short period of time since the Instant Pot was born (and since my first books were published), there have been many new models released—all with slight changes and added bells and whistles. These include upgrades of existing models as well (for instance, the Duo Plus got a facelift in 2021, but still goes by the same model name). While the steps above and in recipes are universal no matter which model you have

(and because I hate confusion), I feel it important to elaborate on and emphasize the evolution of Instant Pot models for crystal-clear clarity:

### THE ADDITION OF THE START BUTTON

If your pot has a Start button, you *must* hit this after selecting a function for it to get going. If you don't, nothing will happen. I say this because if you're used to an earlier model that doesn't have a Start button (no models did when they first came out), you're also used to the pot starting on its own about 5 seconds after selecting the function you wish. So if you have a newer model with a Start button and aren't yet used to it, be mindful of this added step before you hit the Sauté or Pressure Cook buttons and walk away, thinking the process will begin on its own. I don't explicitly state "…and hit the Start button (if your model has one)" in the instructions for my recipes, so make sure to note whether this is a necessary step for your pot.

*Bottom line:* If your Instant Pot doesn't have a Start button, it will begin the process on its own about 5 seconds after selecting a function. If your model does have a Start button, you'll need to hit it to begin.

### THE MANUAL VS. PRESSURE COOK BUTTON

While the pot has acquired new buttons over time, some buttons have been retired or renamed. When the Instant Pot first came out, the original (dare I say, vintage) Lux and Duo models had a button labeled Manual—used for the pressure cooking function—and a Pressure Level function to shift from low pressure

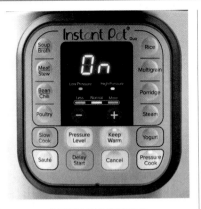

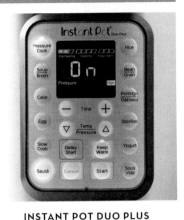

**INSTANT POT DUO**
*(original model)*

**INSTANT POT DUO**
*(updated model)*

**INSTANT POT DUO PLUS**
*(updated model)*

## THE DISPLAY

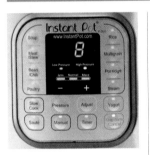

In the older Duo models, the cook time is only displayed in minutes

But in all newer Duos and above, the cook time is displayed with minutes to the right of the colon and hours to the left

The updated Duo Plus uses arrows to adjust the temperature settings and the Start button must be pressed to begin all functions

Some models require a push-dial to set times and functions

When you're done pressure cooking, the display will begin to count up, showing LO:00 or 00:00 for elapsed time

Turn your pot's sound on and off by holding the + and - buttons while the pot is in Off mode

to high. While the word Manual makes sense (since you're manually setting a custom pressure cook time), it seemed to confuse some. So as newer models were released, they just renamed the Manual button as the Pressure Cook button (which makes more sense). But since so many folks still use their original Lux and Duo models (these may show up in the Smithsonian someday), I still mention "hit Manual or Pressure Cook" in my instructions so all bases are covered.

**Bottom line:** Your Instant Pot will have only a Manual *or* Pressure Cook button and they both do the exact same thing.

### THE CANCEL VS. KEEP WARM/CANCEL BUTTON

Speaking of button evolution, my instructions have slightly evolved as well. In this book, I'll tell you to "hit the Cancel button" in most recipes in order to switch functions from Sauté to Pressure Cooking and vice versa. However, in my previous books I said to "hit the Keep Warm/Cancel Button" since the Keep Warm and Cancel functions shared the same button on the original models. But, like the Manual to Pressure Cook button evolution, all newer and upgraded models now have Keep Warm and Cancel functions as their own separate buttons. In this case, you'll only hit the Cancel button to switch functions.

**Bottom line:** When switching functions, hit the shared Keep Warm/Cancel button if your "vintage" model has one. But if it has a separate Cancel button, just hit that to switch functions.

### PRESETS ARE JUST PIZZAZZ

See all those (slightly overwhelming) buttons that say Multigrain, Porridge, Stew, Rice, Steam, and so on? Those are all presets and I never, ever use them. Why? Because not only do they change based on what model Instant Pot you have—which makes including them in recipes nearly impossible—I'd also much rather tailor my recipes by using the customized Pressure Cook (or Manual) button, which gives me full control of the cook time. That way, I'm not relying on a guesstimate from the preset, which, after all, doesn't know which protein I have in my pot or how hearty my stew or porridge is.

**Bottom line:** Skip the presets and stick to the Pressure Cook (or Manual) buttons; once you get used to Instant Potting with these recipes and choose to venture out on your own, you'll have a sense of proper timings for certain foods.

## Invaluable Instant Info

Here's some more simple advice that should prove helpful along your journey, and answer some FAQs.

### LIQUID + HEAT = STEAM + PRESSURE

When pressure cooking, you must have enough liquid in the Instant Pot for it to build steam and come to pressure: This will vary depending on what you're making. To ensure that the proper amount of steam is built, the liquid added prior to pressure cooking should generally be a consistency no thicker than a thin salsa (like Pace Picante sauce). But no need to worry as I've provided for that in all of the recipes in this book.

My passion for cooking goes back fifty-plus years. I was blessed with a great-grandmother and a grandmother who shepherded my family through good times and bad through the love they put in each recipe. I learned about my ancestors while cooking their recipes. I learned about the Depression and my family's struggles while making recipes from that era. Most of all, I learned a valuable lesson about love and how small gifts from my kitchen could change someone's life.

I am blessed to be a part of a blended family now. With no biological children of my own I worried that my family's stories and recipes would be lost. Now my family's history, tales, triumphs, and recipes are being passed on to my eight grandchildren! While we may not share DNA, we share the love and wonders of a family meal shared by so many that came before us.

TAMARA · **MOUNT PLEASANT, SOUTH CAROLINA**

## DEGLAZING IS AMAZING

I can't stress this one enough: It's super important that while sautéing, you ensure the bottom of the pot is deglazed—that is, scraped with a wooden spoon after adding liquid to clear it of any browned bits. Again, the recipes and instructions will remind you to deglaze as you go, so be sure to follow them as written. **Pro tip:** Wine and Worcestershire sauce are magical for deglazing the bottom of a heated pot. Once you swish a tablespoon or two of either around with a wooden spatula, the bottom will clear up within moments.

## THICKNESS AND CREAM COME AFTER THE STEAM

All dairy (with the exception of butter) and very thick tomato products (like a paste) should be added in the final steps, just before serving. Creams tend to curdle under pressure and cheeses and thick tomato products may stick to the bottom of the pot, tampering with the pressure-building. My recipes will call for ingredients at the correct time, but be mindful if attempting your own creations.

## BURN AND LEARN

If you see the word Burn on the screen, don't panic. Again, my recipes shouldn't lead to this notice as all have been rigorously tested, but if for whatever reason you encounter it, simply remove the lid, give the pot a stir, and then add ½ to 1 cup more broth. From there, secure the lid again and restart the pressure cook time. In some cases, when the pot has already come to pressure and you're sure the burn notice is incorrect, you can ignore it and it should go away after a minute, at which point the pressure cooking process continues.

## THAWED MEAT OR FROZEN—WHICH HAVE YOU CHOSEN?

When it comes to cooking meat or poultry under pressure, you can use either thawed or frozen. However, I choose thawed meat every time because when pressure cooking a meat from frozen, the "shock" of cooking it from a solid state can lead to the meat losing tenderness and flavor and having a bit of a strange texture. So if you're asking me, I think taking the extra step to thaw your meats makes a world of difference. Simply take it from the freezer and place it in the fridge about 24 hours before cooking. By dinnertime, it should be thawed and ready to go.

That said, if you're in a pinch and forgot to defrost, you can still definitely cook it from frozen. You'll just need to add more time depending on the cut (see the charts on pages 28 and 29).

## DON'T WANT BEER OR WINE? THAT'S JUST FINE.

Some of my recipes include beer or wine in the ingredients. If you don't wish to cook with alcohol, you can always add an equivalent amount of broth in its place. My recipes generally indicate this but I felt it important to mention here as well.

## TRANSFORMING TOUCHES

With some recipes, the food may not look gorgeous immediately after pressure cooking, and in some cases with veggie- and protein-heavy dishes, you'll notice a lot more liquid in the pot than when you began. This is due to proteins releasing juices and veggies releasing water.

That's what the final touches are for! In recipes that can lead to excess liquid, I've instructed you to incorporate some finishing touches, such as adding a slurry to thicken the sauce, some dairy or tomato paste to bring it together, or letting it rest for a few minutes for the heat to come down a bit. Once everything is stirred together in those final moments, your masterpiece becomes as photo-worthy as it is delicious.

## AS HEAT TAKES WING, FLAVORS WILL SING

When the lid comes off the pot after pressure cooking, it's going to be *hot*. As the food rests in the pot after pressure cooking (and as is the case with most pastas and risottos), the longer it cools, the more the flavors will develop and come together. This is why leftovers can often taste even better the next day after being refrigerated, since the flavors are fusing together under cold temperatures prior to reheating.

To that point, we certainly don't want our food cold when we've just cooked it and are ready to dig in. Sometimes adding colder dairy products at the end of a recipe, such as a large amount of cream (think 1+ cup), can significantly reduce the temperature of a dish—especially in some soups and pastas. If it cools down more than you'd like, simply hit the Sauté button and Adjust the temperature, stir for a few moments, and bring it to a level you're happy with. Then kill the heat and enjoy.

## A CORNSTARCH SLURRY THICKENS IN A HURRY

Many of my poultry (page 152) and meat (page 188) recipes make a *lot* of sauce, which I love because it can be saved and frozen for future meals or served over rice, veggies, or pasta. And since the liquid in a pot

needs to be thin enough for it to produce enough steam and liquid so it can cook and come to pressure, a few recipes in this book call for giving a sauce a little thickening magic in the final moments before serving. This is achieved with a slurry.

Typically, we mix equal parts cornstarch (which is gluten-free) with cold water, and a slurry is born. At first it will have a cement-like consistency, but will become smooth while mixing. It's important to mix the slurry before adding to your sauce, as just dumping the cornstarch into the pot will result in a ball of putty. Once you've created your slurry, pour it into the bubbling pot while stirring continuously for about 30 seconds, and your sauce will thicken up perfectly before your eyes. After that, kill the heat while stirring occasionally; the sauce will continue to thicken as it cools.

***Pro tip:*** My recipes are written to give you what I feel is the perfect thickness for each sauce and soup. However, if you want it thicker start by adding a slurry of 1 tablespoon cornstarch + 1 tablespoon water in the final stages, making sure the sauce or soup is bubbling when you do so. You can always add more slurry should you wish to thicken a dish or more broth if you want to thin it out.

| SAUCE | FLAVOR PROFILE | CONTAINS SOY | CONTAINS GLUTEN |
|---|---|---|---|
| Soy | Salty/savory | Yes | Usually always, but there are some that state they're gluten-free. |
| Tamari | Salty/savory (tastes practically identical to soy) | Yes | Usually not, but just check the label to ensure it states it's gluten-free |
| Coconut aminos | A mix of sweet and savory (as if soy sauce and teriyaki sauce got married—but it does *not* taste like coconut!) | No | No |

## SOY GEVALT!

In many of my recipes I call for either soy sauce (always low-sodium because I personally can't tell the difference between that and regular once mixed into a dish), tamari, or coconut aminos. Now there are many who cannot tolerate soy or who live a gluten-free lifestyle. This simple chart will make you an expert on the differences of the three and which one is right for you.

In a nutshell, in lieu of a classic soy sauce that usually contains soy *and* gluten, tamari will normally give you a gluten-free version and coconut aminos ensure you won't be getting gluten *or* soy in your dish. When shopping and in doubt, always read the label to make sure the product matches your dietary goals.

## I CAN'T FIND THE EXACT SIZE INGREDIENT YOU'RE CALLING FOR. WILL THAT BE A PROBLEM?

Not at all. Based on where I live and the markets I go to, I'm used to specific (and most common) sizes for canned items and packaged frozen foods/veggies. So if a recipe in this book calls for, say, a 10-ounce package of frozen corn and you can only find a 16-ounce package, that's fine! Either just use 10 ounces from the bag and save the rest—or if you really love corn, add all of it in there! Same for canned goods. If you can only find a 16-ounce can of beans and not a 15.5-ounce can, it will make absolutely no difference.

Also, if I call for a certain item like baby bella mushrooms and you can only find white ones, those will do absolutely fine! The same with onions— although I call for specific types in my recipes, it really makes very little difference what kind you use at the end of the day. Want to sub a yellow for a red because you bought that huge netted bag on sale? Have at it!

## WHAT IS A SERVING SIZE?

A good question with a million different answers. To me, "serving size" is simply a suggestion, because the amount of food you eat is fully dependent on your appetite. Sometimes we feel ravenous while other times we just want a few bites. Therefore *serving size* doesn't necessarily equal *portion size*. That said, I am a firm believer in moderation and if you were to make a recipe in my Lighter (blue) cookbook, I'd say my serving sizes are pretty accurate. But in my first (orange) book and this book I give a range. Most recipes will feed *at least* four to six people (and some folks may even claim up to eight). It truly all depends on how large your appetites are. Regardless, the recipes in this book are most certainly "family-style." That means it may all be gone in one shot or you'll have some tasty leftovers (which is a benefit of Instant Pot cooking as the flavors are

## YOU'VE GOT OPTIONS

For each recipe, whenever you see an ingredient marked optional, it means exactly that: You can use it, or not. And because it's not mandatory, it's not reflected in the recipe's lifestyle icons. To that point, I provide many lighter suggestions for each recipe, but you can swap in any desired ingredients to make the dish fit your lifestyle. The flavor and consistency may change a bit from how I intended them, but I'm sure it'll still be lip-smackin'.

often more vibrant after cooling in the fridge before reheating). If you wish to cook for one or two people, go back to page 10 of the introduction and check out #2 of the You Ask, Jeffrey Delivers section.

## CAN THESE RECIPES BE MADE IN ANY SIZE INSTANT POT?

Yes! All the recipes in this book were tested in a 6-quart model but can also be done in an 8-quart or 3-quart just as well. If using an 8-quart, I usually add ½ to 1 cup more broth than called for due to the volume of the pot. Cook time remains the same for 8- or 3-quarts.

The 8-quart will also take longer to come to pressure as there's more space to fill. The opposite holds true for the 3-quart: It'll come to pressure more quickly because it's smaller, but it's also more limited as to how much it can hold. Make sure to *halve all the ingredients when using the smaller model*, but you can keep the cook time the same in most circumstances.

Check out the chart below for easy and general reference.

## WHICH MODEL INSTANT POT SHOULD I GET?

Every model has something great to offer with the same universal functions (with the exception of the Lux since it does not have a Yogurt function) and all models can make all the recipes in this book. That said, there are three Instant Pot models I use the most: the Duo, Duo Crisp, and Duo Plus (which has just been upgraded). I used them to make all the recipes during the photo shoot for this book with no issues whatsoever and for that alone, they are the ones I will continue to suggest as my top picks.

If you want a pot that also has an air fryer lid, the Instant Pot Pro Crisp is the model for you.

## HOW DO I KEEP MY INSTANT POT CLEAN?

Bar Keeper's Friend will be your and your stainless steel liner pot's bestie; just follow the instructions on the label. You can also place the pressure cooking lid on the top rack of your dishwasher, and the liner pot can go on the bottom rack.

To help get any unwanted aromas out of your silicone sealing ring, wash the ring in the top rack of

## COOKING ADJUSTMENTS BY POT SIZE

| POT SIZE | LIQUID AMOUNT | PRESSURE COOK TIME |
|---|---|---|
| **6-quart** (all recipes in this book were made in this size) | As given in the recipes, but if going on your own use 1 cup minimum just to ensure it's enough. | As given in the recipes |
| **3-quart** | ½ cup minimum for roasts and steaming veggies<br>1 cup minimum for rice<br>2 cups minimum for pasta | Same as 6-quart (if halving a roast, shave off 7–10 minutes of cook time) |
| **8-quart** | 1½ to 2 cups minimum for roasts and steaming veggies<br>2 cups minimum for rice<br>3 cups minimum for pasta | Same as 6-quart |

your dishwasher or soak overnight in vinegar and leave outside to air-dry for a day. It's also a good idea to replace the rings every 6 to 12 months to ensure they are supple and don't become loose.

While a sponge could help, I've found the most effective way to get any gunk from under the metal grooves in the outer edges of the top of the pot is to use a Q-tip or those super cheap foam brushes you can get from just about any hardware store.

## The Practical, Well-Stocked Kitchen

### PANTRY STAPLES

When you look at the ingredients lists in each recipe, some will appear longer than others. *Do not let this intimidate you.* Simple, everyday items generally make up one-third to one-half of the ingredients each recipe calls for. I'll bet that many are likely already in your kitchen pantry, cupboards, or fridge. And if they aren't, they can be picked up at most any market or wholesale club—where you'll get more for less (Costco is my happy place). They are well worth the investment and since a little often goes a long way, they will last you for many, many meals to come.

Here is a list of all the pantry staples I strongly suggest keeping on hand—no fancy brands required (though I do specify if I have a favorite)!

### DRIED HERBS, SPICES, AND SEASONINGS

Bay leaves

Black pepper

Cajun/Creole/Louisiana seasoning (I love Tony Chachere's)

Cayenne pepper

Cilantro

Cinnamon, ground

Crushed red pepper flakes

Cumin, both ground and seeds

Dill weed, dried

Garam masala

Garlic powder

Garlic salt

Italian seasoning

Kosher salt

Mustard, ground

Old Bay seasoning

Onion powder

Oregano, dried

Paprika (some like smoked)

Parsley, dried

Poultry seasoning

Rosemary, dried

Saffron (it's the most costly thing on this list, but you use only a pinch at a time and it lasts)

Sage, dried/ground

Salt-free seasoning (such as Dash)

Seasoned salt (I use Lawry's)

Sugars (white/granulated, light brown, and dark brown; you can also use monk fruit sweetener as a substitute)

Thyme, dried

Turmeric, ground

White pepper, ground

Zatarain's Concentrated Shrimp & Crab Boil

### DAIRY

Boursin herb cheese (you can also use Alouette or Laughing Cow)

Butter, salted or unsalted

Cream cheese, by the 8-ounce brick

Ghee (clarified butter)

Greek yogurt, plain

Milk (regular, half-and-half, and heavy cream)

Parmesan cheese, grated

Sour cream

## OILS, VINEGARS, SAUCES, AND OTHER PANTRY STAPLES

All-purpose flour; or coconut flour (gluten-free, keto-friendly, and paleo-friendly); or quinoa flour (gluten-free)

Almond, cashew, oat, or soy milk (all unsweetened and unflavored)

Broth (broths made from all varieties of Better Than Bouillon are my favorite, with low-sodium options if you're watching your sodium intake)

Coconut milk, unsweetened and light (you should be able to shake the can and it should sound like water)

Chili-garlic sauce (my favorite comes from Huy Fong Foods, the same company that makes sriracha)

Cornstarch

Extra-virgin olive oil

Hoisin sauce (check label to ensure brand is gluten-free if necessary)

Honey

Hot sauce (I like Frank's RedHot and Cholula)

Liquid smoke (I prefer hickory flavor but any will do)

Maple syrup, pure

Mustard (Dijon in particular, like Grey Poupon)

Oyster sauce (check label to ensure brand is gluten-free if necessary)

Plum sauce

Red wine (a dry one like a cabernet or pinot noir—use a cheap bottle)

Sesame oil (either toasted or untoasted is fine)

Sherry, dry

Soy sauce (I use low-sodium; you can also use tamari [which is gluten-free] and coconut aminos [gluten-free and soy-free]. See chart on page 20.)

Squeeze ginger (get this at Costco or many markets. It looks like applesauce and is the easiest thing for minced or grated ginger)

Sriracha

Sugar-free steak sauce (Primal Kitchen and G Hughes make good ones)

Tomatoes, canned (crushed, diced, paste, and sauce); use no-salt-added for low-sodium intake

Vinegars (apple cider, balsamic, red wine, rice, and white)

White wine (a dry one like a chardonnay or sauvignon blanc—use a cheap bottle)

Worcestershire sauce (check label to ensure brand is gluten-free if necessary)

## FRUITS & VEGETABLES

Bell peppers (jalapeños and habaneros are also good to have on hand for heat lovers)

Carrots

Garlic (Buying pre-peeled cloves or jars of minced garlic is always a time saver. Also, I often call for 3 cloves of crushed or minced garlic. 1 tablespoon of jarred minced or crushed garlic is about the equivalent of 3 cloves.)

Ginger (see also squeeze ginger, above)

Lemons

Limes

Onions (any kind can be used, but I suggest the one I prefer in each recipe)

Spinach (I use baby)

I grew up around pressure cookers, with my mom and both grandmothers using them to cook and can any number of seasonal vegetables. When my last grandmother passed away, she left me one of her old-school pressure cookers—and whenever I would use it to cook beans or stock, I loved to hear that contraption hiss and rattle, just like it did when I was little.

I first learned about the Instant Pot from *Pressure Luck*. Not only was I not interested, I was aghast at the idea of taking the magic that had been my birthright and replacing it with some automated whiz-bang gadget that didn't even have a rattle on top. That all changed when I learned I was going to be a father. The precise techniques my grandmother and my mom employed would soon prove too time intensive. And my wife wanted in on the pressure action for beans and stews, but, like the rest of her family, she never felt safe using my grandmother's pressure cooker.

I can't remember which of us bought our Instant Pot, but I also can't forget the first meal I made with it: hummus from dry, unsoaked chickpeas. The beans turned out exactly as I'd made them countless times, cleanup was a breeze—and somehow I had time to focus on other things while it cooked. A few pots of beans later, I started trusting the Instant Pot—and I've never looked back. I'll always miss the sights, sounds, and smells of my grandma's kitchen, but judging by the food I've cooked in this Instant Pot, I can guarantee she would approve.

ELI · **BOSTON, MASSACHUSETTS**

### Broth, Bouillon, and Fancy Cream Cheese

If you're familiar with my recipes, you know my obsession with two products: Better Than Bouillon and Boursin. While totally different things, they each bring a very special touch to many of my recipes. These are listed above but I wanted to call extra attention to them here—because they're just that special.

---

**For broth,** you can absolutely make your own (and I have recipes in my first two books). But if you don't have any premade, there's no better option than Better Than Bouillon bases. Not only do they have the household varieties of chicken, beef, and vegetable broth, but they expand to garlic, chili, lobster, ham, and more. They also offer low-sodium and organic options for many of their broth bases, as well as mock-meat if you're vegan! The base is a concentrate that comes in a jar; once opened, it stores in your fridge for quite a long time (taking up very little space). It costs about the same as a quart or two of boxed broth, but makes over 35 cups of broth per 8-ounce jar! To prepare, mix 1 teaspoon of the base with 1 cup water (it doesn't need to be hot while mixing as it'll be pressure cooked)— the result is 1 cup of seriously flavorful broth! Better Than Bouillon is simply a no-brainer for me and is truly one of my favorite products on the market. Find it in your grocery store's soup aisle, online, and in many wholesale clubs in mega-size jars.

Whichever broth you choose, if you live a gluten-free lifestyle, make sure the broth does not contain any wheat. It feels natural to think it doesn't, but some do. Like I've stated earlier (and because it's important to repeat): When in doubt, always read the label.

**NOTE** When I call for a specific broth variety in a recipe, be it chicken, beef, garlic, or even lobster, I'm merely stating that's the one I used when I created it. But it doesn't have to be that way! Whether you only have one kind of broth in your kitchen or if you have a whole collection and simply want to get creative, make your own rules when it comes to types of broth.

**For taking cream cheese to the next level,** give an herb cheese such as Boursin a try. It's usually found in the market near the deli meats and fancy cheeses (as well as in wholesale clubs in packs of three at a great price). Not only does it thicken sauces, pastas, and risottos fantastically, but the smooth and irresistibly unique flavor it adds to my recipes truly sets it apart from the rest. If you can't find Boursin, Alouette, Rondelé, Laughing Cow, or flavored cream cheese works as well. And if you're being more health-conscious, use Greek yogurt instead as a lighter option—roughly ⅓ cup will fill in for a 5.2-ounce package of Boursin. Oh, and guess what? They just released a dairy-free Boursin for those who follow dairy-free and vegan lifestyles! It comes in a 6-ounce tub (instead of a 5.2-ounce package, which my recipes call for as a guideline), but it's perfectly fine to use the whole tub in place of the regular package. The same goes if using Alouette as it comes in a slightly larger size than regular Boursin.

> I cannot express how glad I am to have found the *Pressure Luck* website. For the longest time I dreaded cooking, and maybe part of it was an irrational fear instilled by my mom early on because she never liked cooking. I had a few friends help me out here and there, but I never really embraced it. Even the things I made from recipes I found online were okay at best. What you've done is really speak to someone like me and make everything easy and fun.
>
> A long time ago, I was at the grocery store and saw a gentleman who must've been in his eighties. He had a shopping cart that was absolutely filled with nothing but frozen meals. I couldn't help but wonder about what had happened for him to be in that situation.
>
> At a certain point, I was doing that. I would go to the market and just stock up on frozen or canned meals because I would get too busy to cook. I felt like a prisoner in a cell I created for myself because I could do very limited things.
>
> Now, being able to just have a wonderful pot roast (which I made twice!) and remembering the days I was with my family having dinner has freed me from ever becoming that man I saw in the store.
>
> KEITH • SAN PEDRO, CALIFORNIA

# HERB CHEESE

Now because the fancy cream cheeses aren't available everywhere and because I want you to get that true flavor experience I've intended in these recipes, I'm going to share how to make your own garlic-herb cheese! Not only is this budget conscious, it tastes just as great as the fancy stuff in the market (if not better since it's homemade). All it takes are the following:

**2 (8-ounce) bricks cream cheese,** 2 hours at room temperature so it's softened (don't microwave it)

**2 sticks (8 ounces) salted butter,** 2 hours at room temperature so it's softened (don't microwave it)

**¼ cup grated Parmesan cheese**

**3 cloves garlic, minced or pressed**

**1 teaspoon dried parsley**

**1 teaspoon dried dill weed**

**½ teaspoon garlic powder**

**½ teaspoon dried thyme**

**½ teaspoon dried basil**

**½ teaspoon black pepper**

**½ teaspoon Italian seasoning**

Simply add all the ingredients to a large mixing bowl. Take a silicone, rubber, or wooden mixing spoon and mix it all together, folding it over until well combined with even seasoning distribution. (NOTE: You can also use a hand mixer if that's easier but I find that the familiar consistency is best achieved when mixed by hand.)

**NOTE** This will yield about the equivalent of *five* 5.2-ounce packages of Boursin! You can also use it as a spread for crackers on your charcuterie board. It will last up to three weeks in your fridge and can be frozen for future use.

## THE KEYS TO THE KITCHEN

*While the Instant Pot carries the load of the work, no kitchen would be complete without a few key tools that will become your beloved personal assistants.*

Bundt pan (a 6-cup nonstick pan fits inside the 6- and 8-quart Instant Pot models)

Cheese grater

Fine-mesh strainer/colander

Food processor or blender

Hand or stand mixer

Immersion blender (this is heaven-sent for soups as it eliminates messy batch trips to the blender)

Juicer

Knives (I think an 8-inch chef's knife is best for chopping, slicing, and dicing and a paring knife is great for finely slicing small veggies and getting ribs out of peppers)

Ladle

Measuring cups and spoons

Microplane (amazing for zesting lemons and limes or for topping a dish with some freshly shaved Parmesan)

Mixing bowls

Mixing spoons and spatulas (wooden and silicone are best for the stainless steel liner pot)

Oven mitts/dish towels (to handle a hot pot)

Oven-safe soup crocks (for French Onion Soup, page 58)

Parchment paper rounds

Peeler

Potato masher

Springform pan (7-inch diameter with 3-inch rim is the best size)

Steamer basket

Tongs

Whisk (silicone is best)

## Last Call Advice

As this introduction comes to a close, I hope you find yourself well-equipped and ready to cook some of the simplest, most memorable, and sensational meals you'll ever make.

I want to reiterate what I've always stated: Feel free to make any changes to any of these recipes so they fit your lifestyle and preferences. Instant Pot protocol aside, I believe that when cooking, you make the rules. You control what you put in a dish. Don't like, want, or have a specific ingredient I call for? Leave it out! Most of them are merely supporting players designed to give you an ensemble of flavor results that will lead you to close your eyes and smile with bliss. Once you get used to using your Instant Pot (and it will happen more quickly than you think), it's really like riding a bike. It becomes a very logical science that even the worst chemistry student <raises hand> can master. Simply allow this book to serve as a blueprint for timing and guidance for food-to-liquid ratios. If you're new to cooking, start with something in the 7 Ingredients or Less chapter (page 32). If you're looking for a simple and fun challenge, get cracking on that Wonton Soup (page 75). And if you want to go all out, give that Gumbo (page 224) a whirl.

Speaking of gumbo (which happens to have the longest ingredient list in the book, for those of you who like a challenge), there are as many ways to make this Cajun/Creole classic as there are gators in the bayous of Louisiana. If you see an ingredient that your Gran Gran didn't use and you find it blasphemous, I can't say I blame you for altering it to your preference. After

all, it's the gumbo you grew up on and are comforted by (not to mention, who is this Jewish dude from New York telling you how to make a Southern dish, anyway?). But the point of this book is to introduce ourselves to new comforts, read the stories of others, and discover a trick or two to take a beloved recipe and possibly make it our own. Although I prefer to cook the recipes in this book as written, I encourage you to alter them as you see fit. Adding your own spins and touches will make the recipes that much more personal to you and their stories will evolve and take on a new meaning within a new home.

I have a deep love for cuisines of all cultures and I am excited to help bring some incredible tastes of the world to your kitchen in the best way I know how: in an Instant Pot. Making traditional dishes in an Instant Pot often requires adjustment. Therefore, these recipes aren't exactly the authoritative versions of a classic: Given the more commonly found ingredients I've chosen and this new technique of making a dish come to life, that wouldn't be possible. But whether a dish echoes the flavors of a favorite local eatery, or introduces you to a new flavor profile that spurs you to learn more about a different culture, each recipe honors a cuisine that I love. Many of these dishes have been adapted to American kitchens by others in the best ways they know how, and my take brings them to you with great respect for the originating culture and all the cooks who came before me. I hope these dishes inspire you the way they inspire me.

And with that, my dear reader, let's celebrate the simple comforts and sit down at the table. Dinner is served.

For me, cooking is how I still feel connected to my grandma who raised me and who has been gone for fifteen years now.

The thing that I loved about the time we shared in the kitchen together was the stories she shared about my mom, her youngest, who had passed tragically when I was only 2. She also shared stories about my aunt and uncles and their childhood antics. I had no memories of my mom, but it felt like I knew her from those special moments in the kitchen with Grandma.

I still make her banana bread often, but now it's with my 6-year-old son, whom I've been teaching how to cook. Sharing special moments.

AMBER · EDMONTON, ALBERTA, CANADA

# GENERAL COOKING CHARTS

I have these handy reference charts in my first two books, Volumes 1 and 2, but wanted to include them here as well for when you wish to attempt your own creations. Keep in mind that these are loose guidelines, as the dish or sauce you're making may require slightly altered ratios and times depending on what you're making and adding to each dish (be it meat or veggies).

## PASTA

| PASTA | GRAIN:LIQUID RATIO BY POUND:CUP | PRESSURE COOK TIME AT HIGH PRESSURE | RELEASE |
|---|---|---|---|
| Short pasta (macaroni, rigatoni, penne, ziti, farfalle, rotini, cavatappi, cellentani, campanelle, or medium shells) | 1:4 | 6 minutes | Quick |
| Linguine or egg noodles | 1:4 | 6 minutes | Quick |
| Spaghetti | 1:4 | 8 minutes | Quick |
| Rigatoni | 1:4 | 8 minutes | Quick |
| Bucatini | 1:4 | 12 minutes | Quick |

- *If making whole-wheat pasta, cut the package's suggested minimum cook time in half, then subtract 1 minute for softer pasta or 2 minutes for al dente pasta.*
- *If making gluten-free pasta, halve the suggested Pressure Cook time in the chart above.*
- *You can't pressure cook chickpea or lentil pasta. It will turn to mush. Believe me, I've tried.*
- *If making pasta without a sauce, drain the excess liquid before serving.*
- *If using a long noodle such as spaghetti or linguine, you must break it in half before adding to the pot. True, some Italian grandmothers may chase you with their rolling pins for doing so, but if you don't, it won't fit or cook properly.*
- *Always add 2 tablespoons butter or oil to the pot to prevent sticking.*
- *Be mindful of doubling pasta because that's double the starch, which could cause some bubbly sputtering from the valve when releasing the pressure. Remember, each of my recipes will feed up to six (some would argue eight), but if you really want to double a pasta dish, do it in an 8-quart pot since there's more room. When doubling a pasta—especially if it contains veggies and proteins—I'd only add an additional half of the given amount of broth and seasonings. This will prevent the dish from becoming too soupy from liquids from the veggies and proteins, or too spicy or salty from the seasonings (but this can be a trial and error process depending on the recipe). The cook time would remain the same as written.*

## POULTRY

| MEAT (2–4 POUNDS) | PRESSURE COOK TIME AT HIGH PRESSURE WITH 1 CUP OF LIQUID AND MEAT RESTING ON TRIVET | RELEASE |
|---|---|---|
| Chicken breasts (boneless or bone-in), 1 inch thick | 12 minutes | Quick |
| Chicken breasts (boneless), ¼ inch thick | 8 minutes | Quick |
| Chicken breasts (boneless), cut into bite-size pieces | 5 minutes | Quick |
| Chicken thighs (bone-in or boneless) | 8 minutes | Quick |
| Chicken thighs (boneless), cut into bite-size pieces | 5 minutes | Quick |
| Chicken drumsticks | 6 minutes | Quick |
| Chicken, whole | 25 minutes | 15-minute natural followed by quick |
| Duck breast or leg, confit | 10 minutes | 5-minute natural followed by quick |
| Duck, whole | 30 minutes | 15-minute natural followed by quick |
| Turkey, whole | 40–50 minutes | 12-minute natural followed by quick |
| Turkey breast (boneless or bone-in) | 35 minutes | 12-minute natural followed by quick |

- *All cook times are the suggested general times and will vary based on the quality, cut, and size of meat, as well as the dish you are using it in.*
- *For frozen cuts of meat, add 10–15 minutes of cook time. For a frozen whole chicken, duck, or turkey, thaw before cooking.*

# RICE & GRAINS

| GRAIN (ALL RINSED FOR 90 SECONDS) | GRAIN:LIQUID RATIO BY CUP:CUP | PRESSURE COOK TIME AT HIGH PRESSURE | RELEASE |
|---|---|---|---|
| White rice (jasmine, basmati, or long-grain) | 1:1 | 3 minutes | 10-minute natural followed by quick |
| Brown rice* | 1:1 | 15–25 minutes | 5- to 10-minute natural followed by quick (If going for 15 minutes, do a 10-minute natural release; for 25 minutes, do a 5-minute natural release. As the pressure time increases, the natural release time decreases—so adjust accordingly if cooking within this 10-minute range.) |
| Arborio rice (risotto) | 1:2 | 6 minutes | Quick |
| Wild rice | 1:2 | 25 minutes | 15-minute natural followed by quick |
| Quinoa | 1:1 | 1 minute | 10-minute natural followed by quick |
| Barley | 1:1½ | 15 minutes | 10-minute natural followed by quick |
| Couscous (not quick-cooking) | 1:2½ | 6 minutes | Quick |
| Polenta (not quick-cooking) | 1:4 | 9 minutes | Quick |
| Oats (steel-cut) | 1:2 | 3 minutes | 15-minute natural followed by quick |

- *For brown rice, you can go for 15 minutes with a 5-minute natural release for al dente rice and 25 minutes with a 10-minute natural release for softer rice.
- Cook your grains in broth instead of water to really enhance the flavor!
- Some people use a special rice measuring cup when measuring their rice. I don't. Use a regular measuring cup, the same as you would with liquid, for the ratios above.

# MEAT

| MEAT (3–6 POUNDS) | PRESSURE COOK TIME AT HIGH PRESSURE WITH 1 CUP OF LIQUID AND MEAT RESTING ON TRIVET | RELEASE |
|---|---|---|
| Beef roast (chuck, bottom, rump, round, brisket), whole | 60–75 minutes | 15-minute natural followed by quick |
| Beef roast (chuck, bottom, rump, round, brisket), cut into bite-size pieces | 15–20 minutes | 15-minute natural followed by quick |
| Beef stew meat, cut into bite-size pieces | 10–18 minutes (the longer, the more tender) | 5-minute natural followed by quick |
| Beef short ribs (boneless or bone-in) | 45 minutes | 15-minute natural followed by quick |
| Beef spare ribs (back) | 30 minutes | 15-minute natural followed by quick |
| Pork baby back ribs (back loin) | 30 minutes | 10-minute natural followed by quick |
| Pork spare ribs (St. Louis style) | 30 minutes | 10-minute natural followed by quick |
| Pork shoulder/butt | 60–90 minutes | 10-minute natural followed by quick |
| Pork tenderloin, cut into ½-inch-thick medallions | 8 minutes | 10-minute natural followed by quick |
| Pork chops (boneless or bone-in), ¾ inch thick | 8 minutes | 10-minute natural followed by quick |
| Lamb shanks | 40 minutes | 15-minute natural followed by quick |

- All cook times are the suggested general times and will vary based on the quality, cut, and size of meat, as well as the dish you are using it in.
- For frozen cuts of meat that are bite-size or larger chunks, add 5–10 minutes of cook time. For a frozen whole roast or pork shoulder, I strongly suggest thawing before cooking (see page 18) but if you just don't have the time for that, or simply forgot and have a hungry crew to feed, add another 15–20 minutes of cook time for a roast between 3 and 6 pounds.

# SEAFOOD

| SEAFOOD (1–3 POUNDS) | PRESSURE COOK TIME AT HIGH PRESSURE WITH 1 CUP OF LIQUID AND SEAFOOD RESTING ON TRIVET | RELEASE |
|---|---|---|
| General fish (salmon, halibut, cod, mahi-mahi, haddock, tilapia, etc.), ¼ to 1 inch thick | 3–4 minutes | Quick |
| Large/jumbo shrimp, tail on | 0–1 minute | Quick |
| Lobster tail | 4 minutes | Quick |
| Snow crab legs | 2 minutes | Quick |
| King crab legs | 3 minutes | Quick |
| Mussels, fresh | 2 minutes | Quick |
| Clams, fresh | 2 minutes | Quick |

* All cook times are the suggested general times and will vary based on the quality and size of the seafood, as well as the dish you are using it in.
* If using frozen seafood, increase the Pressure Cook time by 1 minute for shrimp and 2 minutes for everything else.

# BEANS & LEGUMES

| 1 POUND (RINSED) | PRESSURE COOK TIME AT HIGH PRESSURE, SOAKED IN SALTED WATER FOR 6–8 HOURS, THEN COOKED WITH 4 CUPS WATER OR BROTH | PRESSURE COOK TIME AT HIGH PRESSURE, UNSOAKED, COOKED WITH 4 CUPS WATER OR BROTH | RELEASE |
|---|---|---|---|
| Black | 15–20 minutes | 20–25 minutes | 15-minute natural followed by quick |
| Black-eyed peas | 10–15 minutes | 30–35 minutes | 15-minute natural followed by quick |
| Cannellini, great northern, or navy | 10–15 minutes | 35–45 minutes | 15-minute natural followed by quick |
| Chickpea/garbanzo | 15–20 minutes | 40–45 minutes | 15-minute natural followed by quick |
| Kidney | 15–20 minutes | 20–25 minutes | 15-minute natural followed by quick |
| Lima | 15–20 minutes | 25–30 minutes | 15-minute natural followed by quick |
| Pinto | N/A | 30–35 minutes | 15-minute natural followed by quick |
| Red | 15–20 minutes | 25–30 minutes | 15-minute natural followed by quick |
| Lentils (brown) | N/A | 10 minutes | Quick |
| Split peas (green or yellow) | N/A | 6 minutes | 15-minute natural followed by quick |

* All cook times are the suggested general times and may vary based on the dish you are using the beans in.

# VEGETABLES

| VEGETABLE | PRESSURE COOK TIME AT HIGH PRESSURE WITH 1 CUP OF LIQUID AND VEGGIES RESTING ON TRIVET OR IN STEAMER BASKET | RELEASE |
|---|---|---|
| Artichokes, whole | 12 minutes | Quick |
| Asparagus | 1 minute | Quick |
| Beets (larger require more time) | 15–25 minutes | Quick |
| Bell peppers, whole | 3 minutes | Quick |
| Broccoli florets | 1 minute | Quick |
| Brussels sprouts | 2 minutes | Quick |
| Cabbage, whole head | 8 minutes | Quick |
| Carrots | 2 minutes | Quick |
| Cauliflower, whole head | 4 minutes | Quick |
| Celery | 3 minutes | Quick |
| Corn, on the cob | 3 minutes | Quick |
| Eggplant, sliced | 2 minutes | Quick |
| Green beans | 3 minutes | Quick |
| Greens (collards, kale, spinach, etc.) | 4 minutes | Quick |
| Okra | 2 minutes | Quick |
| Onions, sliced | 4 minutes | Quick |
| Peas | 1 minute | Quick |
| Potatoes, peeled and cubed | 6 minutes | Quick |
| Potatoes, whole | 15 minutes | 10-minute natural followed by quick |
| Squash (butternut or acorn), halved | 6–10 minutes | Quick |
| Sweet potatoes | 10–15 minutes | 10-minute natural followed by quick |
| Tomatoes, whole | 3 minutes | Quick |
| Zucchini, sliced | 2 minutes | Quick |

* All cook times are the suggested general times and may vary based on the dish you are using the vegetables in.

* If veggies are frozen, add 1–2 minutes more.

I used to fear cooking. I didn't know how to cook most types of meat or veggies. Once I got the Instant Pot, I got this boost of confidence and excitement for cooking. I'm happy to say I have so much more confidence in the kitchen and actually get excited to put dinner down in front of my partner. I won't say I enjoy cooking itself yet, lol, but I'm getting there and the food is getting better and better. Thank you for inspiring and sharing your amazing recipes! Never had a better chicken and dumpling in my life (don't tell my mama).

LEXI • ROSEBURG, OREGON

When we were first dating, my husband made chicken pot pie. Everything smelled awesome, but the first bite was horrendous. He had thickened the gravy with powdered sugar instead of flour.

CONSTANCE • KEEGO HARBOR, MICHIGAN

# 1

# 7 INGREDIENTS
## · OR LESS ·

While I'm not generally known for using less than ten ingredients in a recipe (even if half are basic spices), I can't count how many requests I've received for recipes with a minimal number of ingredients. I've also seen cookbooks that claim to offer a maximum number of ingredients per recipe, but then include multiple spices that somehow don't count as one of those ingredients. No false advertising here—this chapter was carefully constructed to give you dynamite meals with a true, lucky seven ingredients (along with a few options should you wish to expand them ever so slightly).

One of my favorite things is to go out to dinner with friends and find something at the restaurant that is phenomenal. I'll then go home and research recipes and work at re-creating it. When it's close, everyone is invited over to dinner to have it again and play some cards....There may be a few bottles of wine to share. There's something special about sharing meals that brings back good memories and helps create new, beautiful memories.

CARLA • LOUISVILLE, KENTUCKY

♨ = AIR FRYER LID  = DAIRY-FREE

K = KETO  = GLUTEN-FREE

P = PALEO  = VEGETARIAN

+ = COMPLIANT WITH MODIFICATIONS  = VEGAN

# STRACCIATELLA SOUP
## ALLA ROMANA

**K**

**P** + *(see Lighter Comforts)*

**DF** + *(see Lighter Comforts)*

**GF**

**V** + *(if you're okay with eggs and using vegetable broth)*

If you know and love the classic Chinese egg drop soup, let's travel west to Italy and experience the Roman staple that boasts some of the same characteristics. *Stracciatella* means "rags," and that's exactly what appears once eggs are stirred into the hot broth and glorious trails of cheesy egg form. It's remarkable to me how so few ingredients can make a soup taste so vibrant, yet also remain quite light. Try adding the optional tortellini for extra comfort.

| Prep Time | Pressure Building Time | Pressure Cook Time | Sauté Time | Total Time | Serves |
|---|---|---|---|---|---|
| 2 MIN | 10–15 MIN | 3 MIN | 2–5 MIN | 20 MIN | 4–6 |

**6 cups chicken broth or vegetable broth**

**8 ounces baby spinach**

**4 large eggs, lightly beaten**

**¼ cup grated Parmesan cheese, plus additional for topping**

**1 tablespoon dried basil leaves**

**¼ teaspoon ground nutmeg**

**Seasoned salt, to taste (I use 2 teaspoons)**

**OPTIONAL**

**Black pepper, to taste (I use 1 teaspoon)**

**10–15 ounces fresh tortellini of your choice** (NOTE: You can usually find fresh tortellini in or near the refrigerated dairy section of your local supermarket—and Costco has a *great* one too, near the cheese section! Only add as much tortellini as you'll eat the first go-round—see Jeff's Tips.)

**1** Add the broth and spinach to the Instant Pot (it will seem like a *lot* of spinach in the pot, but it will cook down to practically nothing). Secure the lid and move the valve to the sealing position. Hit Manual or Pressure Cook on High Pressure for 3 minutes. Quick release when done.

**2** Combine the eggs, Parmesan, basil, and nutmeg in a bowl and whisk it all together.

**3** As soon as you remove the lid, stir the pot, hit Cancel, and then hit Sauté and Adjust to the More or High setting to bring the broth to a simmer (which will happen quickly).

**4** **Optional:** If you wish to add tortellini, do it now and cook according to package instructions (usually 3–4 minutes).

**5** Once the pot is simmering (and if you completed Step 4), hit Cancel to turn the pot off. Now, immediately and slowly pour the egg mixture into the Instant Pot in a drizzle-like fashion, using a large fork (**see Jeff's Tips**) to stir it around until the eggs cook and become a frayed and rag-like consistency, 60–90 seconds. Stir in the seasoned salt and pepper (if using) to taste, top with additional Parmesan, and serve.

 **lighter comforts** To make it dairy-free, either leave out the Parmesan or sub in nutritional yeast. This will also make it paleo.

**JEFF'S TIPS** To get the best ribbon-like texture with the egg, use a serving fork to handle the stirring. Pour in a little of the egg mixture at a time while "raking" it through the soup as the egg ribbons form. Repeat until all the egg is added and has formed into ribbons.

Tortellini will soak up a lot of liquid if sitting in soup or broth for a long period of time, so if you plan on adding tortellini to your soup *and* saving some for leftovers, it's best to only add the tortellini you'll need for the first serving. Then, as you reheat the soup, cook any additional tortellini and add them before enjoying!

# CACIO E PEPE

Have you ever wanted to whip something special up but only have a box of spaghetti, pepper, some grated cheese, butter, and broth on hand? Good news: All it takes are these very five ingredients to make my spin on one of the simplest, yet most comforting and beloved Roman dishes ever. *Cacio e pepe* translates as "cheese and pepper" which also translates as "comfort and joy." My version adds additional flavor by using broth in place of water; the pasta absorbs the broth along with the butter while cooking to give it a slightly creamy edge.

 *(if using vegetable or garlic broth)*

| Prep Time | Pressure Building Time | Pressure Cook Time | Total Time | Serves |
|---|---|---|---|---|
| 2 MIN | 10–15 MIN | 8 MIN | 20 MIN | 4–6 |

**4 cups chicken broth, vegetable broth, or garlic broth** (e.g., Garlic Better Than Bouillon)

**1 pound spaghetti**

**8 tablespoons (1 stick) salted butter, divided into 1-tablespoon pats**

**1 cup grated Pecorino Romano or Parmesan (or ½ cup of each), plus more for serving**

**1 tablespoon cracked black pepper** (NOTE: For best results, freshly crack the pepper with a pepper mill), **plus more to taste**

**1** Pour the broth into the Instant Pot, break the spaghetti over it and add to the broth, then follow with 4 tablespoons of the butter.

**2** Secure the lid and move the valve to the sealing position. Hit Manual or Pressure Cook on High Pressure for 8 minutes. Quick release when done. (NOTE: The pasta will appear soupy once the lid comes off. This is what we want because adding the dairy will thicken it up perfectly.)

**3** Stir in the remaining 4 tablespoons butter until melted, then add the cheese and stir until well combined. The sauce will thicken as soon as the cheese is absorbed, which is almost immediately.

**4** Add the cracked black pepper and give it a final stir. Add more pepper to taste.

**5** Transfer the pasta to bowls and top with more cheese and pepper, if desired.

 *lighter comforts* Use ghee instead of butter.

**JEFF'S TIPS** If you want this to be a more traditional cacio e pepe, use water instead of broth and skip the butter. However, you will run the risk of the spaghetti clumping together when pressure cooked without the butter to keep it slick and independent.

If you want the sauce creamier (though less traditional in a cacio e pepe), add ½ cup heavy cream, half-and-half, or an unsweetened nondairy milk and an additional ¼ cup cheese in Step 3.

Due to the heavy buttery/cheesy nature of this dish, it's best eaten immediately and when freshly made.

Any leftovers stored in the fridge will dry out quickly due to the amount of butter and cheese absorbed by the pasta. So if reheating in the microwave or pot, add a little cream or any type of milk, then add a little more cheese after cooking and mix it up!

# RUBY RICE

Like Dorothy's ruby slippers, this simple, savory, tomato-infused rice reminds me of home—along with the countless entrees I've served alongside it. The colorful rice pairs well with nearly any dish, with cumin, chili powder, and paprika adding depth and complex layers of spice throughout. This will go beautifully with the Chicken Mole on page 171 or the Korean Beef Bulgogi Tacos on page 206.

| Prep Time | Pressure Building Time | Pressure Cook Time | Natural Release Time | Total Time | Serves |
|---|---|---|---|---|---|
| 2 MIN | 5–10 MIN | 3 MIN | 10 MIN | 20 MIN | 4–6 |

**2 cups long-grain white rice (jasmine or basmati preferred), rinsed for 90 seconds in cold water**

**2 cups garlic broth (e.g., Garlic Better Than Bouillon) or vegetable broth**

**2 tablespoons extra-virgin olive oil**

**1 tablespoon ground cumin**

**2 teaspoons chili powder**

**2 cups thin, red salsa of your choice (I find Pace Picante perfect for this)**

**1–3 teaspoons paprika (start with less and increase to taste)**

**1** With the exception of the salsa and paprika, add all the ingredients to the Instant Pot and stir. Top with the salsa but *do not stir!* Just gently smooth it out so it's spread evenly over the top.

**2** Secure the lid and move the valve to the sealing position. Hit Manual or Pressure Cook on High Pressure for 3 minutes. When done, allow a 10-minute natural release followed by a quick release.

**3** Stir the rice, add paprika to taste, make sure all is combined, and enjoy.

*lighter comforts* Should you wish to use brown rice instead of white, simply increase the pressure cook time to 15 minutes for a more al dente brown rice, or up to 25 minutes for a softer one (brown rice cooks a bit longer than white). Natural release time would then be 10 minutes and 5 minutes, respectively.

**JEFF'S TIP** If you're craving beans, add 1 to 2 (15.5-ounce) cans beans of your choice (rinsed and drained) in Step 3. You can also give it a squeeze of lime just before serving.

# DRESS-IT-YOURSELF SHREDDED CHICKEN

When it comes to making healthy, juicy, shredded chicken, the Instant Pot is well worth the price of admission. Whether you choose to keep it naked or toss it in a BBQ sauce, or to use it to make chicken salad, top a salad, or add to a soup (like my Potato Leek, page 84), it's laughably easy to achieve. Any way we serve it, we're gonna dress it up in our love!

 K  DF

 P  GF

| Prep Time | Pressure Building Time | Pressure Cook Time | Total Time | Serves |
|-----------|------------------------|--------------------|------------|--------|
| 2 MIN | 5–10 MIN | 12 MIN | 20 MIN | 4–6 |

**1 cup chicken broth**

**½ teaspoon kosher salt**

**½ teaspoon black pepper**

**2 pounds boneless, skinless chicken breasts, about ½ inch thick (see Jeff's Tips)**

### OPTIONAL DRESSINGS

**Any additional sauces or seasonings you wish to mix in with the chicken: barbecue sauce, buffalo wing sauce, mayo, lemon, salad dressing—whatever and how much of anything you like! I start with ½ cup sauce and add more accordingly.**

**1** Add the broth, salt, and pepper to the Instant Pot and stir.

**2** Lay in the chicken breasts. Secure the lid and move the valve to the sealing position. Hit Manual or Pressure Cook on High Pressure for 12 minutes. Quick release when done.

**3** Using tongs, remove the chicken from the pot and place in a large mixing bowl. Shred using two forks—or a hand mixer to make life that much easier.

**4** Once the chicken's shredded, stir in about ¼ cup of the broth the chicken cooked in to keep it moist. Now comes the time to dress it up. Add whatever sauce, seasoning, or condiment you wish—your chicken, your rules. Of course, you don't need to add any sauce. It will taste delicious as is—like a skinless rotisserie chicken!

**5** Serve hot or pop in the fridge in an airtight container and chill before serving.

*lighter comforts* Keeping this naked with a little lemon squeezed over it is as healthy as it gets, folks. It makes for a meal *loaded* with tasty protein.

**JEFF'S TIPS** If using very thick breasts, slice them so they're no more than ½ inch thick. Or, if your breasts are thick and you don't feel like slicing them, go for 17 minutes of pressure cooking.

This will keep for up to 3 days in the fridge, or you can freeze any extra in an airtight container.

# SWEET & SOUR
# CHICKEN

It's amazing how a bottle of Catalina salad dressing, along with a few sweet and a few sour players, can create a truly out-of-this-world sweet and sour sauce. One bite of this super popular, vibrant chicken dish will give you a tropical vibe and may summon some breezy beach vibes—which is good because it's super breezy to make. Make it a spicy sunset with Fire Fried Rice (page 133).

**DF**

**GF**

| Prep Time | Pressure Building Time | Pressure Cook Time | Sauté Time | Total Time | Serves |
|---|---|---|---|---|---|
| 5 MIN | 10–15 MIN | 8 MIN | 3 MIN | 30 MIN | 4–6 |

1 (16-ounce) bottle Catalina salad dressing (or California French—same thing)

2/3 cup honey

2 tablespoons apple cider vinegar

2 red bell peppers, seeded and coarsely diced (optional)

3 pounds boneless, skinless chicken thighs, cut into bite-size pieces

2½ tablespoons cornstarch

1 (20-ounce) can pineapple chunks, drained (optional)

**1** Add the Catalina dressing, honey, and cider vinegar to the Instant Pot. Whisk the mixture together so it forms a sauce.

**2** If using the bell peppers, add them and stir. Lay the chicken thighs on top. Secure the lid and move the valve to the sealing position. Hit Manual or Pressure Cook on High Pressure for 8 minutes. Quick release when done.

**3** Meanwhile, make a slurry in a small bowl by mixing together the cornstarch with 2½ tablespoons cold water until smooth.

**4** Carefully remove the chicken with tongs and place in a serving dish. Hit Cancel and then Sauté so it's on the More or High setting. Once bubbling, add the cornstarch slurry while constantly stirring. Let bubble for 30 seconds. Turn the pot off by hitting Cancel. If using the pineapple chunks, add them now. Let the sauce cool for 3–5 minutes, after which it will thicken nicely.

 **5** Ladle the sauce over the chicken and serve.

*lighter comforts* Feel free to sub light Catalina dressing for regular.

**JEFF'S TIP** The optional pineapple and red peppers really just complement the dish and its flavors perfectly. But if they're not your style and you want more than just the chicken and sauce, feel free to use other veggies in Step 2 (like Vidalia onion) or fruits in Step 4 (like maraschino cherries).

# NAKED EGG ROLLS

If you've been with me for a while, you're well aware that my love for Chinese-American food knows no bounds, and egg rolls are at the top of my list. But say we want to deconstruct the roll and focus on that unmistakable filling: We're about to make that happen, and with a bunch of finishing options. Whether you want it on its own, tucked into a lettuce wrap, served over rice, or scooped up in a crispy wonton skin as we usually know it, there are many ways to rock the flavor of an egg roll.

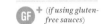

*(if using gluten-free sauces)*

| Prep Time | Sauté Time | Pressure Building Time | Pressure Cook Time | Total Time | Serves |
|---|---|---|---|---|---|
| 5 MIN | 9 MIN | 5–10 MIN | 2 MIN | 25 MIN | 4–6 |

**¼ cup sesame oil (any kind)**

**1 (12- to 14-ounce) bag shredded green cabbage or coleslaw mix**

**1 pound ground pork**

**¼ cup (½ cup if using an 8-quart pot) beef broth or ham broth (e.g., Ham Better Than Bouillon)**

**¼ cup low-sodium soy sauce, tamari, or coconut aminos**

**¼ cup hoisin sauce**

**¼ cup oyster sauce**

**OPTIONAL FINISHES**

**Wonton crisps (<u>see Jeff's Tips</u>)**

**Chow mein noodles**

**Scallions, sliced**

**Bibb lettuce**

**Cooked white or brown rice (see page 29)**

**1** Add the sesame oil to the Instant Pot. Hit Sauté and Adjust so it's on the More or High setting. After 3 minutes of heating, add the cabbage and sauté for 3 minutes, until softened.

**2** Add the pork, breaking it up with a mixing spoon, and sauté for about 3 minutes, until crumbled and lightly browned.

**3** Add the broth and soy sauce and stir, deglazing the bottom of the pot. Secure the lid and move the valve to the sealing position. Hit Cancel and then Manual or Pressure Cook for 2 minutes. Quick release when done.

CONTINUES

**4** Add the hoisin and oyster sauce, stir until combined, and let rest for 5 minutes. Using a slotted spoon (so any excess liquid drains), serve on its own or with any of the optional finishes.

*lighter comforts* If you can't tolerate soy, use coconut aminos instead of the soy sauce.

You can also use gluten-free hoisin and oyster sauce (found in markets or online) and tamari or coconut aminos to make it gluten-free.

**JEFF'S TIP** You can usually find wonton crisps in the same section as croutons, but to make them yourself, simply grab some wonton wrappers from the market (usually in the freezer section), let them thaw, and slice in half so they're triangles (or semi-circles, depending on the shape of your wrappers). Place them on a parchment paper–lined baking sheet, *lightly* brush some canola, vegetable, or soybean oil on each side, and bake in a preheated 400°F oven for 10–15 minutes, until golden brown. If you wish to air fry, brush with oil and bake at 375°F for 3–5 minutes, until crisped. Of course, for the best experience, you can deep fry them at 375°F for about 3 minutes, until crisped.

Cooking is my therapy. If I've had a crap day (or week), I go to the kitchen and cook everything under the sun. I started cooking full meals for my family at 14. I learned a lot by watching my mom and grandma in the kitchen. I'm lucky enough to still have my mom when I get myself into a pickle in the kitchen, even though she's no longer able to cook. Feeding my family makes me happy. Food = Love.

**SUSAN · UNIONTOWN, PENNSYLVANIA**

Cooking is a mental distraction for me. I enjoy it. It makes me focus on just that and helps me forget about my stress for a while. Certain foods also trigger happy memories. Like black raspberry pie for my birthday every year and my mom's porcupines that she makes in her stovetop pressure cooker. Getting *both* of those on my birthday made for a perfect birthday.

KEN · **ROCKFORD, ILLINOIS**

About ten years ago I moved in with my daughter, and my interest in cooking started to wane. Honestly I was bored out of my mind. Then one day my daughter saw an ad for an Instant Pot and talked to me about getting it. I thought, alright, this might be interesting…. Well, the rest is history. I now have three Instant Pots of different sizes, and I have made all kinds of meals in them. It was one of the best things that I have ever bought. I have made your recipes and enjoyed them immensely. I look forward to the batch of recipes from the Blue Book (lol). Thanks for sharing your passion for delicious food.

LOIS · **ONTARIO, OTTAWA, CANADA**

# DULCE DE LECHE

DF⁺ (see Lighter Comforts)

GF

V

VN⁺ (see Lighter Comforts)

*Dulce de leche,* Spanish for "a sweet made of milk," is beyond decadent; and while not the same thing as caramel, it has a similar incredible flavor (but even better). All it takes is a can of sweetened condensed milk and a little vanilla to achieve the simplest, most comforting, silky dessert topping that's perfect for drizzling on cheesecake, cookies, or pretzels or for dipping apples directly into. Don't forget to top it with some sea salt.

| Prep Time | Pressure Building Time | Pressure Cook Time | Cooling Time | Total Time | Serves |
|---|---|---|---|---|---|
| 1 MIN | 10–15 MIN | 40 MIN | 20 MIN | 1 HR 15 MIN | 4 |

**1 (14-ounce) can sweetened condensed milk**

**1 teaspoon vanilla extract**

SERVING SUGGESTIONS

**A sprinkle of sea salt in a ramekin**

**On cheesecake (page 271)**

**In a pie crust, refrigerated and topped with whipped cream**

**Sliced apples, for dipping**

**Pretzel rods, for dipping**

**Shortbread cookies, for dipping**

**Pound cake, for dipping**

**Ice cream, for topping**

**1** Remove the label and lid from the can of condensed milk and securely cover the top of the can with foil. (NOTE: You absolutely must remove the lid from the can, which is why we place foil over it once the lid is removed—it is super dangerous to cook a can with its lid still sealed on.)

**2** Add the trivet to the Instant Pot, place the foil-wrapped can of condensed milk on top, and pour enough water into the pot (*not* directly on top of the can, but on the sides) so that the can is halfway submerged in the water (8–9 cups water in a 6-quart pot).

**3** Secure the lid and move the valve to the sealing position. Hit Manual or Pressure Cook on High Pressure for 40 minutes. Quick release when done.

CONTINUES

**4** Using mitts, carefully remove the can from the pot (it will be hot) and place on the countertop. Remove the foil and let the milk cool for 20 minutes. You'll see it will have transformed from ordinary condensed milk into a beautiful dulce de leche!

**5** Add the vanilla extract directly to the can and stir well for about 2 minutes, until it goes from a lumpy consistency to a creamy one. (The can may still be hot so it's best to hold it with a dish towel while stirring with the other hand.)

**6** And now, the sky's the limit as to what you can do with it.

*lighter comforts* Make it dairy-free and vegan with sweetened condensed coconut milk instead! Pressure cook for 20 minutes with a 10-minute natural release.

**JEFF'S TIP** You can totally do more than one can at once; two or three will fit in the pot. The cooking time will remain the same.

> My mom has always been a great cook and an incredibly talented lady, winning prizes for her sewing and other creations. Sadly, over the past year, she started to manifest signs of dementia and early onset Alzheimer's, which made it very difficult for her to cook, let alone pursue her hobbies.
>
> My dad has been a star taking care of her, but a couple of months ago he suffered a heart attack and had to have heart surgery. That's when I came to stay with them. My mom wants to cook, but she gets easily confused and even cooking things she's made a thousand times before is extremely difficult.
>
> The way you present your recipes has enabled her to cook again, and I can't tell you what it felt like to see her light up because she could prepare food like she used to. She was so happy to regain a measure of her independence. My dad also loves your recipes.
>
> Thank you so much for helping my mom to once again cook and put meals she's prepared on the table. It has given her back some of what her illness has taken from her.
>
> There is an elderly couple in suburban Québec City who are huge fans of "the nice man with the cute little dog that cooks on YouTube."
>
> **MARC · GATINEAU, QUEBEC**

# CORNED BEEF HASH

If you catch me on a day when I'm craving breakfast, corned beef hash is the first thing I want. But sometimes when I'm out for breakfast at a diner, I get served the stuff out of a can and it just about ruins my day. So it became a mission of mine to make the most deluxe and hearty version I could right at home.

  *(if using oil)*

| Prep Time | Pressure Building Time | Pressure Cook Time | Natural Release Time | Sauté Time | Optional Crisping Time | Total Time | Serves |
|---|---|---|---|---|---|---|---|
| 10 MIN | 5–10 MIN | 10 MIN | 5 MIN | 10 MIN | 5–10 MIN | 40 MIN | 4 |

**1 pound uncooked point-cut corned beef brisket (make sure it's corned and not regular brisket), cut into small chunks**

**1 pound unpeeled baby potatoes (I use a mix of white and red), quartered**

**3 tablespoons salted butter or 3 tablespoons vegetable oil**

**1 large yellow onion, diced**

**3 cloves garlic, minced or pressed**

**1/2 teaspoon garlic salt**

**1/2 teaspoon black pepper**

**1** Pour 1 cup water into the Instant Pot. Lay in a steamer basket, add the corned beef, and top with the potatoes. Secure the lid and move the valve to the sealing position. Hit Manual or Pressure Cook on High Pressure for 10 minutes. When done, allow a 5-minute natural release followed by a quick release and hit Cancel to turn the pot off.

**2** Remove the steamer basket followed by the liner pot. Drain the liner pot, wipe it dry, and return it to the Instant Pot.

**3** Hit Sauté and Adjust so it's on the More or High setting. Add the butter or oil. Once bubbling/heated, add the onion and garlic and sauté for 5 minutes, until softened.

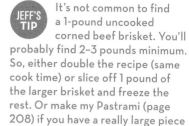

**4** Add the potatoes and corned beef, along with the garlic salt and black pepper. Sauté for another 3–5 minutes, until browned to your liking, and serve.

**5** **Optional:** If you wish to give it all a really nice final roasting crisp, smooth everything out in the pot, add the air fryer lid, hit Broil (400°F) for 5 minutes, and then hit Start. When the time is up, check on it and stir it up. If you want it more well done, add a few more minutes with the air fryer lid.

*lighter comforts* I prefer butter over the oil for this recipe, but you can use ghee instead if that better fits your lifestyle.

**JEFF'S TIP** It's not common to find a 1-pound uncooked corned beef brisket. You'll probably find 2–3 pounds minimum. So, either double the recipe (same cook time) or slice off 1 pound of the larger brisket and freeze the rest. Or make my Pastrami (page 208) if you have a really large piece remaining.

# MUSSELS
## · FRA DIAVOLO ·

 K<sup>+</sup> *(if using sugar-free marinara)*

P<sup>+</sup> *(if using sugar-free marinara)*

DF

GF

It now seems tradition for me to include a mussel recipe in each of my books. But since they're done so quickly, are foolproof, and taste so good in the Instant Pot, can you blame me? This time, I'll focus on a red sauce with a spicy kick. But if a little extra isn't the way you like to roll, simply leave out the hot sauce. Sop up any juices with some garlic toast or Italian bread.

| Prep Time | Pressure Building Time | Pressure Cook Time | Total Time | Serves |
|---|---|---|---|---|
| 5 MIN | 5–10 MIN | 3 MIN | 15 MIN | 4–6 |

1 cup vegetable broth

¼ cup hot sauce (optional)

1 teaspoon crushed red pepper flakes or Zatarain's Concentrated Shrimp & Crab Boil (optional)

3–5 pounds mussels, rinsed and debearded (toss out any that have opened before cooking)

2 cups marinara sauce, at room temperature (I like Victoria and Rao's brands)

10 cloves garlic, sliced

1 cup loosely packed fresh basil

**1** Add the broth, hot sauce (if using), and pepper flakes or Zatarain's (if using) to the Instant Pot. Stir until combined.

**2** Add the mussels and top with the marinara, garlic, and basil, but *do not stir.*

 *lighter comforts* This is already a pretty light dish, but feel free to use a low-salt marinara sauce.

 **JEFF'S TIP** To make this a complete dinner, serve over angel hair pasta.

**3** Secure the lid and move the valve to the sealing position. Hit Manual or Pressure Cook on High Pressure for 3 minutes. Quick release when done. Serve immediately.

# MELT-IN-YOUR-MOUTH POTATOES

 *(see Jeff's Tip)*

 DF + *(see Lighter Comforts)*

 GF

 V

Potatoes are probably the most comforting vegetable around—and you can do as much to them as what Bubba Gump can do with shrimp. One of my favorite ways to serve them is to give them a bit of a crispy exterior with a melt-in-your-mouth interior, and I'll even up the ante by coating them in a buttery Parmesan sauce. Melts in your mouth like butta!

| Prep Time | Sauté Time | Pressure Building Time | Pressure Cook Time | Optional Crisping Time | Total Time | Serves |
|---|---|---|---|---|---|---|
| 5 MIN | 15 MIN | 5–10 MIN | 2 MIN | 5–10 MIN | 25–30 MIN | 4 |

- ¾ cup (1½ sticks) salted butter, plus more if needed
- 2 pounds unpeeled white or Yukon Gold potatoes, rinsed and sliced into ½-inch disks

- 6 cloves garlic, minced or pressed
- 1 cup garlic broth (e.g., Garlic Better Than Bouillon) or vegetable broth

- 2 teaspoons dried thyme
- 1 teaspoon ground sage
- ¼ cup grated Parmesan cheese
- 2 sprigs fresh rosemary (optional)

**1** Add the butter to the Instant Pot, hit Sauté, and Adjust so it's on the Normal or Medium setting. Once the butter's melted and bubbling, add a layer of potatoes (you'll do this in about two batches). Allow to brown for 5 minutes, then flip over to sear the other side of each potato for 1–2 minutes. Use tongs to transfer the potatoes to a plate and repeat the process for the remaining potatoes, adding more butter if needed.

**2** Add the garlic and sauté in the remaining butter for 1 minute. Add the broth, thyme, and sage and stir well, deglazing the bottom of the pot.

**3** Place the steamer basket or trivet in the pot with the handles facing up and stack the seared potatoes on it. Secure the lid and move the valve to the sealing position. Hit Cancel, and then Manual or Pressure Cook on High Pressure for 2 minutes. Quick release when done.

**4** Carefully remove the trivet or steamer basket along with the potatoes and place the potatoes in a serving dish.

**5** Hit Cancel, then hit Sauté and Adjust so it's on the More or High setting. Once bubbling, stir the Parmesan into the sauce left in the pot and allow it to bubble for 3–5 minutes. Hit Cancel to turn the pot off. Drape some of the butter sauce (you won't use it all) over the potatoes and serve topped with fresh rosemary, if desired.

*lighter comforts* To make it dairy-free, you can use about ½ cup extra-virgin olive oil instead of butter and sub nutritional yeast for the Parmesan (or just leave it out).

**JEFF'S TIP** As implied in Step 5, this sauce is very butter-laden. It's designed to be more of a drizzle over the potatoes than a slather. That said, any leftover sauce would be wondrous over rice, pasta, or veggies.

**6** **For an optional, crispier finish:** After removing the potatoes in Step 4 and after finishing the sauce in Step 5, in batches, carefully add the potatoes to the top tier of the air fryer basket and lay it in the liner pot. Add the air fryer lid, hit Broil (400°F) for 5 minutes, and hit Start. When the time is up, see if you've attained the desired crispiness. If not, broil for up to 5 more minutes, until crisped to your desire. Then, transfer the potatoes to a serving dish, drape the sauce over them, and serve.

# 2

# SOUPS & STEWS

I could write an entire cookbook on soups and stews. I love sitting on my couch with a ladled helping in an oversized mug or crock. Whether they're light or rich or creamy or clear, to me soups are the epitome of comfort food. This chapter is a treasure chest of some of my best and favorites. My suggestion? Try them all. One spoonful of any and you'll be wrapped up in a blanket of love and comfort.

> My sister made a cake from scratch. It called for cinnamon, but she accidentally used cumin. She was going to throw the cake away. Dad wouldn't let her. He eventually ate the whole, disgusting cake.
> JENNIFER • NEW LONDON, IOWA

 = AIR FRYER LID    DF = DAIRY-FREE

K = KETO    GF = GLUTEN-FREE

P = PALEO    V = VEGETARIAN

⁺ = COMPLIANT WITH MODIFICATION    VN = VEGAN

# FRENCH ONION SOUP

K + (see Lighter Comforts)

P + (see Lighter Comforts)

DF + (see Lighter Comforts)

GF + (if using gluten-free croutons)

V + (see Lighter Comforts)

In my first book, I made French Onion Chicken that became an instant household staple. Now it's time to pay homage to the soup that inspired it. The iconic French soup can vary greatly based on who makes it. Mine is loaded with deep, rich flavor and has the perfect balance of fork-tender onions and a sweet and savory broth. Serving it in a crock allows us to top it with a rink of cheese resting on bread (in my case, croutons—which are far easier and less messy to eat in this soup). Then, it's broiled so the cheese is bubbly-brown as it cascades down the sides, making it as drool-worthy as this headnote.

| Prep Time | Sauté Time | Pressure Building Time | Pressure Cook Time | Broiling Time | Total Time | Serves |
|---|---|---|---|---|---|---|
| 10 MIN | 10–15 MIN | 10–15 MIN | 8 MIN | 3–5 MIN | 45 MIN | 4–6 |

**4 tablespoons (½ stick) salted butter**

**4 large onions (I used one of each: Vidalia [sweet], red, yellow, and Spanish), sliced into long strips**

**2 tablespoons light brown sugar, divided**

**4 cups beef broth, vegetable broth, or onion broth (e.g., Sautéed Onion Better Than Bouillon)**

**1 cup dry red wine (like a pinot noir)**

**1 tablespoon Worcestershire sauce**

**2 teaspoons dried thyme**

**3 teaspoons seasoned salt, divided**

**1 teaspoon garlic powder**

**1 teaspoon black pepper, divided**

**2 bay leaves**

**Croutons of your choice (buy a small bag of your favorite)**

**Provolone and Swiss/Gruyère slices**

**Shaved Asiago (optional)**

**Paprika, for topping**

**1** Add the butter to the Instant Pot, hit Sauté, and Adjust so it's on the More or High setting.

**2** Once the butter is melted and bubbling, add the onions and 1 tablespoon of the brown sugar and stir regularly for 10–15 minutes, until the onions have cooked down by about half, become translucent, and have a pasta-like consistency. Make sure they aren't too firm or too mushy!

**3** Add the broth, red wine, Worcestershire sauce, thyme, 1½ teaspoons of the seasoned salt, garlic powder, and ½ teaspoon of the pepper and stir. Top with the bay leaves. Secure the lid and move the valve to the sealing position. Hit Cancel, and then hit Manual or Pressure Cook on High Pressure for 8 minutes. Quick release when done. Preheat the oven to broil.

CONTINUES

**4** Remove and discard the bay leaves. Stir in the remaining 1 tablespoon brown sugar, 1½ teaspoons seasoned salt, and ½ teaspoon pepper. Taste the soup and, if desired (although I think it's perfect as is), add additional sugar, seasoned salt, and pepper as you see fit.

**5** Place oven-safe crocks on a baking sheet. Ladle the soup into the crocks (**see Jeff's Tips**) until it comes up just below the brim of each. Layer the croutons on top of the soup so that they stick up just above the surface of the brim and serve as a foundation for the cheese. Seal the crock with one slice of provolone and then layer one slice of Swiss/Gruyère and a few flakes of the Asiago (if using). Sprinkle lightly with some paprika.

**6** Pop the baking sheet into the oven. Watch carefully for 3–5 minutes, until the cheese begins to bubble, turns bubbly-brown, and forms a cheese-like crust. Don't let it overcook, as you don't want the cheese to burn!

**7** Using oven mitts, carefully remove the sheet from the oven and let rest for 2 minutes. Keeping the mitts on, gently place each crock (they will be super hot) on a plate, then savor every slurping second.

*lighter comforts* If you want a keto-friendly soup, use 1 tablespoon monk fruit sweetener in place of the brown sugar, sub sugar-free steak sauce for the Worcestershire, and leave out the croutons. Try to add as much onion to each crock as possible so the cheese has something to rest on, otherwise it'll sink.

If you want it paleo, use ghee instead of butter, replace the brown sugar with 2 tablespoons pure maple syrup, sub sugar-free steak sauce for the Worcestershire, and leave out the croutons and cheese.

To make it dairy-free, sub ¼ cup vegetable oil for the butter and leave out the cheese (or use a plant-based one).

To make it vegetarian, use a vegetable-based broth and sugar-free steak sauce in place of the Worcestershire.

**JEFF'S TIPS** There are a few different crock sizes that can be found online in sets of four or six. If you have 10- to 12-ounce crocks (standard), follow the cheese-topping as written in Step 5. But if you have larger, 16- to 18-ounce crocks (which typically have handles and are designed for a full meal), you'll want to double the cheese so it fits properly (any excuse for more cheese, right?). In this case, seal with two slices of provolone so they overlap on the edges and in the center and lay in two slices of Swiss in a crisscross fashion. Then, top with the optional Asiago flakes and paprika.

When layering the cheese, leave some of the Swiss a little over the edges so when it bakes, it coats the sides of the crock for drool-factor. Peeling the cheese off is one of the best parts of the French onion soup experience!

# THE BEST
# BEEF STEW

 K <sup>+</sup> *(see Lighter Comforts)*

 P <sup>+</sup> *(see Lighter Comforts)*

DF

 GF <sup>+</sup> *(see Lighter Comforts)*

If you thought the best way to make the grandest beef stew was in a slow cooker, the Instant Pot will make you rethink that. You'll have this ready in a fraction of the time, but with even richer flavor, making this stew one of the easiest, tastiest, and most tender dishes you can create. This classic, hearty dinner is a total winner.

| Prep Time | Sauté Time | Pressure Building Time | Pressure Cook Time | Natural Release Time | Total Time | Serves |
|---|---|---|---|---|---|---|
| 10 MIN | 10 MIN | 15–20 MIN | 20 MIN | 10 MIN | 1 HR 10 MIN | 6–8 |

- 3 pounds chuck roast (nice and marbled), sliced into 1-inch bite-size chunks; or beef stew meat
- 2 teaspoons garlic salt
- 2 teaspoons black pepper
- 1 teaspoon Italian seasoning
- 1 teaspoon garlic powder
- 1 teaspoon onion powder
- ¼ cup extra-virgin olive oil
- 1 large yellow onion, diced
- 2 ribs celery, diced, with leafy tops reserved

- 8 ounces baby bella mushrooms, sliced (optional)
- 3 cloves garlic, minced or pressed
- 2 tablespoons Worcestershire sauce
- ¼ cup all-purpose flour
- 4 cups beef broth
- 1 cup dry red wine (like a pinot noir), or additional 1 cup beef broth
- 1 teaspoon dried rosemary
- 1 teaspoon dried thyme

- 1 tablespoon light or dark brown sugar
- 2 bay leaves
- 1 (16-ounce) bag baby carrots, halved
- 1 pound unpeeled baby red and/or white potatoes, rinsed and halved
- 10 ounces frozen cut green beans (optional)
- 1 (6-ounce) can tomato paste
- 1 (1-ounce) packet au jus dip or beefy onion dip mix (optional)

**1** Place the meat in a large bowl and add the garlic salt, black pepper, Italian seasoning, garlic powder, and onion powder. Mix by hand until well-coated and set aside.

**2** Add the oil to the Instant Pot, hit Sauté, and Adjust so it's on the More or High setting. After 3 minutes, add the onion, celery, and mushrooms (if using) and sauté for 3 minutes, until slightly softened. Add the garlic and sauté for 1 minute longer.

**3** Add the Worcestershire, scrape up any browned bits, and let simmer with the veggies for 1 minute.

CONTINUES

**4** Add the seasoned meat and sauté, stirring often, for about 3 minutes, until the edges are just lightly browned.

**5** Add the flour and stir until everything is coated.

**6** Add the broth, wine, rosemary, thyme, and brown sugar and stir well, deglazing the bottom of the pot. Top with the bay leaves, carrots, potatoes, and green beans (if using) but *do not stir them in.* Just rest them on top of everything in the pot.

**7** Secure the lid and move the valve to the sealing position. Hit Cancel followed by Manual or Pressure Cook on High Pressure for 20 minutes. When done, allow a 10-minute natural release followed by a quick release.

**8** Discard the bay leaves and add the tomato paste, leafy celery tops, and seasoning packet (if using). Stir well and let rest for 10 minutes. As it cools down a bit, it will thicken into the perfect consistency and allow the flavors to really come together. Ladle into bowls and serve with some crusty French or garlic bread.

Eating is a necessity, dining is an art form. I remember as a child feeling a house transition to a home when guests were coming. Food preparation became a delicate dance of flavors, each course interacting with another to tell a story.

Recently we had friends over for "formal sweatpants Sunday." Everyone was comfortable and the table was set to the nines!

JIM • **PORT JEFFERSON, NEW YORK**

 *lighter comforts* If you want this to be keto or paleo, leave out the brown sugar and potatoes and use coconut flour instead of all-purpose. Using coconut flour will also make it gluten-free.

For less sodium, use low-sodium broth and salt-free tomato paste and leave out the au jus mix.

 **JEFF'S TIP** Some also love this with Guinness beer in place of the wine. Feel free to give it a shot.

# BROCCOLI CHEDDAR SOUP

 **K** + *(if using coconut flour and sugar-free steak sauce)*

**GF** + *(if using coconut flour)*

**V** + *(if using garlic or vegetable broth and sugar-free steak sauce)*

If there's a soup that's more eye-catching, enticing, and familiar than this one, I've yet to find it. As spectacular as it is silky, as cheesy as it is creamy, and as classic as it is comforting, this gold standard of broccoli-cheddar soup reigns "soup"reme and delivers on all fronts. Go on, slurp away.

| Prep Time | Sauté Time | Pressure Building Time | Pressure Cook Time | Total Time | Serves |
|---|---|---|---|---|---|
| 10 MIN | 10 MIN | 10–15 MIN | 5 MIN | 40 MIN | 4–6 |

- 8 tablespoons (1 stick) salted butter
- 1 Spanish or red onion, diced
- 1 red bell pepper, seeded and diced
- 2 medium carrots, peeled and diced
- 3 ribs celery, diced
- 8 ounces baby bella mushrooms, sliced (optional, but adds some serious flavor)

- ½ cup all-purpose, whole-wheat, quinoa, or coconut flour
- 6 cups chicken broth, vegetable broth, or garlic broth (e.g., Garlic Better Than Bouillon)
- 32–48 ounces (2–3 pounds) frozen or fresh broccoli florets, divided
- 1 cup heavy cream or half-and-half
- 1 tablespoon dried thyme
- 2 teaspoons seasoned salt or Cajun/Creole/Louisiana Seasoning (I use Tony Chachere's), or 1 teaspoon of each

- 1 teaspoon garlic powder
- 1 pound shredded sharp Cheddar cheese
- 1 (5.2-ounce) package Boursin herb cheese (optional, any flavor), cut into small chunks
- 1 tablespoon Worcestershire sauce or sugar-free steak sauce
- Croutons, for topping (optional)

**1** Add the butter to the Instant Pot, hit Sauté, and Adjust so it's on the More or High setting. Once the butter's melted, add the onion, pepper, carrots, celery, and mushrooms (if using). Sauté for 7 minutes, stirring often.

**2** Add the flour and stir well so it coats all the veggies.

**3** Immediately pour in the broth and stir well, scraping the bottom to make sure no flour is stuck on it. Add 16 ounces (1 pound) of the broccoli florets. Secure the lid and move the valve to the sealing position. Hit Cancel and then hit Manual or Pressure Cook on High Pressure for 5 minutes. Quick release when done.

**4** Meanwhile, as the soup is cooking, place the remaining 16–32 ounces (1–2 pounds) broccoli florets in a microwave-safe bowl and add ¼ cup water. Cover with plastic wrap and microwave for 9–10 minutes if frozen, 3–4 minutes if fresh. Remove the plastic wrap and drain the broccoli. If you want smaller pieces of broccoli, cut them into the desired size. Set aside.

**5** When the lid comes off the pot, give everything a stir. Pour in the cream and add the thyme, seasoned salt, and garlic powder. In batches, whisk in the Cheddar until nicely combined. Take an immersion blender (or, in batches, transfer to a blender) and blend everything until it becomes silky smooth.

**6** If you're using the Boursin (which I suggest for even more outrageous flavor), add it now along with the Worcestershire sauce and give it a final blend with the immersion blender.

*lighter comforts* This soup is a veritable dairy barn between all the cheese and cream it includes, but you can lighten it up a bit by swapping out the cream for an unsweetened nondairy milk such as almond, oat, or soy. Feel free to use a low-sodium broth as well.

**7** Add the microwaved broccoli florets and stir well. Ladle into bowls and top with croutons, if desired.

 **JEFF'S TIP** The reason we add some broccoli before pressure cooking and the rest afterward is to create wonderful layers and textures in the soup. Once pureed with the other veggies, the broccoli that is cooked in the IP sets the texture for this complex soup. In the final step, we add microwaved florets to give the soup plenty of volume and additional texture, with broccoli you can bite into. How much you wish to add at the end is up to you but I strongly suggest 2 pounds (and definitely nothing less than 1 pound).

# JAPANESE STEAKHOUSE · SOUP ·

 K
 P
 DF
 GF
 VN+ *(see Lighter Comforts)*

Confession: I've gone to Japanese steakhouses here in the States just to order the amazing "clear soup" with mushrooms, scallions, and crispy onions that is common on many hibachi and teppanyaki menus. Not only is this soup full of flavor, it's packed with nutrients and the perfect remedy for a cold evening (or to help with a sore throat). When I fed my take of this soup to my hibachi-loving friends, their slurps said it all. It's great as a starter for my Chicken Teriyaki (page 160).

| Prep Time | Sauté Time | Pressure Building Time | Pressure Cook Time | Total Time | Serves |
|-----------|-----------|------------------------|--------------------|-----------|--------|
| 10 MIN | 13 MIN | 10–15 MIN | 15 MIN | 50 MIN | 4–6 |

1 tablespoon sesame oil (any kind)

1 medium (or 2 small) yellow onions, quartered into wedges

1 large carrot, peeled and cut into large chunks

3 cloves garlic, crushed or smashed

2- to 3-inch piece fresh ginger, peeled and cut into chunks

2 cups vegetable broth, garlic broth, or onion broth (e.g., Garlic or Sautéed Onion Better Than Bouillon)

2 cups chicken broth

2 cups beef broth

1 teaspoon onion powder

½–2 teaspoons seasoned salt (to taste)

**TOPPING**

1 bunch scallions, sliced

2–4 ounces white mushrooms, thinly sliced

Fried onions (optional, I use French's)

**1** Add the sesame oil to the Instant Pot, hit Sauté, and Adjust so it's on the More or High setting. After 3 minutes of heating, add the onion, carrot, garlic, and ginger and sauté for 8–10 minutes, until the onion and garlic are nicely browned and just slightly charred on the edges.

**2** Use a mixing spoon to transfer the sautéed veggies to a steamer basket (**see Jeff's Tip**) and lower it into the pot.

**3** Pour the broths in the pot, secure the lid, and move the valve to the sealing position. Hit Cancel and then Manual or Pressure Cook on High Pressure for 15 minutes. Quick release when done.

**4** Remove the steamer basket with the veggies from the broth and discard them. Stir the onion powder into the broth and then the seasoned salt, more or less to taste (the salt flavor comes out more as it cools).

**5** Ladle into bowls and top with the scallions, sliced mushrooms, and some fried onions (if using).

*lighter comforts* This soup is already pretty light as is! I would only suggest sticking to low-sodium broths to cut down on sodium.

To make it vegan, use 6 cups of vegetable, garlic, or onion broth—or a mix.

**JEFF'S TIP** If you don't have a steamer basket, skip Step 2 and pour the broth into the pot with the sautéed veggies in Step 3. Then, in Step 4, you'll need a large pot with either a strainer or colander over it; strain the broth through it to catch the veggies. *Or* you can fish them all out with a slotted spoon (but that will take way more time and may cause more of a mess).

# BUFFALO CHILI

With Blue Ribbon Chili and Green Chicken Chili appearing in my first two books, I had to continue the tradition and include a chili in this one. If you're a lover of buffalo wing sauce, get ready to do a happy dance like one of the Peanuts characters! And if spicy food isn't your thing, not to worry—this one is actually on the milder side since I use a tame hot sauce.

 <sup>+</sup> *(see Lighter Comforts)*

| Prep Time | Sauté Time | Pressure Building Time | Pressure Cook Time | Total Time | Serves |
|---|---|---|---|---|---|
| 10 MIN | 10 MIN | 10–15 MIN | 5 MIN | 35 MIN | 4–6 |

- 2 tablespoons (¼ stick) salted butter
- 1 Spanish or red onion, diced
- 3 cloves garlic, minced or pressed
- 2 pounds ground chicken, turkey, or beef
- 4 cups chicken broth
- 1 (14.5-ounce) can diced tomatoes (I like the ones with zesty jalapeños for an extra kick), drained
- 1 (10-ounce) can Ro-Tel diced tomatoes and chilies

- ½ cup buffalo wing sauce (I like Frank's RedHot)
- 1 (1-ounce) package ranch dip mix (not the same as dressing mix but you can use that if necessary)
- 1 teaspoon celery salt
- 1 teaspoon Cajun/Creole/Louisiana seasoning (I use Tony Chachere's)
- 1 teaspoon dried cilantro (optional)
- 10 ounces frozen corn (optional)
- 2 (15.5-ounce) cans navy, cannellini, or great northern beans, drained and rinsed

- ¼ cup cornstarch
- ¼ cup cold water
- 4 ounces brick cream cheese, cut into small chunks
- 1 (5.2-ounce) package Boursin herb cheese (any flavor), cut into small chunks
- 8 ounces shredded sharp Cheddar cheese (or any cheese blend of your choice)

**OPTIONAL TOPPINGS**
- Blue or feta cheese crumbles
- Oyster crackers

**1** Add the butter to the Instant Pot, hit Sauté, and Adjust to the More or High setting. Once the butter is melted and bubbling, add the onion and sauté for 3 minutes, until lightly softened and the color begins to dull. Add the garlic and sauté for 1 minute longer.

**2** Add the ground meat and break up with a mixing spoon or spatula. Sauté for 3 minutes, until crumbled and lightly browned.

**3** Add the broth, diced tomatoes, Ro-Tel, buffalo wing sauce, ranch mix, celery salt, Cajun seasoning, dried cilantro (if using), and frozen corn (if using). Stir well.

**4** Top with the beans but *do not stir*. Just let them rest on top of everything in the pot.

**5** Secure the lid and move the valve to the sealing position. Hit Cancel and then hit Manual or Pressure Cook on High Pressure for 5 minutes. Quick release when done.

**6** In a small bowl, mix together the cornstarch and cold water to form a smooth slurry. Hit Cancel and then hit Sauté and Adjust to the More or High setting. Once bubbling, stir in the cornstarch slurry followed by the cream cheese, Boursin, and Cheddar. Stir well until all is melded and incorporated into the chili.

**7** Ladle into bowls and top with blue cheese crumbles and oyster crackers, if desired.

 *lighter comforts* You can skip some or all of the dairy in Step 6 if you wish, or instead add ½ cup of an unsweetened nondairy milk such as almond or oat milk for a touch of creaminess. To make it totally dairy-free, sub extra-virgin olive oil for the butter in Step 1.

 **JEFF'S TIPS** Want to make this the ultimate party dip? Add double the shredded Cheddar cheese until it's super thick and dip-like!

In lieu of the Boursin, feel free to up the cream cheese to 8 ounces.

# ITALIAN WEDDING SOUP

My favorite soup in Italian cuisine would have to be the one that involves a wedding. Except the origins of this one aren't about two humans tying the knot, but rather celebrating the union of meats and greens. With tiny meatballs and pasta pearls playing together in a stunning, basil-laden broth, what's not to love? The secret to the soup's special flavor is using sausage for the meatballs.

| Prep Time | Sauté Time | Pressure Building Time | Pressure Cook Time | Total Time | Serves |
|---|---|---|---|---|---|
| 30 MIN | 18 MIN | 15–20 MIN | 5 MIN | 1 HR 5 MIN | 4–6 |

### THE MEATBALLS

- 1 pound Italian sausage (sweet, hot, or a mix; see Lighter Comforts), casings removed
- 1/2 pound ground beef (the less lean, the better)
- 1/2 cup grated Parmesan cheese
- 1/3 cup breadcrumbs
- 6 cloves garlic, minced or pressed
- 2 tablespoons dried parsley
- 2 teaspoons seasoned salt
- 1 teaspoon black pepper
- 1 teaspoon dried oregano
- 1/3 cup whole milk
- 1 large egg, lightly beaten
- 2 tablespoons extra-virgin olive oil

### THE SOUP

- 2 tablespoons extra-virgin olive oil
- 2 large shallots, diced
- 2 medium carrots, peeled and diced
- 3 ribs celery, diced (green, leafy tops reserved)
- 3 cloves garlic, minced or pressed
- 1 bunch fresh basil leaves (about 1 packed cup), stems removed
- 1 cup sherry wine (if you wish to leave this out, simply add another cup of broth)
- 7 cups chicken broth or garlic broth (e.g., Garlic Better Than Bouillon)
- 1 1/2 teaspoons Italian seasoning
- 1 1/2 teaspoons dried oregano
- 1 1/2 teaspoons garlic powder
- 1 1/2 teaspoons black pepper
- 1/4–1/2 cup acini di pepe (pearl) pasta (see Jeff's Tip)
- 5–8 ounces baby spinach
- 1/2 teaspoon seasoned salt (optional)

## THE MEATBALLS

**1** In a large mixing bowl, combine all the meatball ingredients except the olive oil and mix together well by hand (almost like making a dough) until it binds together nicely and forms one large meatball. From there, grab enough meat to roll a meatball about the size of a pinball and set aside on a plate. Repeat to make 35–40 meatballs.

**2** Add the olive oil to the Instant Pot, hit Sauté, and Adjust so it's on the More or High setting. After 3 minutes of the oil heating, add half of the meatballs (we don't want them overcrowding the bottom of the pot) and flash-sear for about 30 seconds on each side. Carefully remove the meatballs with tongs or a slotted spoon when done. Repeat with the remaining meatballs.

**3** Add the olive oil to the pot and then the shallots, carrots, and diced celery (reserve the leafy tops) and sauté for 5 minutes, scraping the bottom of the pot to get any browned bits up. Add the garlic and sauté for 1 minute longer. Add the basil leaves and stir until wilted, about 1 minute longer.

**4** Add the sherry and simmer the veggies for 2 minutes. Add the broth, reserved celery tops, Italian seasoning, oregano, garlic powder, pepper, and pasta and stir.

**5** Carefully return the flash-seared meatballs to the pot. Top with the spinach *but do not stir*. Secure the lid and move the valve to the sealing position. Hit Cancel and hit Pressure Cook or Manual on High Pressure for 5 minutes. Quick release when done.

**6** Give everything a stir and give the soup a taste. If you feel it needs some seasoned salt (many likely won't), *now* is the time to add it. Ladle into bowls and serve with Italian bread.

**lighter comforts** While the Italian sausage does infuse the soup with special flavor, you can use a different meat for your meatballs. I suggest chicken sausage or ground beef, chicken, or turkey. You can even use a crumbled vegan-style "meat"! Just make sure you use 1½ pounds of meat total.

**JEFF'S TIP** Use ¼ cup of acini di pepe if you want minimal pasta in your soup (there will still be plenty) and *no more than ½ cup* if you want a substantial amount. Just keep in mind that you don't want to go overboard on the pasta, otherwise it will absorb too much of the broth—which means less slurping for you. If you're worried about your pasta portion and want more control, simply boil about ¼ cup separately on the stove according to package directions and add to individual soup bowls when serving.

# CREAM OF  BACON SOUP

No, this isn't an April Fool's joke: You read the title of this soup correctly. If you ever wanted to take the "cream of" soups to a level that truly sizzles, this recipe is all you need. Feel free to pig out on this one for dinner, but I'm going to go rogue and suggest enjoying it for breakfast as well—you could even dip a waffle in as an inventive garnish. Crazy? Maybe a little. Delicious? Completely.

**K** + *(see Lighter Comforts)*

**GF** + *(see Lighter Comforts)*

| Prep Time | Sauté Time | Pressure Building Time | Pressure Cook Time | Total Time | Serves |
|---|---|---|---|---|---|
| 10 MIN | 25–30 MIN | 10–15 MIN | 10 MIN | 55 MIN | 4–6 |

- 2 tablespoons (¼ stick) salted butter
- 1½ pounds thick-cut bacon, diced (see Jeff's Tips)
- 2 Vidalia (sweet) onions, cut into strips
- ½ cup sherry wine (you can use another ½ cup of chicken broth if you don't want to use wine)

- 3 cloves garlic, minced or pressed
- 3 cups ham broth (e.g., Ham Better Than Bouillon), chicken broth, or vegetable broth
- 2 cups chicken broth
- 2 pounds Idaho (russet) potatoes, peeled and cut into chunks
- 2 teaspoons dried thyme
- ⅓ cup all-purpose flour

- 1 cup heavy cream or half-and-half
- ¼ cup pure maple syrup, plus more for serving
- Up to 1 tablespoon seasoned salt (optional, to taste)

**TO SERVE**
- ⅓ cup thinly sliced fresh chives
- Waffles, for dipping (I use Eggos and toast them separately)

**1** Place the butter in the Instant Pot and hit Sauté and Adjust so it's on the More or High setting. Once the butter's melted and bubbling, add the bacon, coat well with the butter, and sauté for 15–20 minutes, until nice and crispy. Remove with a slotted spoon and set aside in a paper towel–lined bowl.

**2** With the bacon grease still in the pot, add the onions, coat well with the bacon grease, and sauté for 5 minutes.

**3** Add the sherry and garlic and let simmer for 1 minute longer, deglazing the bottom of the pot and getting any browned bits up.

*lighter comforts* Sub 1 head of chopped cauliflower for the potatoes in Step 4. If you do that, and sub coconut flour for the all-purpose, leave out the maple syrup, and let go of that Eggo—you'll have a keto dish.

Make it gluten-free by omitting the flour. If you want it thicker, once you've added the seasoned salt in Step 7, hit Sauté, bring the pot to a bubble, and stir in a cornstarch slurry made of 2 tablespoons cornstarch + 2 tablespoons cold water. If you don't want to miss out on the waffle, shop for frozen gluten-free ones and heat according to package instructions.

**4** Add the ham broth, chicken broth, potatoes, and thyme and stir well. Secure the lid and move the valve to the sealing position. Hit Cancel and then hit Manual or Pressure Cook on High Pressure for 10 minutes. Quick release when done.

**5** Once the lid comes off, whisk in the flour and then add three-fourths of the bacon, which will have crisped from resting. (NOTE: Don't worry: The flour will be cooked by the heat of the soup and won't taste raw at all.)

**6** Now it's time to make this an unforgettable soup. Take an immersion blender and blend everything in the pot together for 1–2 minutes, until it's pureed. The soup will thicken nicely once done.

**7** Add the cream and maple syrup and stir well. Add seasoned salt to taste, if desired.

**8** Ladle into bowls and top with the remaining bacon, the chives, and perhaps a few extra drops of maple syrup. Oh, and dip in that waffle to really make things exciting!

 **JEFF'S TIPS** Here's an easy way to dice bacon: Don't separate the strips from one another, but slice the slab perpendicularly into ⅛-inch-thick strips. You'll have little rectangular strips that you can then feel free to dice up even further. Don't worry if they still stick together as they'll separate once sautéed.

Add more texture by adding some drained canned corn or beans in Step 7.

# WONTON SOUP

As in many Long Island Jewish households, it was tradition for my dad to bring home dinner from our local Chinese restaurant for the family every Sunday night, and wonton soup was always a given. Now I've had hundreds, if not thousands, of bowls of this iconic soup, and the most important thing to me is that the broth be full of deep flavor with a wonton that is delicate, yet filled with meat. You're going to get that here with easy-to-find ingredients and—although this is a slightly more involved recipe than most of my others—simple techniques. Enjoy with Mongolian Beef (page 200) and Fire Fried Rice (page 133). The recipe yields a ton of wontons that you can freeze for the future, and is well worth the time!

| Prep Time | Boil Time | Pressure Building Time | Pressure Cook Time | Total Time | Serves |
|---|---|---|---|---|---|
| 40 MIN | 10 MIN | 10–15 MIN | 1 MIN | 1 HR 5 MIN | 4–6 |

## THE WONTONS

- 1 pound ground pork (or see Lighter Comforts)
- 1 large shallot, finely chopped
- 1/3 bunch scallions, finely chopped
- 4 large shiitake mushrooms, stemmed and finely chopped (optional, or you can use white or baby bella mushrooms)
- 2 tablespoons Shaoxing wine (or sherry wine, but I do suggest using Shaoxing, which can be found in many major or international markets and online)
- 2 tablespoons sesame oil (any kind)
- 1 tablespoon low-sodium soy sauce
- 1½ teaspoons minced or grated ginger (I use squeeze ginger), optional
- ½ teaspoon seasoned salt
- 1 (14-ounce) package frozen wonton wrappers (square-shaped is preferable; usually found in the frozen section of many major or international markets; the thicker the wrapper the better, but the thin ones will work fine), thawed

## THE SOUP

- 1 pound chicken tenderloins, sliced into thin strips about ¼ inch long (optional, but I love this in my wonton soup)
- 6 cups chicken broth
- 1½ teaspoons minced or grated ginger (I use squeeze ginger)
- 1 teaspoon sugar
- 1 teaspoon turmeric
- ½ teaspoon garlic powder
- 2 tablespoons Shaoxing wine (or sherry wine)
- 2 tablespoons low-sodium soy sauce
- 2 teaspoons sesame oil
- 2 teaspoons seasoned salt
- 5–8 ounces baby spinach
- 2/3 bunch scallions (remaining from above), sliced
- Chow mein noodles, for serving (optional)

### THE WONTONS

**1** Combine all of the wonton ingredients (except for the wrappers, of course) in a large mixing bowl and mix well by hand for 1–2 minutes.

CONTINUES

**2** Take a wrapper and lay it on the counter so it's in a diamond position. With your index finger, rub the upper perimeter/edges of the wrapper with cold water (this serves as a glue).

**3** Spoon a pinball-size portion of the filling mixture into a ball and place in the center of the wrapper.

**4** Take the bottom edges of the diamond to meet the top edges, and tightly press to seal together so that the meat is nice and tucked in, forming a triangular pocket with enough wrapper to spare on the edges, with three corners—left, right, and at top.

**5** Fold the right corner over so it's resting on the center of the meat-filled wonton and dab some water on it.

**6** Now gently pull the left corner so it's snugly overlapping the right corner. With your index finger slid under the corners serving as a buffer between them and the meaty pouch of the wonton, use your other index finger to firmly pinch the two corners together. They will fuse with the triangular corner remaining at the top. Remove your index finger from the buffer position and you've got yourself a wonton!

**7** As the wontons are fully wrapped, place them one-by-one into a container; place an airtight lid on it when done. You should have 40–50 wontons when all's said and done.

 **NOTE** You'll get the hang of it after two or three wontons. I suggest you have two people do this: one person to roll the meat into a pinball-size ball and place it into the center of the wonton skin, and the other to do the wrapping. It will be faster and a lot less messy this way, and you'll avoid getting the filling meat on the outside of the wonton wrapper.

> When I was a kid, we had some friends spend the night. In the morning my mom made waffles. We told her they tasted burnt. She told us to shut up and eat them, they weren't burnt. When she finished cooking all the batter, she sat down to finally eat. She took one bite and said, "OMG! These are disgusting. How did you all eat them?" She realized she'd used baking soda instead of baking powder. It's thirty years later and we still won't let her live that one down!
>
> ELLEN · **SURPRISE, ARIZONA**

**8** Add all the soup ingredients to the Instant Pot *except* for the spinach, scallions, and chow mein noodles. Stir well. Hit Sauté and Adjust so it's on the More or High setting. We want the soup to come to a bubble (this will take about 10 minutes) so the wontons cook in a timely fashion as they are delicate and we don't want them overdone.

**9** Once the soup is bubbling, add 20–25 wontons, one-by-one, but *do not stir*, as the wontons are delicate and we don't want to pester them too much. Top with the spinach.

**10** Secure the lid and move the valve to the sealing position. Hit Cancel and then hit Manual or Pressure Cook for 1 minute on High Pressure. Quick release when done.

**11** Give the soup a gentle stir (the wontons are still a bit delicate) so the spinach gets evenly dispersed. Add the scallions, give another light stir, and immediately spoon into bowls with desired wontons and soup in each. Top off each bowl with some chow mein noodles if you like.

*lighter comforts* Don't want pork for the wonton filling? Use ground turkey, ground chicken, or chopped raw shrimp instead! You can also add some chopped raw shrimp to the pork mixture: About ¼ pound should do nicely.

> One of the best Christmas presents my mom ever gave my sister and me was our Instant Pots! I would call my mom and tell her about the recipes that I made in it. She died last July from complications from a simple heart surgery, and every time I cook I can't help but think of her. I hung up one of her ancient, battered mixing spoons in my kitchen so she's always with me while I cook.
>
> **KRISTIN · LAKE FOREST PARK, WASHINGTON**

**JEFF'S TIPS** For firmer, less delicate wontons, add them in Step 11 after pressure cooking. Hit Sauté and Adjust so it's on the More or High setting. Once bubbling, follow Step 9 but let them simmer for 4–5 minutes. They will be cooked through in that time.

This makes a *lot* of wontons, which are great to have on hand for when the mood strikes. Simply leave any leftover wontons in the container and seal with an airtight lid. Pop them in the fridge if you plan to use the rest the next day, *or* in the freezer where they'll last for a few months. If you don't want any leftover wontons, simply halve the wonton recipe.

Don't feel like making the wontons at all? Get a bag of frozen ones from your favorite market and just focus on the soup ingredients and steps. Add the frozen wontons in Step 9 in place of the fresh wontons and increase the pressure cook time to 2 minutes.

# CHICKEN GNOCCHI SOUP

Picture the perfect, classic chicken noodle soup (like in my first book), but instead of a clear broth, we make it creamy, and instead of the noodles, we have the fluffy potato dumplings known as gnocchi. What you'll get is the most comforting Tuscan-style gnocchi soup, unlike any soup you've had. It's one of my most popular recipes, and you're just 60 minutes from finding out why.

| Prep Time | Sauté Time | Pressure Building Time | Pressure Cook Time | Simmer Time | Total Time | Serves |
|---|---|---|---|---|---|---|
| 10 MIN | 14 MIN | 15–20 MIN | 10 MIN | 3–5 MIN | 1 HR | 6–8 |

- 4 tablespoons (½ stick) salted butter
- 8–10 ounces pancetta, diced (optional, or you can use ½ pound of bacon cut into bits)
- 1 yellow onion, diced
- 2 medium carrots, peeled and diced
- 3 ribs celery, diced (leafy tops reserved)
- 3 cloves garlic, minced or pressed
- ½ cup sherry wine (optional)

- 5½ cups chicken broth or garlic broth (e.g., Garlic Better Than Bouillon)
- 1 tablespoon seasoned salt
- 2 teaspoons black pepper
- 2 teaspoons dried thyme
- 1 teaspoon dried oregano
- 1 teaspoon Italian seasoning
- 1 whole chicken (4–5 pounds), chopped into quarters (leg, breast, thigh, and wing; your market's butcher will usually do this for you if you ask nicely)

- 8–10 ounces baby spinach or chopped kale
- 2 cups heavy cream or half-and-half
- ½ cup all-purpose flour
- 1–2 pounds gnocchi of your choice (see Jeff's Tips)
- ⅓ cup grated Parmesan cheese
- 1 (5.2-ounce) package Boursin or any spreadable herb cheese (any flavor), cut into small chunks (optional)

**1** Add the butter to the Instant Pot, hit Sauté, and Adjust so it's on the More or High setting.

**2** Once the butter's melted, add the pancetta or bacon and sauté for 6–8 minutes, until cooked and slightly crispy. Remove with a slotted spoon to a paper towel–lined bowl and set aside, but leave the bacon grease and melted butter in the pot.

**3** Add the onion, carrots, and diced celery to the bacon grease and sauté for 3 minutes. Deglaze/scrape the bottom of the pot and get any browned bits up. Add the garlic and sauté for 1 minute longer.

CONTINUES

JEFF'S TIPS

For this recipe, I like cooking the chicken with the skin on as it creates a richer, more colorful broth, but if you don't wish to use a whole chicken, you can use 2–3 pounds of boneless, skinless breasts or thighs instead.

I used potato gnocchi, usually found in the market at either room temperature near the deli section in an airtight container or frozen in a bag—either is fine! How much gnocchi you wish to add is up to you. One pound is good for many but some (me) like as much as 2 pounds, which is perfectly grand.

**4** Add the sherry (if using) and let simmer for 1 minute.

**5** Add the broth, seasoned salt, black pepper, thyme, oregano, and Italian seasoning. Stir well.

**6** Add the chicken and make sure it's submerged in the broth. Top with the spinach but *do not stir*. Secure the lid and move the valve to the sealing position. Hit Cancel and then hit Pressure Cook or Manual on High Pressure for 10 minutes. Quick release when done.

**7** Using tongs, slide the spinach off the chicken and into the soup. Transfer the chicken to a bowl and let cool for 10 minutes. Pull off the meat and discard any cartilage, skin, and bones.

**8** Meanwhile, in a bowl, whisk together the cream and flour until thickened (it should look a little curdled and slightly lumpy). Add to the soup and stir for about a minute to get any small lumps out. (NOTE: Not to worry, the flour will cook from the heat of the soup and smooth out perfectly as the steps go on.)

**9** Hit Cancel and then hit Sauté and Adjust so it's on the More or High setting. Once bubbling, add the gnocchi and let boil for 2–3 minutes, until the gnocchi float (but if they don't, just check to make sure they're tender). Hit Cancel to turn the pot off and switch to Keep Warm.

**10** Add the pancetta or bacon, the shredded chicken, the reserved leafy tops from the celery, Parmesan, and Boursin (if using) and stir until the dairy is melded into the soup. Ladle into bowls and enjoy with some crusty bread!

*lighter comforts* This is quite a rich soup: To lighten it up a bit, sub a nondairy unsweetened milk (such as almond or cashew) for the cream, use whole-wheat gnocchi, and/or omit the bacon or Boursin.

# POZOLE ·VERDE·

K+ *(see Lighter Comforts)*

P+ *(see Lighter Comforts)*

DF

GF

Pozole is an iconic, vibrant stew common across Mexico that is full of intense yet simple flavors, all derived from either chiles (red/rojo-style pozole) or tomatillos (green/verde-style). Due to the resounding success of the red pork pozole from my lighter book, I wanted to represent its green sibling in this one. Rather than pork, the protein of choice here is chicken, and instead of chiles we use tomatillos. The hominy, of course, is here to stay.

| Prep Time 10 MIN | Sauté Time 7 MIN | Pressure Building Time 15–20 MIN | Pressure Cook Time 10 MIN | Total Time 45 MIN | Serves 4–6 |
| --- | --- | --- | --- | --- | --- |

1/4 cup extra-virgin olive oil

1 large Spanish or yellow onion, diced

1 poblano pepper, seeded and diced

3 cloves garlic, minced or pressed

6 cups chicken broth or water

1 tablespoon dried oregano (see Jeff's Tips)

4 teaspoons seasoned salt

1 teaspoon ground cumin

1 teaspoon garlic powder

4 pounds boneless, skinless chicken (I use 2 pounds thighs and 2 pounds breasts)

3 (15-ounce) cans white hominy, rinsed and drained

1 pound tomatillos (green Mexican tomatoes), husks and stems removed and halved

4 cloves garlic, peeled

1/2 cup fresh cilantro leaves, chopped

Juice of 1 lime

1 teaspoon kosher salt

2 teaspoons chili powder (optional)

2 jalapeño peppers, roughly chopped with seeds intact (optional)

2 (7-ounce) cans diced green chiles

**OPTIONAL TOPPINGS**

Shredded green cabbage or lettuce

Sliced radishes

Avocado slices

Lime wedges

Chopped fresh cilantro

**1** Add the oil to the Instant Pot, hit Sauté, and Adjust so it's on the More or High setting. After 3 minutes of heating, add the onion and poblano and sauté for 3 minutes, until slightly softened. Add the minced garlic and sauté for 1 minute longer.

**2** Add the broth, oregano, seasoned salt, cumin, and garlic powder. Stir well.

CONTINUES

**3** Place the chicken in the pot so it's submerged in the broth. Top with the hominy and tomatillos.

**4** Secure the lid and move the valve to the sealing position. Hit Cancel and then hit Manual or Pressure Cook on High Pressure for 10 minutes. Quick release when done.

**5** Using tongs or a slotted spoon, transfer what's left of the tomatillos to a food processor or blender and the chicken to a bowl. Shred the chicken with two forks or with a hand mixer until shredded.

**6** Those tomatillos in the food processor are lonely, so add the peeled garlic cloves, cilantro, lime juice, salt, chili powder (if using), and jalapeños (if using) and ladle in 1 cup of the broth. Blend until pureed.

**7** Pour the puree back into the pot along with the shredded chicken and diced green chiles. Stir well. Ladle into bowls and let everyone choose their favorite toppings.

*lighter comforts* This is already a pretty light dish, but feel free to leave out the hominy if you want it keto-, paleo-, and low carb–compliant. But keep in mind that leaving hominy out of a pozole is like leaving chicken out of chicken soup.

**JEFF'S TIPS** If you can find Mexican oregano instead of regular, go for it as it will be truer to the traditional flavor profile. To that point, the same goes for a poblano pepper—but if you can't find one, use a green bell pepper instead.

For milder spice, either remove the seeds and ribs from the jalapeños or leave the peppers out completely.

I gave my 80-year-old parents an Instant Pot a year ago last Christmas. Due to Mom's health, Dad is now the sole cook in the house and I thought this would be a big help. Well, he was afraid of it until I started sharing some of your recipes and showing him how easy your steps are to follow. I just gave him your book, and he's been using the Instant Pot with much pride and success. Thank you so much!

**KATHERINE · CLEARWATER, FLORIDA**

# POTATO LEEK
## SOUP

 K⁺  *(see Lighter Comforts)*

GF

V

There are few things as satisfying as a good old-fashioned, cheesy, creamy, bacon-y, and all-around loaded baked potato. The only thing better is turning it into a soup that will sit right at the top of your recipe rotation.

| Prep Time | Sauté Time | Pressure Building Time | Pressure Cook Time | Total Time | Serves |
|---|---|---|---|---|---|
| 10 MIN | 20 MIN | 15–20 MIN | 8 MIN | 55 MIN | 4–6 |

4 tablespoons (1/2 stick) salted butter

2–3 leeks (middle section only with hard green tops and roots removed), rinsed and roughly chopped

8–10 ounces pancetta or thick-cut bacon, diced (optional)

1 medium yellow onion, diced

6 cloves garlic, minced or pressed

1/2 cup dry white wine (like a chardonnay)

6 cups garlic broth (e.g., Garlic Better Than Bouillon) or vegetable broth

2 pounds Idaho (russet) potatoes, peeled and cut into 1-inch chunks

3 pounds unpeeled baby red and white potato combo, rinsed and quartered

1 1/2 teaspoons dried thyme

1 teaspoon black pepper

1 (5.2-ounce) package Boursin herb cheese (any flavor) or 4 ounces brick cream cheese, cut into small chunks

8 ounces shredded cheese of your choice (I used half Gouda and half sharp Cheddar), plus more for topping, if desired

1 cup heavy cream or half-and-half

1 1/2 teaspoons seasoned salt

1/3 cup sliced chives, plus more for topping, if desired

Frozen soft pretzels, thawed and heated, for dipping (optional)

**1** Add the butter to the Instant Pot and hit Sauté and Adjust so it's on the More or High setting. Once melted and bubbling, add the leeks and sauté for 8–10 minutes, until crispy but not burned. Remove the leeks and set aside.

**2** Add the pancetta (if using), onion, and garlic and sauté for 5 minutes.

**3** Add the white wine and allow to simmer for 1 minute, deglazing the bottom of the pot to remove any browned bits from the pancetta and butter. Add the broth, potatoes, thyme, and black pepper. Stir well.

**4** Secure the lid and move the valve to the sealing position. Hit Cancel followed by Manual or Pressure Cook on High Pressure for 8 minutes. Quick release when done.

**5** When the lid comes off, use a slotted spoon to remove half the potatoes and set aside in a bowl (**see Jeff's Tips**). Stir the Boursin (or cream cheese) and shredded cheese into the soup. Then take an immersion blender and blend until completely smooth.

**6** Stir in the crispy leeks (reserving some for garnish), reserved potatoes, cream, seasoned salt, and chives. Ladle into bowls, top with more cheese, leeks, and chives as desired, and serve. Enjoy with a hot soft pretzel for dipping!

*lighter comforts* Sub two heads of chopped cauliflower for the potatoes. Then it'll be Cauliflower Leek Soup *and* keto!

You can also sub Greek yogurt for the Boursin or cream cheese.

**JEFF'S TIPS** In Step 5, you control the thickness of your soup prior to blending. I like to remove half the potatoes as suggested, but the less you remove, the thicker the soup base will be and the fewer chunks you'll have once you return the potatoes in Step 6. It's wiser to start by removing more potatoes, blending, and then adding and blending more potatoes until you hit the desired consistency. If you made it thicker than you wish, you can always thin it out with more cream.

No one who loves to make soups should be without an immersion blender. It makes life so much easier than transferring the soup to a blender in messy batches!

To reheat any leftovers, add a little cream or milk and stir while heating.

# PASTA E FAGIOLI

Pasta e fagioli (sometimes pronounced *fah-zool*) is a classic Italian soup with many variations. I love it every time I order it in a restaurant, but I've never had the same experience twice—so as long as you have the beans, pasta, and a tomato base, it's pasta e fagioli. After many bowls of this deliciousness, I've found the perfect balance, with some of the beans blended into a wonderfully smoky tomato undertone.

 **DF** <sup></sup> *(see Lighter Comforts)*

 **V**

 **VN** <sup></sup> *(see Lighter Comforts)*

| Prep Time | Sauté Time | Pressure Building Time | Pressure Cook Time | Total Time | Serves |
|---|---|---|---|---|---|
| 10 MIN | 15 MIN | 15–20 MIN | 8 MIN | 50 MIN | 4–6 |

- 1½ cups ditalini (small tube-shaped pasta)
- Pinch of kosher salt
- 2 tablespoons (¼ stick) salted butter
- 8 ounces pancetta or thick-cut bacon, diced (optional)
- 1 yellow onion, diced
- ½ cup dry white wine (like a sauvignon blanc)
- 1 teaspoon liquid smoke
- 4 cups vegetable broth or garlic broth (e.g., Garlic Better Than Bouillon)
- 1 (8-ounce) can tomato sauce (not the same as pasta sauce)
- 2 (15.5-ounce) cans cannellini beans, divided (one can drained and rinsed)
- 2 (15.5-ounce) cans red kidney beans, divided (one can drained and rinsed)
- 2 bay leaves
- 1 cup grated Parmesan cheese, plus more for serving
- 2 (14.5-ounce) cans stewed tomatoes, drained and roughly chopped

**1** Add the pasta to the Instant Pot and cover with enough water (about 2 cups) so all of it is just submerged. Add a pinch of salt and stir. Secure the lid and move the valve to the sealing position. Hit Manual or Pressure Cook on High Pressure for 4 minutes. Quick release when done. Drain the cooked pasta in a strainer, rinse with cold water, and set aside. Dry the liner pot, return it to the Instant Pot, and hit Cancel.

**2** Add the butter to the Instant Pot, hit Sauté, and Adjust so it's on the More or High setting. After 3 minutes of heating, add the pancetta (if using) and sauté for 5–8 minutes. Add the onion and sauté for 3 minutes longer.

*lighter comforts* Want it vegan and dairy-free? Use 2 tablespoons extra-virgin olive oil instead of butter and sub nutritional yeast for the Parmesan.

**3** Add the wine and liquid smoke and deglaze (**see Jeff's Tips**), getting up any browned bits from the pancetta. Add the broth, tomato sauce, the undrained can of cannellini beans, and the undrained can of kidney beans. Stir well and top with the bay leaves.

**4** Secure the lid and move the valve to the sealing position. Hit Cancel and then Manual or Pressure Cook on High Pressure for 4 minutes. Quick release when done.

**5** Discard the bay leaves, add the Parmesan, and stir well.

**6** Using an immersion blender, blend everything in the pot together until pureed.

**7** Add the drained pasta (**see Jeff's Tips**), stewed tomatoes, and remaining two cans of drained cannellini and kidney beans. Mix well and let set for a few minutes to thicken as it cools down a little. Serve with additional Parmesan.

**JEFF'S TIPS** If you prefer not to use wine, add another ½ cup of broth in its place in Step 3. If using the pancetta and *not* using wine, use 1 tablespoon Worcestershire sauce to deglaze in Step 3.

If you're serving the whole pot at once, you're good to add all the cooked pasta to the pot in Step 7. But because pasta always continues to absorb liquid and expand when it's in a broth or soup, if you anticipate leftovers, I suggest adding the cooked ditalini to each serving bowl directly and then ladling in the soup. Then store the leftover pasta and soup separately.

# THAI-STYLE CHICKEN SOUP

My favorite soup in Thai cuisine is tom kha gai, which usually features chicken in a coconut milk base with a wonderful sweet/savory blend of flavors and an optional spicy touch. My spin varies from the traditional preparation as it doesn't use galangal or makrut lime leaves, and has been adapted for the ease of the Instant Pot. Yet completed in just four simple steps, it's loaded with that familiar comforting flavor. The lemongrass is pretty key, but I offer an alternative.

DF

GF

V **+** *(see Lighter Comforts)*

| Prep Time | Pressure Building Time | Pressure Cook Time | Total Time | Serves |
|---|---|---|---|---|
| 10 MIN | 15–20 MIN | 6 MIN | 33 MIN | 4–6 |

2 cups chicken broth or garlic broth (e.g., Garlic Better Than Bouillon)

2 (14-ounce) cans unsweetened coconut milk (it should be thin like water and not thick and lumpy)

1½ pounds chicken breast cutlets (about ¼ inch thick), cut into 1-inch squares

1 bunch scallions, sliced

8 ounces baby bella mushrooms, sliced

2 stalks lemongrass, sliced and cut into thin 1½-inch strands (use the bottom third of the stalk and the 4–5 closest inner layers from each) (NOTE: If you cannot find lemongrass, use the grated zest of 1 lemon and 1 tablespoon of its juice.)

Juice of 1 lime

2 tablespoons fish sauce

1 tablespoon sesame oil (any kind)

1 tablespoon minced or grated ginger (I use squeeze ginger)

1 tablespoon dried tarragon

1½ teaspoons white granulated sugar

¼ teaspoon crushed red pepper flakes (optional)

2 bay leaves

¼ cup pad thai sauce

½–1 tablespoon hot sauce (optional)

2–4 tablespoons chopped fresh cilantro, plus more for garnish

2–3 teaspoons seasoned salt

**1** Add the broth, coconut milk, chicken, scallions, mushrooms, lemongrass, lime juice, fish sauce, sesame oil, ginger, tarragon, sugar, red pepper flakes (if using), and bay leaves to the Instant Pot. Secure the lid and move the valve to the sealing position. Hit Manual or Pressure Cook on High Pressure for 6 minutes. Quick release when done.

**JEFF'S TIP** Fish sauce is a bit pungent in its aroma, but it's an essential ingredient in this dish. If you're a bit thrown off by the scent, don't worry: Once added, it won't overpower, but will blend into the wonderfully complex background, making the soup a flavor bomb.

**2** Remove the bay leaves and add the pad thai sauce, hot sauce (if using), and fresh cilantro.

**3** Add the seasoned salt to taste.

**4** Stir well, ladle into bowls, and top with additional cilantro.

*lighter comforts* Want shrimp instead of chicken? Omit the chicken, but follow Step 1 as directed. In Step 2, after stirring, hit Sauté and Adjust to the More or High setting and bring the pot to a simmer. Add 1 pound peeled and deveined shrimp and cook until they're curled and opaque.

To make it vegetarian but still keep the protein, use garlic broth, omit the chicken, and add 12 ounces extra-firm tofu cut into cubes: Stir in at the end of Step 2. No simmering required as the tofu will heat quickly in the finished soup.

# BIG EASY CORN CHOWDER

What can I say? I love soup with a dreamy, creamy richness—typically known as chowder. And with the success of the classic New England Clam Chowder from my first book, I couldn't pass up the chance to make a New Orleans–style corn chowder featuring the holy trinity of onion, pepper, and celery along with some Louisiana seasoning. But make no mistake, calling this Big Easy Corn Chowder was definitely a double entendre since it brings the flavors of the Big Easy to your mouth with little effort at all.

**DF** + *(see Lighter Comforts)*

**GF**

**V** *(if not doing the Seafood Finish)*

| Prep Time | Sauté Time | Pressure Building Time | Pressure Cook Time | Total Time | Serves |
|---|---|---|---|---|---|
| 10 MIN | 10 MIN | 5–10 MIN | 5 MIN | 30 MIN | 4–6 |

2 tablespoons (¼ stick) salted butter

1 medium onion, diced

1 red bell pepper, seeded and diced

2 ribs celery, diced

3 cups garlic broth (e.g., Garlic Better Than Bouillon) or vegetable broth

¼ cup sherry wine (if not using, add another ¼ cup broth)

1 pound Idaho (russet) potatoes, peeled and cut into small cubes

16 ounces frozen sweet corn kernels

2 bay leaves

2 tablespoons cornstarch

2 tablespoons cold water

1½ cups heavy cream or half-and-half

1 tablespoon Cajun/Creole/Louisiana seasoning (I use Tony Chachere's) or seasoned salt

½ teaspoon black pepper

Croutons (I use cornbread style) or oyster crackers, for serving (optional, see Jeff's Tips)

**OPTIONAL SPICY SEAFOOD FINISH**

1 teaspoon Old Bay seasoning

2 (6-ounce) cans white, pink, or lump crabmeat, drained

⅛–½ teaspoon Zatarain's Concentrated Shrimp & Crab Boil, for a kick (NOTE: Start with ⅛ teaspoon and see if the spice level is okay. Do not use more than ½ teaspoon: Since it's a concentrate it may become spice overkill!)

**1** Add the butter to the Instant Pot, hit Sauté, and Adjust so it's on the More or High setting. When melted and bubbling, add the onion, bell pepper, and celery and sauté for 5 minutes.

**2** Add the broth, sherry, potatoes, and corn. Stir well and top with the bay leaves. Secure the lid and move the valve to the sealing position. Hit Cancel and then Manual or Pressure Cook on High Pressure for 5 minutes. Quick release when done.

**3** Make a slurry by mixing together the cornstarch and cold water in a small bowl until smooth.

**4** Remove the lid and discard the bay leaves. Hit Cancel and then hit Sauté and Adjust to the More or High setting and bring to a bubble. Stir in the cornstarch slurry and let bubble for about 30 seconds before turning off the pot by hitting Cancel.

**5** Add the cream, Creole seasoning, and black pepper. As you stir it will become a chowder.

**6** If you wish to seafood it up, stir in the Old Bay, crabmeat, and Zatarain's (if you're okay with some spice) and let the heat of the soup heat it up for 2 minutes. Ladle into bowls and top with some cornbread croutons or oyster crackers for a lovely crunch factor, if desired.

 *lighter comforts* To make it dairy-free, swap in 2 tablespoons vegetable oil for the butter and use an unsweetened nondairy milk in place of the cream (almond milk works best).

**JEFF'S TIPS** If you don't want the Cajun flavor or can't find the proper seasoning, sub seasoned salt for the Cajun seasoning.

For the croutons, you can also make the garlic bread from my Steak Tidbits on Garlic Bread recipe (page 190): Follow Step 6 and cut them into croutons.

As someone who has fought depression and anxiety far too many times, I have to say the Instant Pot has simplified meal prep for me, especially when I'm going through a rough patch. From only using one "dish" to cook an entire meal, to not having to stand there and babysit different components of a meal, I have found the Instant Pot can greatly reduce the amount of overwhelm I experience.

KRISTEN • **BEAVERTON, OREGON**

# 3

# PASTA

The ability to make complete pasta dishes in the Instant Pot is revolutionary. We're talking a true one-pot, no-drain situation that cooks noodles to a perfect Goldilocks grade of "just right." I actually have a hard time making pasta any other way now. Here is a chapter to give you a slew of some of the greatest and most creative pasta dishes to ever grace your fork.

♨ = AIR FRYER LID    DF = DAIRY-FREE

K = KETO    GF = GLUTEN-FREE

P = PALEO    V = VEGETARIAN

+ = COMPLIANT WITH MODIFICATIONS    VN = VEGAN

# THE BEST SPAGHETTI & MEATBALLS

Mamma mia! Spaghetti and meatballs cooked together at the same time? In *one* pot?! With *no* draining?!? Not only has this spaghetti received the nod of approval from kids of all ages, it's customizable to be as spicy and/or creamy as you like. I prefer making my own meatballs (see Jeff's Tips), but you can just as easily simplify things and use packaged frozen ones.

 **DF** + *(see Lighter Comforts)*

 **V** + *(see Lighter Comforts)*

 **VN** + *(see Lighter Comforts)*

| Prep Time | Sauté Time | Pressure Building Time | Pressure Cook Time | Total Time | Serves |
|---|---|---|---|---|---|
| 5 MIN | 6 MIN | 10–15 MIN | 8 MIN | 30 MIN | 4–6 |

2 tablespoons extra-virgin olive oil

2 tablespoons (¼ stick) salted butter

2 large shallots or 1 large yellow or Vidalia (sweet) onion, diced

3 cloves garlic, minced or pressed

2 cups garlic broth (e.g., Garlic Better Than Bouillon) or vegetable broth

3 cups marinara sauce (I like Victoria or Rao's), at room temperature, divided

1 teaspoon dried oregano

1–1½ pounds frozen or raw meatballs (about the size of Ping-Pong balls, see Jeff's Tips)

1 pound spaghetti

10 ounces grape or cherry tomatoes

¼ cup grated Parmesan cheese (optional)

**OPTIONAL SPECIAL TOUCHES**

½ cup hot sauce of your choice

1 teaspoon Cajun/Creole/Louisiana seasoning (I use Tony Chachere's)

¼ teaspoon crushed red pepper flakes (or more to taste)

1 (5.2-ounce) package Boursin cheese (any flavor) or 4 ounces brick cream cheese, cut into small chunks

 **JEFF'S TIPS** For a thinner sauce, add an additional cup of broth in Step 2.

If you're feeling lazy and/or are looking to save time, any meatballs from the frozen section of the market will do (Costco has good ones). Same cook time as raw meatballs.

**1** Add the oil and butter to the Instant Pot, hit Sauté, and Adjust so it's on the More or High setting. Once heated (about 3 minutes), add the shallots and garlic and sauté for 3 minutes, until slightly softened.

**2** Add the broth, 1½ cups of the marinara sauce, and the oregano. Then add any of the optional touches: hot sauce, Cajun seasoning, crushed red pepper. Stir well and gently add the meatballs (frozen or raw).

CONTINUES

**3** In batches, break the spaghetti in half and place in the pot in a crisscross fashion. (NOTE: I know it's a sin for some to break spaghetti, but for it to cook properly and fit in the pot, this needs to be done!) *Do not stir the spaghetti,* but smooth it out with a spatula so it's mostly submerged under the broth (it's fine if not all is). Top with the grape or cherry tomatoes.

**4** Secure the lid and move the valve to the sealing position. Hit Cancel and then hit Manual or Pressure Cook on High Pressure for 8 minutes. Quick release when done.

**5** Give the spaghetti a stir. (NOTE: If noodles appear to clump together a bit, they will quickly detach once stirred and while they should be perfectly al dente, they will also soften in a few moments of resting. If the sauce appears a bit thin, not to worry as that will soon change!) Add the remaining 1½ cups of marinara sauce along with the Parmesan (if using) and the Boursin or cream cheese (if using). Give it a final stir and let rest for 3–5 minutes to thicken the sauce even more.

**6** Place in bowls and serve with additional Parmesan cheese, if desired.

**JEFF'S TIP** If you want to make this using my meatballs, simply follow Steps 1 and 2 of the Meatballs Marinara recipe on page 213. Just make sure they're the size of Ping-Pong balls *and no larger,* as they can clog the pot when pressure cooking along with the spaghetti.

*lighter comforts* These Spaghetti & Meatballs are easily tailored to taste:

- If you want it creamy *and* spicy, add all the optional ingredients.

- If you want just spicy, omit the Boursin or cream cheese.

- If you want just creamy, omit the spicy ingredients.

- If you want just classic spaghetti and no meatballs, leave the meatballs out and it will be vegetarian. And if you add another 2 tablespoons olive oil in place of the butter, this will make it dairy-free and vegan. Of course, if you're vegan or vegetarian and wish to have a form of "meat"balls, you can use frozen plant-based ones.

- *Same cook time no matter what you choose!*

Cooking brings me great comfort. It takes me back to when I was a very little girl, standing next to my great-grama, in the same kitchen I stand in now, and listening to her hum a wordless tune and speak words of wisdom and instructions on how to make the perfect potato soup.

Today, I find myself standing next to my 6-year-old son and 4-year-old daughter, humming the same wordless tune, speaking the same words of wisdom and the same instructions of "don't stop stirring...not too fast, not too slow...yes, just like that" to them. I've learned it's not the foods themselves that are comforting...it's the memories that are attached to these foods.

KAYLA • GARFIELD HEIGHTS, OHIO

# SESAME PEANUT NOODLES

One of my all-time favorite things to eat is sesame noodles, the modern-classic Asian fusion dish that provides as much comfort as it does flavor. After many attempts at testing and tweaking my original spin on this recipe, I finally struck the perfect peanut-to-noodle ratio and the ideal sauce consistency to make sure you'll go (pea)nuts for it.

| Prep Time | Pressure Building Time | Pressure Cook Time | Total Time | Serves |
|-----------|----------------------|-------------------|-----------|--------|
| 5 MIN | 10–15 MIN | 6 MIN | 25 MIN | 4–6 |

1 pound linguine

2½–3½ cups garlic broth (e.g., Garlic Better Than Bouillon) or vegetable broth (see Jeff's Tips)

¼ cup sesame oil (any kind), plus more for serving

¼ cup low-sodium soy sauce

½ cup peanut butter (smooth or chunky)

2 tablespoons hoisin sauce

2 tablespoons honey

1 tablespoon minced or grated ginger (I use squeeze ginger)

½–1 cup peanuts, crushed, plus more for serving

1 bunch scallions, sliced, plus more for serving

2 tablespoons sesame seeds (I use a mix of black and white), plus more for serving

½–1 teaspoon crushed red pepper flakes (optional, or more or less to taste)

**1** Break the linguine in half and layer it in the Instant Pot in a crisscross fashion.

**2** Add the broth, sesame oil, and soy sauce, making sure the noodles are mostly submerged in the broth but *do not stir*. Secure the lid and move the valve to the sealing position. Hit Manual or Pressure Cook on High Pressure for 6 minutes. Quick release when done. (NOTE: When the lid comes off the pot, it may appear a bit soupy with some of the noodles clumped together. Have no fear! This is normal and will soon change.)

CONTINUES

**3** While the linguine's cooking, microwave the peanut butter in a bowl for 30 seconds, until softened and thinned out. Add the hoisin sauce, honey, ginger, peanuts, scallions, sesame seeds, and crushed red pepper flakes (if using) and whisk until combined.

**4** When the lid comes off, grab a mixing spoon/spatula and stir the pasta for a few moments until the noodles become freed up and springy. Pour the sauce over the cooked noodles and toss until well coated.

**5** Serve either hot or chilled, topped with additional sesame oil, peanuts, scallions, sesame seeds, and crushed red pepper flakes, if desired.

*lighter comforts* In case peanut butter is too heavy for you or you are allergic to peanuts and tree nuts, try sunflower butter instead and sub shelled sunflower seeds for the peanuts; they have a comparable flavor.

**JEFF'S TIPS** How thick your final sauce will be all depends on how much broth you use to pressure cook the noodles. Go with 2½ cups if you want a thicker sauce, and up to 3½ or even 4 cups if you want it thinner. I personally go for 3½ cups.

If using spaghetti instead of linguine, cook for 8 minutes instead of 6.

> As a 22-year-old newlywed I made my very first lasagna. I was so proud, and new hubby was all excited to try it. While pulling it out of the oven I burned my arm and then dropped the pan of lasagna, which landed upside-down on the oven door and then spilled onto the floor. I was crying because my arm was burned, dinner was ruined, and there was a mess everywhere. Hubby calmly turned off the oven, treated my burn, cleaned up the entire mess, and never ever mentioned it again.
>
> MELISSA • **PHOENIX, ARIZONA**

> I am 81 years old. I lived in an assisted living facility for six years until they told me I couldn't cook in my Instant Pot. That's the day I said "I'm out of here." When I moved into a new apartment I gave myself a housewarming present of my second Instant Pot. We are living happily ever since.
>
> EVELYN • **HOUMA, LOUISIANA**

> While my grandma made delicious latkes for Chanukah, we the adorable grandchildren would try to steal one as they were placed on a big platter. Grandma would yell, playfully, "Aveck!" telling us to go away from the kitchen. I am 71 but the memories are vivid.
>
> PEGGY • **COLUMBUS, OHIO**

# GODFATHER PASTA

I'm about to give you a pasta you can't refuse. Since I thrive off wild ideas for how to marry dishes, I decided to take the best and richest flavors of what Americans know as an Italian hero/sub/grinder/hoagie and transform it into the most decadent, creamy, tangy, cheesy, and meaty pasta dish ever. Folks, this one's called Godfather Pasta and it's only fitting as this is a dish to make the Don himself proud.

| Prep Time | Sauté Time | Pressure Building Time | Pressure Cook Time | Total Time | Serves |
|---|---|---|---|---|---|
| 10 MIN | 15 MIN | 10–15 MIN | 6 MIN | 45 MIN | 4–6 |

- **2 tablespoons (¼ stick) salted butter**
- **4 ounces diced prosciutto, pancetta, or thick-cut bacon**
- **1 red onion, diced**
- **1 (8-ounce) bottle Italian salad dressing** (NOTE: Use a dressing that is clear like an oil and not creamy.)
- **3 cups garlic broth (e.g., Garlic Better Than Bouillon) or chicken broth**

- **1½ teaspoons Italian seasoning**
- **1 pound cellentani or cavatappi (pigtail-shaped pasta)**
- **1 (12-ounce) jar sliced banana peppers, drained, plus more for serving (optional for spice)**
- **1 (12-ounce) jar roasted red peppers, drained and cut into bite-size pieces**
- **4 ounces dry salami or soppressata, sliced thin and then into quarters (you can add more if you want it super meaty)**

- **4 ounces pepperoni, sliced thin and then into quarters (you can add more if you want it super meaty)**
- **½ cup heavy cream or half-and-half**
- **1 (5.2-ounce) package Boursin cheese (any flavor) or 4 ounces brick cream cheese, cut into small chunks**
- **1 cup shredded Asiago cheese**

**1** Add the butter to the Instant Pot, hit Sauté, and Adjust so it's on the More or High setting. Once the butter's melted and sizzling, add the diced prosciutto (or pancetta or bacon) and sauté for 5–10 minutes, until it begins to become well-cooked and crispy. Remove with a slotted spoon and let rest in a paper towel–lined bowl.

**2** Add the onion to the pot and sauté for 3 minutes.

**3** Add the Italian dressing and deglaze (scrape the bottom of the pot until it's cleared of any browned bits from the prosciutto). Add the broth and Italian seasoning and stir well.

*lighter comforts* Don't tell the Don I told you this, but to lighten this one up use a low-fat Italian dressing, sub fat-free half-and-half for the cream, sub ¼ cup Greek yogurt for the Boursin, and/or only use half the meat.

**4** Add the pasta but *do not stir.* Just allow it to be as submerged as possible in the liquid by smoothing it out with a mixing spoon (it is okay if some of the pasta is sticking out above the liquid). Top it off with the banana peppers.

**5** Secure the lid and move the valve to the sealing position. Hit Cancel and then hit Manual or Pressure Cook on High Pressure for 6 minutes. Quick release when done.

**JEFF'S TIPS**

It's totally up to you how much meat you want in this pasta. I suggest 4–5 ounces of each but if you feel you want more, add more! Easy to do as we don't add the salami or pepperoni until the final steps after pressure cooking.

If you'd like your banana peppers to have more volume, add them after pressure cooking with the roasted red peppers. *Or* you can double the amount of banana peppers, adding half before pressure cooking (which infuses a kick into the sauce) and half after! To me, you can never have too many banana peppers!

**6** Stir in the crisped prosciutto, roasted red peppers, salami, and pepperoni. Then, add the cream (or half-and-half), Boursin (or cream cheese), and Asiago cheese and stir until melded into the sauce. Plate it up and top with additional banana peppers if you desire. Of course, this goes great with some crusty Italian bread.

# FETTUCCINE ALFREDO

Perhaps the creamiest, cheesiest, most beloved pasta sauce ever, Alfredo is a delicious gift from Italy to the rest of the world. As familiar as it is decadent, my version of this white-sauced fettuccine classic is an undeniable go-to for when you need some good old-fashioned, creamy comfort.

| Prep Time | Pressure Building Time | Pressure Cook Time | Total Time | Serves |
|-----------|------------------------|--------------------|-----------|--------|
| 5 MIN | 10–15 MIN | 7 MIN | 25 MIN | 4–6 |

3 cups garlic broth (e.g., Garlic Better Than Bouillon), vegetable broth, or chicken broth

1 pound fettuccine

8 tablespoons (1 stick) salted butter, divided into 1-tablespoon pats

1½–2 cups heavy cream (preferred) or half-and-half (see Jeff's Tips)

1 cup grated Parmesan cheese

1 (5.2-ounce) package Boursin herb cheese (any flavor) or 4 ounces brick cream cheese, cut into small chunks

1 teaspoon garlic powder

1 teaspoon black pepper

**OPTIONAL TOUCHES**

½–1 pound Shredded Chicken (page 40)

½–1 pound diced ham

10 ounces frozen peas

**1** Add the broth to the Instant Pot. In batches, break the fettuccine in half so it fits in the pot and layer in a crisscross fashion. (NOTE: Sorry, nonnas! I'm aware that breaking pasta in half is an Italian sin, but I assure you the noodles will still feel plenty long. This simply ensures even cooking and creates more portions!) *Do not stir* the noodles, but rather just press down on them until they're mostly submerged in the broth (it's okay if some of the noodles stick above the broth). Top with 4 tablespoons of the butter.

**2** Secure the lid and move the valve to the sealing position. Hit Manual or Pressure Cook on High Pressure for 7 minutes. Quick release when done.

**3** When the lid comes off, give everything a stir. (NOTE: If any noodles seem slightly fused together, keep stirring and lightly separating with a wooden spatula. The noodles should separate easily.) Hit Sauté and Adjust so it's on the More or High setting.

**4** Add the remaining 4 tablespoons butter and stir everything in the pot with the spatula until the butter's melted.

**5** Lastly, add the cream, Parmesan, Boursin (or cream cheese), garlic powder, and pepper. If adding any of the optional touches, do so now. Stir until the dairy is totally melded. Hit Cancel to turn the pot off, then let rest for 5 minutes to fully come together and thicken. Serve, topped with freshly cracked black pepper, if desired.

 *lighter comforts* Sub ¼ cup Greek yogurt for the Boursin and use fat-free half-and-half for the cream.

**JEFF'S TIPS** Start with 1½ cups cream or half-and-half but go up to 2 cups to make it even creamier with a slightly thinner sauce.

If you have refrigerated leftovers you wish to heat up, some splashes of cream will do the trick to get it smooth and creamy again while heating.

Due to all the dairy in the sauce, this dish is best eaten *immediately* after making it. When a dish of this nature sits in the pot for a while, the sauce is prone to separate. If you have leftovers, store in the fridge immediately after serving. When reheating in the microwave for 1–2 minutes, add a little more cream to revive and stir halfway through. Once heated, stir in more Parmesan as desired to thicken.

# TOMATO-FETA (FRISBEES)

Like everyone else, I saw the TikTok videos that turned internet denizens into tomato-feta pasta fanatics, and for good reason. This is my own take on that Greek-style pasta dish, made even easier by using an Instant Pot. I chose orecchiette because they look like little Frisbees and I love how they create a pocket for holding the creamy tomato-feta sauce that's about to go down.

| Prep Time | Sauté Time | Pressure Building Time | Pressure Cook Time | Total Time | Serves |
|---|---|---|---|---|---|
| 10 MIN | 8 MIN | 10–15 MIN | 5 MIN | 35 MIN | 4–6 |

3 tablespoons extra-virgin olive oil

1 large red onion, diced

6 cloves garlic, sliced into slivers

3 cups garlic broth (e.g., Garlic Better Than Bouillon) or vegetable broth

1½ cups marinara sauce (I like Victoria or Rao's), at room temperature

½–1 tablespoon hot sauce (optional)

2 teaspoons Italian seasoning

1½ teaspoons seasoned salt or Greek seasoning (I use Cavender's)

1 teaspoon black pepper

1 pound orecchiette

12 ounces cherry or grape tomatoes

Leaves from 1 bunch fresh basil, some reserved for serving

12 ounces crumbled feta cheese, some reserved for serving

⅓ cup tzatziki (optional)

**1** Add the olive oil to the Instant Pot, hit Sauté, and Adjust so it's on the More or High setting. After 3 minutes of the oil heating, add the onion and garlic and sauté for 5 minutes, until lightly softened.

**2** Add the broth, marinara, hot sauce (if using), Italian seasoning, seasoned salt, and black pepper. Stir everything together well.

**3** Add the pasta but *do not stir.* Just smooth it out so it's lightly submerged in the sauce. Top with the cherry tomatoes and basil.

**4** Secure the lid and move the valve to the sealing position. Hit Cancel and then hit Manual or Pressure Cook for 5 minutes on High Pressure. Quick release when done.

**5** Stir in the feta and tzatziki (if using) until they're mostly combined with the pasta and sauce. Serve topped with additional feta and basil, if desired.

## GIVE IT A CHEESY BROILED TOP

Sprinkle additional feta cheese over the finished pasta and add the air fryer lid. Hit Broil (400°F) for 3–5 minutes, then hit Start. When the cheese begins to melt and become bubbly, you're done. If you don't have an air fryer lid, transfer the finished pasta to a casserole dish, top with feta, and broil until slightly melted and bubbly-brown.

*lighter comforts* — Feel free to use a low-sodium broth and/or reduced-fat feta.

**JEFF'S TIP** — If you wish to give this an extra Greek-style touch, add some Pork Gyros (page 198) along with the feta in Step 5 and stir.

# ·CREAMY CAJUN·
# TORTELLINI

Inspired by the bayou, and soon to be made *by you*, this creamy pasta dish with a Southern touch always does the trick. Once that addictive Cajun-style sauce gets tossed with the little stuffed rounds of pasta known as tortellini, shield yourself from any gators—because they'll want some. This one can be made spicy or mild to your liking.

 **V**+ *(see Lighter Comforts)*

| Prep Time | Sauté Time | Pressure Building Time | Pressure Cook Time | Total Time | Serves |
|---|---|---|---|---|---|
| 10 MIN | 9 MIN | 5–10 MIN | 1–2 MIN | 35 MIN | 4–6 |

- 4 tablespoons (1/2 stick) salted butter
- 1 large shallot, diced
- 1 1/2 pounds andouille (or any smoked) sausage, sliced into 1/4-inch-thick disks
- 6 cloves garlic, minced or pressed
- 2 1/2 cups ham broth (e.g., Ham Better Than Bouillon) or vegetable broth
- 2 teaspoons Italian seasoning

- 1 teaspoon Cajun/Creole/Louisiana seasoning (I use Tony Chachere's)
- 1 teaspoon black pepper, plus more for serving
- 1/8 teaspoon ground nutmeg
- 20 ounces fresh tortellini of your choice (I use cheese tortellini; look for it in the refrigerated section of your market, usually near the dairy)
- 1/2 cup heavy cream or half-and-half

- 1 cup grated Parmesan cheese, plus more for serving
- 1/2 cup shredded Cheddar cheese

OPTIONAL TOUCHES
- 1/2–1 tablespoon hot sauce
- 1/2 teaspoon cayenne pepper
- 1/4 teaspoon crushed red pepper flakes
- 10 ounces frozen okra, thawed and rinsed (NOTE: It will thaw as you rinse it.)

**1** Add the butter to the Instant Pot, hit Sauté, and Adjust so it's on the More or High setting. Once the butter's melted, add the shallot and sauté for 3 minutes, until lightly softened.

**2** Add the sausage and garlic and sauté until lightly browned, about 3 minutes.

**3** Add the broth, Italian seasoning, Cajun seasoning, black pepper, and nutmeg. Stir everything together well.

**4** Add the tortellini but *do not stir.* Just smooth them out so they're lightly submerged in the broth.

**5** Secure the lid and move the valve to the sealing position. Hit Cancel and then hit Manual or Pressure Cook on High Pressure for 1 minute (for slightly firmer pasta) or 2 minutes (for softer). Quick release when done.

**6** Remove the lid, hit Cancel, and then hit Sauté and Adjust so it's on the More or High setting. Add the cream, Parmesan, and Cheddar, then any (or all) optional touches. Gently stir (the tortellini will be fragile) until the dairy is melded into the sauce. Hit Cancel to turn the pot off. Serve topped with additional sprinklings of cracked black pepper, crushed red pepper flakes, and Parmesan, if desired.

 *lighter comforts* Sub an unsweetened nondairy milk (such as almond or soy) for the cream, or just use light cream or fat-free half-and-half.

You can use chicken sausage if avoiding red meat. To make it vegetarian, use cheese tortellini and a vegetarian sausage (such as Beyond brand)—or leave the sausage out completely.

**JEFF'S TIPS** Since taste greatly varies from one palate to another, the hot spices are all optional. That said, feel free to go nuts and add more than I suggest if you're feeling fiery.

Want shrimp? Toss in up to 1 pound of peeled and deveined raw shrimp in Step 6 and stir until opaque and curled.

# CHEESEBURGER DELUXE PASTA

Picture your favorite diner or coffee shop. Now, picture a cheeseburger deluxe, loaded with all the fixin's, being placed right in front of you. And finally, picture that burger being deconstructed into a pasta. What you're about to experience is pure magic; you won't even be upset you missed out on the classic diner accompaniment of a milkshake (which I've yet to learn how to pressure cook).

| Prep Time | Sauté Time | Pressure Building Time | Pressure Cook Time | Total Time | Serves |
|---|---|---|---|---|---|
| 10 MIN | 9 MIN | 10-15 MIN | 6 MIN | 35 MIN | 4-6 |

3 tablespoons extra-virgin olive oil

1 large red onion, diced, divided (see Jeff's Tips), plus more for serving

1½ pounds ground beef (the less lean, the better)

3 cloves garlic, minced or pressed

1 tablespoon Worcestershire sauce

3 cups beef broth

1 (28-ounce) can crushed tomatoes

1 (8-ounce) can tomato sauce (not the same as pasta sauce)

½-1 tablespoon hot sauce (optional)

1 teaspoon liquid smoke (optional)

2 teaspoons Italian seasoning

1½ teaspoons seasoned salt

1 teaspoon black pepper

1 pound large elbow macaroni

½ cup Thousand Island dressing (I like Ken's Steakhouse brand)

¼ cup diced dill pickles, plus more for serving (optional)

2 tablespoons sweet relish (optional)

2 tablespoons barbecue sauce (I like Sweet Baby Ray's)

1 tablespoon yellow mustard (optional)

1 pound shredded Cheddar cheese

Fried onions, for serving (I use French's, optional)

**1** Add the olive oil to the Instant Pot, hit Sauté, and Adjust so it's on the More or High setting. After 3 minutes of the oil heating, add half the onion and sauté for 3 minutes, until lightly softened.

**2** Add the ground beef and garlic and, using a mixing spoon or spatula, break up the meat until it begins to crumble and lightly brown, about 3 minutes. It shouldn't be fully cooked at this point (that's what the pressure cooking is for). *Do not drain any juices released*—we want them in there for more flavor!

**3** Add the Worcestershire sauce and deglaze (scrape the bottom of the pot to free it of any browned bits).

**4** Add the broth, crushed tomatoes, tomato sauce, hot sauce (if using), liquid smoke (if using), Italian seasoning, seasoned salt, and black pepper. Stir everything together well.

**5** Add the pasta but *do not stir. (Why? Well, there's lots of meat in there. If you stir the pasta in, you run the risk of clogging the pot when it tries to come to pressure.)* Just smooth the pasta out so it's slightly submerged in the sauce.

**6** Secure the lid and move the valve to the sealing position. Hit Cancel and then hit Manual or Pressure Cook for 6 minutes on High Pressure. Quick release when done.

**JEFF'S TIPS** If you only like your onions cooked and don't mind missing out on the nice crunch of raw onion, add all the diced onion in Step 1 while sautéing.

However crazy you like your burger is how crazy you can get with this recipe. Be it black olives, sliced jalapeño, or even pastrami (see page 208), add whatever toppings you love in Step 7!

**7** Add the remaining red onion, the Thousand Island dressing, pickles (if using), relish (if using), barbecue sauce, mustard (if using), and Cheddar cheese. Stir until the cheese is melded into the pasta. Serve topped with additional red onion, dill pickles, and fried onions, if desired.

*lighter comforts* Try a low-fat cheese instead of the Cheddar here.

# CHICKEN PICCATA PASTA

If there were a dish that was sunshine in a bowl, it would be this recipe. In this piccata-inspired pasta, we have chicken in a lemon-Parmesan sauce adorned with a burst of savory capers and buttery leeks. It's a dish that can part the dreariest of clouds and pave the way for culinary happiness.

GF + *(see Lighter Comforts)*

V + *(see Lighter Comforts)*

| Prep Time | Sauté Time | Pressure Building Time | Pressure Cook Time | Total Time | Serves |
|---|---|---|---|---|---|
| 15 MIN | 13 MIN | 10–15 MIN | 6 MIN | 45 MIN | 4–6 |

4 tablespoons (½ stick) salted butter

1 large leek, tough tops, bottoms, and outer layers removed, diced

1 large shallot, diced

3 cloves garlic, minced or pressed

1½ pounds boneless, skinless chicken breasts, sliced into ¼-inch-thick cutlets and cut into bite-size pieces

3 cups chicken broth

Juice of 2 lemons

1 pound farfalle (bow tie–shaped pasta)

⅓ cup heavy cream or half-and-half

1 cup grated Parmesan cheese, plus more for serving, if desired

½ cup capers (try to use the smaller ones rather than larger ones), drained, plus more for serving, if desired

1 (14-ounce) can artichoke hearts, drained and ripped up by hand (optional)

**1** Add the butter to the Instant Pot, hit Sauté, and Adjust so it's on the More or High setting.

**2** Once the butter's melted and bubbling, add the leek and sauté for 5–8 minutes, until crispy. Remove with a spoon and let rest in a bowl.

**3** Add the shallot and garlic to the pot and sauté for another 2 minutes, until softened. Add the chicken and sauté for 3 minutes longer, until the chicken is pinkish-white in color.

**4** Add the broth and lemon juice and stir until all is combined.

**5** Add the pasta so it's lying on top of the broth, but *do not stir*. Instead, gently smooth and push it down with a spatula so it's submerged. (It's okay if some of the pasta is sticking up above the water.)

**6** Secure the lid and move the valve to the sealing position. Hit Cancel and then hit Manual or Pressure Cook for 6 minutes on High Pressure. Quick release when done.

**7** Stir in the cream, Parmesan, capers, artichoke hearts (if using), and leeks, reserving some for garnish. Transfer to a serving bowl, plate it up, and sprinkle with extra Parmesan cheese and/or capers, if desired.

*lighter comforts* You can make this vegetarian by leaving out the chicken and using a vegetable-based broth.

Want whole-wheat or gluten-free pasta? Use any short-form pasta such as penne, farfalle, or rotini and go for 4 minutes instead of 6.

 **JEFF'S TIP** If you're in love with artichokes, feel free to double the amount.

# ★ AMERICAN MAC

When you combine perfectly cooked macaroni with a richly seasoned tomato-based meat sauce, you have what's come to be known as a classic American pasta dish. Depending on the region of the U.S. in which one resides, the version you're familiar with may be called American goulash, American chop suey, Johnny Marzetti, slumgullion, hot dish, or a slew of other names. Whatever you wanna call it, this dish is quick, easy, flavorful, and a home run for the entire family.

 DF

 GF + *(see Lighter Comforts)*

| Prep Time | Sauté Time | Pressure Building Time | Pressure Cook Time | Total Time | Serves |
|-----------|------------|------------------------|---------------------|------------|--------|
| 10 MIN | 10 MIN | 10–15 MIN | 5 MIN | 35 MIN | 4–6 |

- 3 tablespoons extra-virgin olive oil
- 1 yellow onion, diced
- 1 green bell pepper, seeded and diced
- 3 cloves garlic, minced or pressed
- 1½ pounds ground beef or meatloaf mixture (veal/pork/beef)

- 1 (28-ounce) can crushed tomatoes
- 1 (8-ounce) can tomato sauce (not the same as pasta sauce)
- 3 cups low-sodium beef broth
- 1–2 tablespoons hot sauce (optional)
- 1 tablespoon seasoned salt

- 2 teaspoons Italian seasoning
- 1 teaspoon black pepper
- 1 teaspoon dried basil
- ¼ teaspoon ground nutmeg
- 1 pound elbow or large elbow macaroni

**1** Add the olive oil to the Instant Pot, hit Sauté, and Adjust so it's on the More or High setting. After 3 minutes of the oil heating, add the onion and bell pepper and sauté for 3–5 minutes, until slightly softened. Add the garlic and sauté for 1 minute longer.

**2** Add the ground beef and, using a mixing spoon or spatula, break it up until the meat begins to crumble and lightly brown—about 3 minutes. It shouldn't be fully cooked at this point (that's what the pressure cooking is for). Do not drain any juices released—we want them in there for more flavor!

**3** Add the crushed tomatoes, tomato sauce, broth, hot sauce (if using), seasoned salt, Italian seasoning, black pepper, dried basil, and nutmeg. Stir everything together well.

**4** Add the macaroni but *do not stir. (Why? Well, there's lots of meat in there. If you stir the pasta in, you run the risk of clogging the pot when it tries to come to pressure.)* Just smooth the pasta out so it's lightly submerged in the sauce.

**5** Secure the lid and move the valve to the sealing position. Hit Cancel and then hit Manual or Pressure Cook for 5 minutes on High Pressure. Quick release when done.

**6** Give everything a final good stir and serve.

**lighter comforts** For a gluten-free alternative, sub gluten-free macaroni and pressure cook for 4 minutes instead of 5.

**JEFF'S TIP** Some like this with a chili flair and then it becomes Chili Mac. Add a 1-ounce packet of chili seasoning or 1–2 tablespoons Chili Better Than Bouillon in Step 6. You can also add a 15.5-ounce can of rinsed and drained beans of your choice.

# SHELLEY STROGANOFF

The Beef Stroganoff in my first book is one of my most popular recipes. Stroganoff is now most widely known as a protein dish served over noodles in a sour cream–infused sauce, but I felt it would work really nicely with ground meat cooked directly alongside pasta shells. Since I love alliteration and my mom's name is Shelley, this one's named after her (whether she likes it or not).

 **V** + *(see Lighter Comforts)*

| Prep Time | Sauté Time | Pressure Building Time | Pressure Cook Time | Total Time | Serves |
|---|---|---|---|---|---|
| 10 MIN | 15 MIN | 10–15 MIN | 6 MIN | 45 MIN | 4–6 |

- 2 tablespoons extra-virgin olive oil
- 1 large yellow onion, diced
- 2 tablespoons (¼ stick) salted butter
- 1 pound baby bella or white mushrooms, sliced (optional; if you hate 'shrooms, don't use them and omit the butter)
- 3 cloves garlic, minced or pressed
- 1 tablespoon Worcestershire sauce

- 1½ pounds ground meat of your choice (beef, chicken, turkey)
- ½ cup dry white wine (like a chardonnay), or additional ½ cup broth
- 1 tablespoon Dijon mustard (like Grey Poupon), optional
- 3½ cups beef broth
- 1 teaspoon seasoned salt
- 1 teaspoon dried thyme
- 1 pound medium pasta shells

- 1 (1-ounce) packet dry onion dip/ soup mix
- 1 cup sour cream
- 1 (5.2-ounce) package Boursin herb cheese (any flavor) or 4 ounces brick cream cheese, cut into small chunks
- ¼ cup grated Parmesan cheese (optional)
- 1 tablespoon truffle oil (any kind, optional)

**1** Add the olive oil to the Instant Pot and hit Sauté and Adjust so it's on the More or High setting. After 3 minutes of heating, add the onion and sauté for 2 minutes. Add the butter and mushrooms and sauté for 3 minutes.

**2** Add the garlic and sauté for 1 minute, then add the Worcestershire sauce. Deglaze the bottom of the pot so it's free of any dark brown spots.

**3** Add the meat and break up with a spatula for 3 minutes, until it crumbles and lightly browns.

*lighter comforts* Make this vegetarian by using plant-based "meat" (such as Impossible brand) for the ground meat and use a vegetable-based broth in lieu of the beef broth.

Sub low-fat sour cream for regular.

**4** Add the white wine followed by the Dijon mustard and simmer for 2 minutes. Stir well and deglaze (scrape the bottom of the pot so nothing's stuck to it).

**5** Add the broth, seasoned salt, and thyme and stir well.

**6** Add the pasta but *do not stir*. Just smooth it out so it's mostly submerged in the broth (it's okay if some sticks up above).

**7** Secure the lid and move the valve to the sealing position. Hit Cancel followed by Manual or Pressure Cook on High Pressure for 6 minutes. Quick release when done.

**8** When the lid comes off, stir in the onion mix, sour cream, Boursin (or cream cheese), Parmesan (if using), and truffle oil (if using). Stir well until all is totally melded into the sauce.

**JEFF'S TIP** You can season up the final product with any additions you'd like. If you want it a little spicy, add a few shakes of your favorite hot sauce. If you want it even creamier, add a few splashes of half-and-half or cream in the final step and stir until combined.

# SPICY SAUSAGE TWISTS

My Sausage & Shells (from my orange book) has become one of my most popular, sought-after (and imitated) recipes. To build on that success, I thought it was time to create another sausage pasta—this time, with a spicy, marinara-based sauce (think a fra diavolo/arrabbiata combo) paired with twisty gemelli pasta—and creamy perfection to send it home.

DF $^+$   *(see Lighter Comforts)*

| Prep Time | Sauté Time | Pressure Building Time | Pressure Cook Time | Total Time | Serves |
|---|---|---|---|---|---|
| 10 MIN | 8 MIN | 10–15 MIN | 6 MIN | 35 MIN | 4–6 |

- 4 tablespoons (½ stick) salted butter
- 2 large shallots, diced
- 3 cloves garlic, minced or pressed
- 2 pounds Italian sausage (sweet, hot, or mixed), removed from its casing (see Jeff's Tips)
- 2 bunches scallions, cut into ½-inch pieces, divided (optional)

- 2 cups garlic broth (e.g., Garlic Better Than Bouillon) or chicken broth
- 3½ cups marinara sauce (I like Victoria or Rao's), at room temperature, divided
- ½ cup hot sauce (I use Frank's RedHot)
- 1 teaspoon Italian seasoning
- 1 teaspoon dried basil

- ½ teaspoon crushed red pepper flakes
- 1 pound gemelli pasta (campanelle or cavatappi works well too)
- 5–8 ounces baby spinach
- 4 ounces brick cream cheese, cut into cubes (optional)
- 1 (5.2-ounce) package Boursin herb cheese (any flavor), cut into small crumbles (optional)

**1** Add the butter to the Instant Pot and hit Sauté and Adjust to the More or High setting. Once the butter's melted, add the shallots and sauté for 2 minutes. Add the garlic and sauté for 1 minute longer.

**2** Add the sausage meat and ¾ of the scallions (if using) and sauté for 3 minutes, until it crumbles/breaks apart and lightly browns. (NOTE: It's easiest to do this with a wooden spoon or spatula.)

**3** Add the broth, 1½ cups of the marinara, the hot sauce, Italian seasoning, dried basil, and crushed red pepper flakes. Stir everything together well.

 **JEFF'S TIPS** Sometimes you can find bulk Italian sausage (i.e., without casings) in larger grocery stores. Otherwise, removing the casing yourself is easy-peasy. Using the sharp tip of a knife, slice the surface of the sausage casing lengthwise, spread the casing open, and remove the meat. Discard the casing when done.

Don't want it spicy? Leave out the hot sauce and red pepper flakes and use sweet Italian sausage instead of hot.

**4** Add the pasta but *do not stir*. Just allow it to be as submerged under the liquid as possible by smoothing it out with a mixing spoon (it is okay if some of the pasta is sticking out above the liquid). Top with the spinach. (NOTE: It's going to feel like there's a lot of spinach in there and it will come up to the brim of the pot, but don't worry—it cooks down to nothing!)

**5** Secure the lid and move the valve to the sealing position. Hit Cancel followed by Manual or Pressure Cook on High Pressure for 6 minutes. Quick release when done.

**6** Stir in the remaining 2 cups marinara sauce and the remaining scallions (if using).

**7** Lastly, stir in the cream cheese and Boursin (if using) and stir until completely melded into the sauce. Let rest for 5 minutes before transferring to a serving dish.

*lighter comforts* I prefer this pasta with a creamy finish, but you can sub ½ cup Greek yogurt for the cream cheese and Boursin. To make it dairy-free, leave out the creamy cheeses (or try a vegan sub like dairy-free Boursin, Miyoko's, or Treeline) and sub 3 tablespoons extra-virgin olive oil for the butter.

# DRUNKEN SPAGHETTI

This pasta is inspired by the popular Thai rice-noodle dish known as drunken noodles or pad kee mao. But despite the name, there's actually no alcohol in it; as the story goes, the name comes from the noodles being spicy and folks swigging some beer to drown the heat, leading to a jolly time. But since rice noodles don't cook well under pressure, I'm using spaghetti instead. I also give you options on the spice level so everyone can enjoy my take on this outrageously comforting masterpiece.

(see Lighter Comforts)

| Prep Time | Sauté Time | Pressure Building Time | Pressure Cook Time | Total Time | Serves |
|---|---|---|---|---|---|
| 15 MIN | 10 MIN | 10–15 MIN | 8 MIN | 45 MIN | 4–6 |

¼ cup sesame oil (any kind)

1 medium yellow onion, diced

1 large red bell pepper, seeded and sliced into matchsticks

1–2 jalapeño peppers, diced (optional)

1 red or green chile pepper, diced (optional)

1 cup loosely packed fresh Thai basil or fresh tarragon leaves (I use tarragon and it works like a charm)

1½ pounds boneless, skinless chicken thighs, cut into ¼-inch-thick strips

6 cloves garlic, minced or pressed

1 teaspoon crushed red pepper flakes, plus more for serving (optional)

2½ cups garlic broth (e.g., Garlic Better Than Bouillon) or vegetable broth

1 pound spaghetti

2 tablespoons (¼ stick) salted butter, cut into two pats

¼ cup hoisin sauce

¼ cup oyster sauce

3 tablespoons low-sodium soy sauce

2 tablespoons pad thai sauce

2 tablespoons chili-garlic sauce or sriracha (optional)

2 teaspoons fish sauce

1 pound frozen or fresh broccoli florets (optional)

1 bunch scallions, sliced, some reserved for serving

**1** Place the sesame oil in the Instant Pot and hit Sauté and Adjust to the More or High setting. Once the oil's heated, add the onion, bell pepper, jalapeño (if using), red chile pepper (if using), and Thai basil or tarragon. Sauté for 5 minutes, until lightly softened.

**2** Add the chicken, garlic, and red pepper flakes (if using) and sauté until the chicken is pinkish-white in color, about 3 minutes.

**3** Add the broth and stir. Break the spaghetti in half and add it to the pot, layering it in a crisscross fashion but *do not stir*. Top with the butter.

**4** Secure the lid and move the valve to the sealing position. Hit Cancel followed by Manual or Pressure Cook on High Pressure for 8 minutes. Quick release when done.

**5** While the spaghetti's cooking, combine the hoisin sauce, oyster sauce, soy sauce, pad thai sauce, chili-garlic sauce, and fish sauce in a bowl. Whisk together until combined.

**6** If using the broccoli, place the florets in a microwave-safe bowl, add ¼ cup water, cover with plastic wrap, and microwave for 9–10 minutes (if frozen) or 3–4 minutes (if fresh). Remove the plastic wrap and drain. If you want smaller pieces of broccoli, cut them into the desired size.

**7** Give the cooked pasta a stir. Add the broccoli (if using), sauce, and scallions to the pot and toss until the noodles are coated. Serve topped with reserved scallions and a sprinkle of red pepper flakes, if desired.

*lighter comforts* You can use gluten-free hoisin sauce, oyster sauce, and pasta (shave 2 minutes off the cook time) to make this gluten-free. But also make sure the pad thai sauce and fish sauce are gluten-free—most are but some are not.

 **JEFF'S TIP** You'll notice I list all the spicy ingredients as optional. Personally, I like this dish *spicy*, as it's known to be, but I know that's not everyone's game. Feel free to spice it up as you wish!

# ⫴ STRAW ⫴
# ⫴ & HAY ⫴

I simply love this rich and indulgent pasta. It's so beautiful (not to mention delicious) to see the egg (straw) and spinach (hay) pastas tangle themselves together when tossed in the pork-y, Parmesan cream sauce. Sold yet? If not, give it a twirl on a spoon and prepare to swoon. (Yes, this dish is as cheesy as that previous sentence.)

**V** + *(see Lighter Comforts)*

| Prep Time | Sauté Time | Pressure Building Time | Pressure Cook Time | Total Time | Serves |
|---|---|---|---|---|---|
| **10** MIN | **15** MIN | **10–15** MIN | **7** MIN | **45** MIN | **4–6** |

2 tablespoons (¼ stick) salted butter

¼ cup extra-virgin olive oil

8 ounces prosciutto or pancetta, diced

2 large shallots, diced

3 cloves garlic, sliced into slivers

½ cup dry white wine (like a sauvignon blanc)

3½ cups garlic broth (e.g., Garlic Better Than Bouillon) or chicken broth

½ pound regular (egg) fettuccine or linguine

½ pound spinach fettuccine (see Jeff's Tip) or linguine

1 (5.2-ounce) package Boursin herb cheese (any flavor) or 4 ounces brick cream cheese, diced into small cubes

¼ cup heavy cream

¼ cup grated Parmesan cheese, plus more for serving, if desired

10 ounces frozen peas, thawed by rinsing (optional)

**1** Add the butter and oil to the Instant Pot. Hit Sauté and Adjust to the More or High setting. Once the butter's melted, add the prosciutto and sauté for 5–8 minutes, until it begins to get a bit crispy. Remove with a slotted spoon and set aside in a bowl lined with a paper towel.

**2** Add the shallots and garlic to the pot and sauté for 5 minutes, until softened and browned.

**3** Add the wine and deglaze the bottom of the pot to get up any browned bits. Once the wine's simmering, add the broth.

**4** Break the fettuccine in half and place in the pot, layering in a crisscross fashion and submerging it under the liquid as best as possible but *do not stir*.

**5** Secure the lid and move the valve to the sealing position. Hit Cancel followed by Manual or Pressure Cook on High Pressure for 7 minutes. Quick release when done.

**6** Return the prosciutto to the pot and add the Boursin or cream cheese, cream, and Parmesan. Once melded, add the thawed peas (if using). Let sit for 3–5 minutes for the pasta to thicken perfectly. Transfer to a large bowl and serve.

*lighter comforts*
While I love the prosciutto in this dish, you can go vegetarian and omit it completely; just start by sautéing the shallots and garlic once the butter and oil are heated. You can also sub tempeh for the prosciutto to make it vegetarian. Add 8 ounces of sliced mushrooms during this step as well, if that's your thing.

**JEFF'S TIP**
If you can't find spinach fettuccine, it's not the end of the world. Just use 1 pound of regular fettuccine. True, you won't get that two-tone color, but it'll taste just as grand.

# REUBEN ROTINI

My favorite sandwich is the Reuben, which is comprised of pastrami (or corned beef), sauerkraut, Swiss cheese, and Russian (or Thousand Island) dressing on caraway-studded rye bread. The only thing better than this gem in sandwich form is when it's magically transformed into to-die-for pasta.

| Prep Time | Pressure Building Time | Pressure Cook Time | Total Time | Serves |
|---|---|---|---|---|
| 10 MIN | 10–15 MIN | 5 MIN | 25 MIN | 4–6 |

1 pound rotini

3 cups beef broth

2 cups chicken broth

1–2 teaspoons caraway seeds, plus more for serving

½ cup Russian or Thousand Island dressing (make sure it's a creamy-orange color and not burgundy—I like Ken's Steakhouse brand for both Russian and Thousand Island)

1 (5.2-ounce) package Boursin herb cheese (any flavor) or 4 ounces brick cream cheese, cut into small crumbles (optional)

1 pound pastrami or corned beef (either the recipe on page 208 or from the deli), sliced ¼ inch thick and then diced up

1 pound sauerkraut, drained and squeezed

2 cups shredded Swiss or mozzarella cheese (or more, see Step 6)

**1** Add the rotini, broths, and caraway seeds to the Instant Pot. Make sure the pasta is mostly submerged under the broth (it's okay if some sticks up above the top).

**2** Secure the lid and move the valve to the sealing position. Hit Manual or Pressure Cook on High Pressure for 5 minutes. Quick release when done.

**3** Stir in the dressing and Boursin or cream cheese (if using) until fully melded into the pasta.

**4** Add the pastrami or corned beef, sauerkraut, and Swiss cheese and stir until the cheese becomes stretchy and one with the pasta.

**5** Serve immediately, topped with additional caraway seeds for garnish, if desired.

**6** **Optional:** To give it that broiled cheese goodness, add another 1–2 cups shredded cheese to the top of the pasta just before serving in Step 5 and place the air fryer lid on top. Hit Broil (400°F) for 3–5 minutes and hit Start. Once the cheese is bubbly-brown to your liking, it's done.

*lighter comforts* The Boursin (or cream cheese) is used here for extra creaminess. Given that it is optional, there's no need to include either of them. But if you want a light creaminess, you can sub in Greek yogurt.

**JEFF'S TIP** If you can find only thin-sliced pastrami or corned beef at the market, you can just cut it into smaller pieces before adding in Step 4.

# JALAPEÑO POPPER PENNE

One of my all-time favorite appetizers is the classic cheese-filled, deep-fried jalapeño popper. Sometimes I like mine stuffed with melty cheese, and other times I prefer the cream cheese. Here, we'll deconstruct this iconic appy and transform it into a pasta that gives you the best of all worlds.

| Prep Time | Sauté Time | Pressure Building Time | Pressure Cook Time | Total Time | Serves |
|-----------|------------|------------------------|--------------------|------------|--------|
| 10 MIN | 10 MIN | 15–20 MIN | 6 MIN | 45 MIN | 4–6 |

¼ cup extra-virgin olive oil or vegetable oil

1 large Vidalia (sweet) onion, sliced lengthwise into strips about ¼ inch thick

3 jalapeño peppers, ribs and seeds removed, sliced into disks

1 red bell pepper, seeded and sliced lengthwise into strips about ¼ inch thick

1 green bell pepper, seeded and sliced lengthwise into strips about ¼ inch thick

3 cloves garlic, minced or pressed

1–2 (1-ounce) packet(s) fajita or taco seasoning

3 cups garlic broth (e.g., Garlic Better Than Bouillon) or vegetable broth

1 pound penne rigate or mezze penne pasta

1 teaspoon ground cumin

1 teaspoon chili powder

½ teaspoon Cajun/Creole/ Louisiana seasoning (I use Tony Chachere's) or seasoned salt

½ teaspoon garlic powder

½ teaspoon onion powder

2 cups shredded Mexican cheese blend, some reserved for serving

1 (8-ounce) brick cream cheese, cut into small chunks (see Jeff's Tips)

¼ cup hot sauce or taco sauce (optional)

1 (12-ounce) jar sliced jalapeños, drained (optional)

Up to 1 cup heavy cream or half-and-half (optional, see Jeff's Tips)

**1** Add the oil to the Instant Pot, hit Sauté, and Adjust so it's on the More or High setting. After 3 minutes of heating, add the onion, jalapeño, and bell peppers and sauté for 5 minutes, until slightly softened. Add the garlic and sauté for 2 minutes longer.

**2** Add the fajita or taco seasoning and coat everything with it. Scrape the bottom of the pot to make sure nothing is sticking.

**3** Pour in the broth and give everything a good stir, again scraping the bottom of the pot to ensure nothing's stuck on it and that everything is submerged in the broth. Add the pasta but *do not stir*. Simply smooth it out so it's submerged in the broth the best it can be.

**4** Secure the lid and move the valve to the sealing position. Hit Cancel and then hit Manual or Pressure Cook on High Pressure for 6 minutes. Quick release when done.

**5** Give the finished pasta a final stir. You'll see some extra liquid in the pot—this is what we want, as it serves as the base for the sauce!

**6** Add the cumin, chili powder, Cajun seasoning or seasoned salt, garlic powder, onion powder, shredded cheese, cream cheese, hot sauce or taco sauce (if using), and jarred sliced jalapeños (if using). Stir until fully melded and combined.

**7** Serve in bowls and feel free to top with fixin's such as additional jarred jalapeño slices, shredded cheese, and hot sauce, along with fresh salsa or diced tomatoes, and avocado or guacamole.

**_lighter comforts_** Sub light cream cheese (or even Greek yogurt) for the full-fat version.

**JEFF'S TIPS** Like the inside of a jalapeño popper, this pasta is designed to have a very thick and creamy consistency. For a thinner and creamier sauce, add up to 1 cup heavy cream in Step 6 after all the cheese is melded into the sauce (start with ½ cup and you can always increase). You can also use only 4 ounces of the brick of cream cheese instead of all 8.

Feel free to add shredded chicken (see page 40) or raw shrimp in Step 6. The chicken will already be cooked so it'll be ready to eat; the shrimp will cook very quickly from the heat of the pot: Once curled and opaque (3–5 minutes), they're done.

# 4

# RICE

Whether you like your rice fluffy, creamy, or sticky, the Instant Pot is a prodigy when it comes to cooking these beloved grains. And so I'm supplying you with a chapter that gives you a slew of Instant Pot rice recipes ranging from simple comfort classics to downright bold and fresh creations of my own.

I have always loved being in the kitchen. I started off as a young child watching my grandmothers and mom cook traditional Filipino foods.

Now my 4-year-old and I bond in the kitchen. She loves helping. Seeing the joy it brings her the way it did me fills my heart.

KIMBERLEY • RALEIGH, NORTH CAROLINA

 = AIR FRYER LID
 = KETO
 = PALEO
+ = COMPLIANT WITH MODIFICATIONS

 = DAIRY-FREE
 = GLUTEN-FREE
 = VEGETARIAN
VN = VEGAN

# JEWISH DELI FRIED RICE

If there's one thing we Jewish folk are known for, it's delicatessens, where it's not at all uncommon to order an omelet loaded with pastrami—in fact, egg and meat is a frequent pairing. So one day as I was eating some Chinese-American fried rice and noticed all that egg and protein, I was inspired to create Jewish Deli Fried Rice. L'chayim.

**DF** + *(see Lighter Comforts)*

**V** + *(see Lighter Comforts)*

| Prep Time | Pressure Building Time | Pressure Cook Time | Natural Release Time | Sauté Time | Total Time | Serves |
|---|---|---|---|---|---|---|
| 10 MIN | 5–10 MIN | 3 MIN | 10 MIN | 10 MIN | 40 MIN | 4–6 |

2 cups jasmine rice, rinsed for 90 seconds and drained

2 cups chicken broth or onion broth (e.g., Sautéed Onion Better Than Bouillon)

8 large eggs

½ cup whole milk or half-and-half

2 tablespoons vegetable oil

1 Spanish (or yellow) onion, diced

1 bunch scallions, sliced (some reserved for garnish)

1 pound pastrami, thinly sliced and diced (easy to get at any market deli, or use my recipe on page 208)

¾ cup teriyaki sauce (I like Soy Vay for this one, for obvious reasons)

⅓ cup Russian or Thousand Island dressing (make sure it's a creamy-orange color and not burgundy—I like Ken's Steakhouse brand for both Russian and Thousand Island), optional

**1** Add the rinsed rice to the Instant Pot along with the broth and stir. Secure the lid and move the valve to the sealing position. Hit Manual or Pressure Cook on High Pressure for 3 minutes. When done, allow a 10-minute natural release followed by a quick release.

**2** While the rice is cooking, whisk together the eggs and milk in a bowl and set aside.

**3** After opening the pot, hit Cancel. Fluff the rice with a fork and transfer to a bowl. You can either rinse the liner pot and return it to the Instant Pot (just make sure it's totally dry before returning) or leave as is (it will be more prone to things getting stuck to the bottom in the next step, but not a big deal).

**4** Add the vegetable oil to the pot and hit Sauté and Adjust to the More or High setting. After 3 minutes of heating, add the onion and scallions and sauté for 5 minutes. Add the pastrami and sauté for 3 minutes longer.

**5** Add the egg mixture and cook, stirring constantly and scraping the bottom of the pot, until it becomes cooked into broken-down bits, 4–5 minutes. Turn off the pot by hitting Cancel.

**6** Return the rice to the pot, pour the teriyaki sauce over the rice and eggs, and stir until fully combined. Lastly, stir in the Russian dressing (if using), garnish with scallions, and serve.

*lighter comforts* If you wish to make it kosher and dairy-free, replace the cream with an unsweetened nondairy milk such as almond or oat milk.

You can make this vegetarian by leaving out the pastrami or subbing in a meat replacement such as diced tempeh or ground Impossible meat. Of course, you'd also use the onion broth instead of chicken. If eggs are off-limits, leave them out.

**JEFF'S TIP** If you want it saucier, add more teriyaki sauce and/or Russian dressing to taste.

When my twin daughters were little (they are 36 now), they would make me breakfast in bed for Mother's Day. Kati was attentive to making my fave scrambled eggs with cream cheese and chives in them. One year, she dutifully went to the garden to get the chives, and made the eggs. Unfortunately, she used some weeds, not the chives. We still joke around every year that she should make that again for me. It was cooking from the heart and yes, I ate it anyway.
LAURA • HALF MOON BAY, CALIFORNIA

# CHICKEN SHAWARMA RICE

Shawarma is a classic Middle Eastern street food, composed of spiced meat or poultry roasted on a rotisserie, thinly sliced, and often served in a pita (not unlike a gyro). I included a recipe for it in my orange book and due to its great popularity I decided to make my own take on shawarma as a complete rice dish. The flavors will make you think you're eating some of the best street rice in the world while using the most affordable and accessible ingredients to make it come to life. See Jeff's Tips for information on making it spicy or mild.

  *(see Lighter Comforts)*

| Prep Time | Sauté Time | Pressure Building Time | Pressure Cook Time | Natural Release Time | Total Time | Serves |
|---|---|---|---|---|---|---|
| 10 MIN | 10 MIN | 10–15 MIN | 3 MIN | 10 MIN | 45 MIN | 4–6 |

2 tablespoons extra-virgin olive oil

2 tablespoons (¼ stick) salted butter

1 large red onion, diced

2 pounds boneless, skinless chicken thighs, cut into ¼-inch-thick strips

3 cloves garlic, minced or pressed

3 cups garlic broth (e.g., Garlic Better Than Bouillon) or chicken broth

1 tablespoon paprika

1 tablespoon curry powder

1 tablespoon seasoned salt

1–2 teaspoons black pepper (see Jeff's Tips)

1½ teaspoons ground cumin

1 teaspoon turmeric

1 teaspoon ground cinnamon

½–1 teaspoon crushed red pepper flakes (optional)

½ teaspoon cayenne pepper (optional)

2 cups basmati rice, rinsed for 90 seconds and drained

**OPTIONAL WHITE GARLIC SAUCE**

1 cup plain whole-milk yogurt (not Greek or flavored)

¼ cup mayonnaise

2 tablespoons tahini (optional)

Juice of ½ lemon

3 cloves garlic, minced or pressed

1 tablespoon garlic powder

½ teaspoon lemon pepper seasoning

½ teaspoon cayenne pepper (optional, for heat)

⅛–¼ teaspoon garlic salt, to taste

**OPTIONAL TOPPINGS**

Tzatziki (if not using the white garlic sauce and you want a shortcut)

Dill pickles, diced

**1** Add the olive oil and butter to the Instant Pot. Hit Sauté and Adjust to the More or High setting. Once the butter's melted, add the onion and sauté for 3 minutes, until softened and the color begins to fade.

**2** Add the chicken and garlic and sauté until the chicken is pinkish-white in color, about 3 minutes.

CONTINUES

**3** Add the broth, paprika, curry powder, seasoned salt, black pepper, cumin, turmeric, cinnamon, crushed red pepper flakes (if using), and cayenne pepper (if using). Stir until well combined and the bottom of the pot is clear of any browned bits. Add the rice and *do not stir,* but rather just smooth it out on top.

**4** Secure the lid and move the valve to the sealing position. Hit Cancel followed by Manual or Pressure Cook on High Pressure for 3 minutes. When done cooking, allow a 10-minute natural release followed by a quick release.

**5** If using, combine the white garlic sauce ingredients in a large mixing bowl, mix together, and set aside.

**6** Mix the rice up, transfer to a serving dish, and enjoy topped with the white garlic sauce (or tzatziki) and dill pickles, if desired.

*lighter comforts* Should you wish to use brown rice instead of white, simply increase the pressure cook time to 15 minutes for a more al dente brown rice, or up to 25 minutes for a softer one (brown rice cooks a bit longer than white). Natural release time would then be 10 minutes and 5 minutes, respectively.

Make this dairy-free by omitting the butter and using a total of ¼ cup olive oil.

**JEFF'S TIPS** In case spice isn't your thing, start with 1 teaspoon of black pepper. You can always add more in Step 6 to taste.

You'll notice the cayenne and red pepper flakes are optional; this is because adding them as written will make this a spicier dish (even more so than my Chicken Shawarma in the orange book, because all the spices are absorbed into the rice rather than just serving as a marinade). So if you want something with just a touch of spice, only use ¼ teaspoon of each, or just one or the other. To that point, you can keep it mild by simply not adding them at all. It's also worth noting that as a dish cools, the spice level usually does as well.

> When I moved out of my parents' house, my father was concerned that I'd starve. I didn't cook well at all, but I didn't have to when it was just me. Fast forward a few years and add a husband and four kids to the mix. I learned to make some staples that were in constant rotation, and we'd eat out fairly frequently. In an attempt to eat at home more often to save money, my husband bought me an Instant Pot and your cookbook. Because of the kids' schedules, I use the IP at least five days a week. My 4-year-old thinks I'm a gourmet chef. Her favorite is your French onion chicken. My favorite part of the IP, though, is the bonding time I have with my daughter making dinner together and then playing while it cooks!
>
> JESSICA • **SHAVERTOWN, PENNSYLVANIA**

# FIRE FRIED RICE

I obviously love fried rice and I especially love when some heat graces those grains. So I created a fierce fried rice with a creamy and optionally spicy yum yum sauce finish for my fellow spicy lovers. I'm not saying you'll breathe fire (I don't like when spice dominates the flavors of a dish), but you'll definitely want to keep a glass of milk nearby. But if you'd rather it be mild, I've got you covered in Jeff's Tip.

DF

GF⁺ (see Lighter Comforts)

V⁺ (see Lighter Comforts)

| Prep Time | Pressure Building Time | Pressure Cook Time | Natural Release Time | Sauté Time | Total Time | Serves |
|---|---|---|---|---|---|---|
| 10 MIN | 5–10 MIN | 3 MIN | 10 MIN | 15 MIN | 45 MIN | 4–6 |

2 cups jasmine rice, rinsed for 90 seconds and drained

2 cups water or garlic broth (e.g., Garlic Better Than Bouillon)

¼ cup low-sodium soy sauce

2 tablespoons chili-garlic sauce

2 tablespoons sriracha

2 tablespoons hoisin sauce

2 tablespoons oyster sauce

1½ teaspoons minced or grated ginger (I use squeeze ginger)

¼ cup sesame oil (any kind)

1 pound ground pork

1 large white or yellow onion, diced

1 bunch scallions, sliced (some reserved for topping)

1 jalapeño pepper, seeded and diced

3 cloves garlic, minced or pressed

10 ounces frozen peas and carrots mix

10 ounces frozen corn

4 large eggs, lightly beaten

Sesame seeds, for serving

### OPTIONAL JAPANESE-STYLE YUM YUM FIRE SAUCE

1 cup mayonnaise

1 tablespoon melted butter

1 teaspoon tomato paste

1 teaspoon sugar

½ teaspoon garlic powder

¼ teaspoon seasoned salt

2 tablespoons sriracha or chili-garlic sauce (optional)

1 teaspoon cayenne pepper (optional)

1 teaspoon crushed red pepper flakes (optional)

**1** Add the rinsed rice to the Instant Pot along with the water or broth and stir. Secure the lid and move the valve to the sealing position. Hit Manual or Pressure Cook on High Pressure for 3 minutes. When done, allow a 10-minute natural release followed by a quick release, then fluff the rice with a fork.

 **JEFF'S TIP** As the name suggests, this is designed to be a spicy rice. If you want less spice or none at all, simply omit the jalapeño and go easier on (or nix) the chili-garlic sauce and the optional spicy ingredients for both the main recipe and the yum yum sauce. To that point, if you want it spicier, add more to your heart's content (and pour a second glass of milk).

CONTINUES

**2** While the rice is cooking, combine the soy sauce, chili-garlic sauce, sriracha, hoisin sauce, oyster sauce, and ginger in a bowl and whisk until combined. If making the optional yum yum sauce, combine all the ingredients in a separate bowl now as well. The last three ingredients for this optional sauce will make it nice and spicy, making this dish live up to its name (see Jeff's Tip, page 133).

**3** Hit Cancel and transfer the rice from the pot to a bowl. You can either rinse the liner pot and return it to the Instant Pot (just make sure it's totally dry before returning) or leave as is (it will be more prone to things getting stuck to the bottom in the next step, but not a big deal).

**4** Add the sesame oil to the pot and hit Sauté and Adjust to the More or High setting. After 3 minutes of heating, add the ground pork and sauté for 5–10 minutes, until browned.

**5** Add the onion, scallions, jalapeño, and garlic and sauté for 5 minutes, until softened. Add the peas and carrots and corn and sauté for 2 minutes longer, until heated through.

**6** Move the meat and veggies to one side of the pot. Pour the eggs into the other side and stir constantly to scramble and cook. Once the eggs are cooked, mix them up with the meat and veggies. Turn off the pot by hitting Cancel.

**7** Return the rice to the pot, add the soy sauce mixture from Step 2, and stir until fully combined with the meat, eggs, and veggies. Serve topped with yum yum sauce, sliced scallions, and sesame seeds, if desired.

 *lighter comforts* Make it vegetarian by omitting the pork—if you're okay with using eggs. If not, nix them.

If you want it to be gluten-free, be sure to sub tamari or coconut aminos for the soy sauce and use gluten-free hoisin and oyster sauces. Keep it soy-free by using coconut aminos.

# BREAKFAST

FRIED RICE

GF

V + *(see Lighter Comforts)*

Picture a breakfast plate with all the fixin's: I'm talking cheesy eggs, bacon, sausage, potatoes, peppers, and onions. Now let's take it to the next level and turn this plate into the ultimate fried rice. This recipe will literally give you a reason to get out of bed in the morning, and just may inspire you to live a bit on the wild side.

| Prep Time | Pressure Building Time | Pressure Cook Time | Natural Release Time | Sauté Time | Total Time | Serves |
|---|---|---|---|---|---|---|
| 10 MIN | 5–10 MIN | 3 MIN | 10 MIN | 15 MIN | 45 MIN | 4–6 |

- 2 cups jasmine rice, rinsed for 90 seconds and drained
- 2 cups ham broth (e.g., Ham Better Than Bouillon) or chicken broth
- 1/2 pound unpeeled baby potatoes, rinsed and quartered
- 8 large eggs

- 1/2 cup whole milk or half-and-half
- 3 tablespoons salted butter
- 8 ounces thick-cut bacon, diced
- 1 pound breakfast sausage (use your favorite), crumbled or sliced into 1/4-inch-thick disks
- 1 medium yellow onion, diced

- 1 green bell pepper, seeded and diced
- 1/4 cup pure maple syrup (trust me)
- 2 cups shredded Cheddar cheese (or more, see Step 8)
- Hot sauce and/or ketchup, for serving (optional)

**1** Add the rinsed rice to the Instant Pot along with the broth and stir. Top with the potatoes. Secure the lid and move the valve to the sealing position. Hit Manual or Pressure Cook on High Pressure for 3 minutes. When done, allow a 10-minute natural release followed by a quick release, then fluff the rice with a fork.

**2** While the rice is cooking, whisk together the eggs and milk in a bowl and set aside.

**JEFF'S TIP** I know adding maple syrup to the rice may seem a bit strange, but is anything about this recipe normal? If you love syrup on your breakfast, you'll love it in this rice as it provides a wonderful sweet touch to balance out the savory!

**3** Hit Cancel and transfer the rice and potatoes to a bowl. You can either rinse the liner pot and return it to the Instant Pot (just make sure it's totally dry before returning) or leave as is (it will be more prone to things getting stuck to the bottom in the next step, but not a big deal).

**4** Add the butter to the pot and hit Sauté and Adjust to the More or High setting. After 3 minutes of heating, add the bacon and sauté for 5–10 minutes, until crispy. Use a slotted spoon to transfer the bacon to the same bowl with the rice and potatoes.

**5** Add the sausage, onion, and bell pepper to the pot and sauté in the bacon grease for 5 minutes, until softened and browned. As the veggies release liquid, scrape the bottom of the pot to get any browned bacon bits up.

**6** Add the egg mixture to the pot and cook, stirring constantly and scraping the bottom of the pot, until it becomes cooked into broken-down bits, 4–5 minutes. Turn off the pot by hitting Cancel.

**7** Return the rice, potatoes, and bacon to the pot, add the maple syrup, fold in the cheese (wink), and stir until fully combined. Serve with hot sauce or ketchup, if desired.

**8** **Optional:** To give the rice a melty, cheesy top, sprinkle on another 1–2 cups cheese just before serving in Step 7, add the air fryer lid, hit Broil (400°F) for 3–5 minutes, and hit Start. Check to make sure it's as bubbly-brown and/or melty as you want it and serve.

 *lighter comforts* If you feel you don't need both bacon and sausage, choose your preferred meat and let the other one sit it out. You can also use tempeh or plant-based sausage instead of the meats to make it vegetarian (if you're okay with eggs).

# FAJITA JAMBALAYA

One day, I was craving both jambalaya and fajitas at the same time. And so I took the best of both worlds and combined the two into an unforgettable dish where Mexico and Louisiana dance together. Whether wrapped in a tortilla or served in a bowl with a side of cornbread, it's one of my (and my sister's) favorite creations and embodies comfort in every way.

  *(see Lighter Comforts)*

| Prep Time | Sauté Time | Pressure Building Time | Pressure Cook Time | Total Time | Serves |
|---|---|---|---|---|---|
| 15 MIN | 15 MIN | 10–15 MIN | 15 MIN | 1 HR | 4–6 |

¼ cup vegetable oil

2 tablespoons salted butter

3 large green bell peppers, seeded, sliced into ¼-inch-thick strips, and halved

1 large Spanish or yellow onion, chopped

2 ribs celery, diced

1 bunch scallions, sliced thin

1½ pounds boneless, skinless chicken breasts/cutlets (about ¼ inch thick), sliced into ¼-inch-thick strips

3 cloves garlic, minced or pressed

2 tablespoons paprika

1 tablespoon ground cumin

1 teaspoon seasoned salt

½ teaspoon black pepper

¼ teaspoon cayenne pepper (optional)

1 (14.5-ounce) can diced tomatoes, with their juices

4 cups chicken broth

1 fajita box kit (should contain one 1-ounce packet fajita mix, one 1-ounce packet sauce, and about 10 tortillas)

1 (14-ounce) box yellow rice (arroz amarillo)

**OPTIONAL TOPPINGS**

Shredded Mexican cheese blend

Salsa

Guacamole

Sour cream

**1** Add the olive oil and butter to the Instant Pot. Hit Sauté and Adjust to the More or High setting. Once the butter's melted, add the bell peppers, onion, celery, and scallions. Sauté for 5 minutes, until softened.

**2** Add the chicken and garlic and sauté until the chicken becomes pinkish-white in color, about 3 minutes.

**3** Add the paprika, cumin, seasoned salt, black pepper, and cayenne (if using). Mix the spices with the chicken for 1 minute, then add the canned tomatoes with their juices. Stir well.

**4** Add the broth and fajita mix packet. Stir *very well* and do a final scrape at the bottom of the pot with a mixing spoon. Bring to a bubble.

**5** Add the rice but *do not stir*—just use a mixing spoon to lightly submerge it in the liquid.

**6** Secure the lid and move the valve to the sealing position. Hit Cancel followed by Manual or Pressure Cook on High Pressure for 15 minutes. Quick release when done.

**7** When you take the lid off, it will look a little soupy. That's normal after pressure cooking—especially with all the ingredients in this dish that produce liquids once cooked! Don't you worry as that will soon change. Add the packet of fajita sauce and stir occasionally for 5–7 minutes, until thickened. Hit Cancel to turn the pot off.

**8** Serve in tortillas or in bowls topped with shredded cheese, salsa, guacamole, and/or sour cream, if desired.

**JEFF'S TIPS** If you can't find a fajita box kit, you can make your own with a 1-ounce packet of fajita seasoning, ¼ cup taco sauce or salsa of your choice, and fajita- or burrito-sized flour (or corn) tortillas.

If you want it more jambalaya-like, in Step 7 hit Cancel followed by Sauté and Adjust to the More or High setting. Add the raw shrimp and a pre-cooked packaged sausage such as chorizo or andouille. Once the shrimp is curled and opaque and the sausage is heated (2–4 minutes), it's done.

*lighter comforts* Although yellow rice is strongly preferred, brown or long-grain white rice is absolutely fine to use. Same cook time for brown rice, but lower to 10 minutes if using white rice.

Make it dairy-free by replacing the butter with 2 additional tablespoons vegetable oil.

# ·RICE·
# PILAF

This classic Middle Eastern culinary comfort is a very simple and mild dish, yet loaded with buttery and savory flair. I've often seen it combined with very short pasta, and so I wanted to showcase that in my version. This makes it perfect as a side to a trove of dishes as well as in a bowl all on its own. No longer will you ever be hungry for the pilaf in someone else's pot when you make your own—simply, perfectly, and deliciously.

| Prep Time | Sauté Time | Pressure Building Time | Pressure Cook Time | Natural Release Time | Total Time | Serves |
|---|---|---|---|---|---|---|
| 5 MIN | 8 MIN | 5–10 MIN | 3 MIN | 10 MIN | 35 MIN | 4–6 |

- **4 tablespoons (½ stick) salted butter or ¼ cup extra-virgin olive oil**
- **1 medium yellow onion, diced**
- **½ cup orzo or fideo (which is a cut spaghetti)**

- **6 cloves garlic, minced or pressed**
- **1½ cups jasmine or any long-grain white rice, rinsed for 90 seconds and drained**

- **2 cups garlic broth (e.g., Garlic Better Than Bouillon) or vegetable broth**
- **1 tablespoon Greek seasoning (I use Cavender's—see Jeff's Tip)**
- **2 teaspoons dried parsley**

**1** Add the butter or olive oil to the Instant Pot. Hit Sauté and Adjust to the More or High setting. Once heated, about 3 minutes, add the onion and sauté for 2–3 minutes, until slightly softened.

**2** Add the orzo or fideo and garlic and sauté for another 3 minutes until the pasta begins to lightly brown.

**3** Add the rice, broth, Greek seasoning, and parsley and stir well, deglazing the bottom of the pot. Secure the lid and move the valve to the sealing position. Hit Cancel and then hit Manual or Pressure Cook on High Pressure for 3 minutes. When done, allow a 10-minute natural release followed by a quick release.

 *lighter comforts* Sub brown rice for white. Pressure cook time will increase to 25 minutes with the same 10-minute natural release.

 **JEFF'S TIP** If you can't find Cavender's, or any Greek seasoning for that matter, sub the following spice mix:

- 1 teaspoon seasoned salt
- 1 teaspoon garlic powder
- 1 teaspoon onion powder

**4** Fluff the rice with a fork before serving.

# GINGER-SCALLION CHICKEN & RICE

Flushing, Queens, is the home to many of the best Asian cuisines and eateries the States have to offer. It was at a Cantonese restaurant in Flushing that I first tasted the most amazingly fragrant dressing that typically accompanies steamed chicken. It's an oil-based delight that's filled with finely chopped ginger and crunchy scallions, then kissed with a touch of soy sauce and salt. It's remarkable how something so simple and light can taste so flavorful. When drizzled over a chicken and rice dish, it's quite special.

 DF + *(see Lighter Comforts)*

 GF + *(if using tamari or coconut aminos)*

 V + *(see Lighter Comforts)*

| Prep Time | Sauté Time | Pressure Building Time | Pressure Cook Time | Natural Release Time | Total Time | Serves |
|---|---|---|---|---|---|---|
| 10 MIN | 8–10 MIN | 10–15 MIN | 3 MIN | 10 MIN | 45 MIN | 4–6 |

## THE CHICKEN & RICE
- 2 tablespoons vegetable oil
- 2 tablespoons (¼ stick) salted butter
- 2 large shallots, diced
- 6 cloves garlic, sliced into slivers
- 2 pounds boneless, skinless chicken thighs or breasts, cut into bite-size chunks
- 3 cups garlic broth (e.g., Garlic Better Than Bouillon) or water
- 2 cups jasmine rice, rinsed for 90 seconds and drained

## THE GINGER-SCALLION OIL
- 4 inches ginger, peeled and roughly diced
- 1 bunch scallions, sliced and roughly diced, white parts (lower one-third of the scallions) separated from green parts
- 2/3 cup vegetable oil
- 2 teaspoons low-sodium soy sauce, tamari, or coconut aminos
- ½ teaspoon kosher salt

### THE CHICKEN & RICE

**1** Add the vegetable oil and butter to the Instant Pot. Hit Sauté and Adjust to the More or High setting. Once the butter's melted, add the shallots and garlic and sauté for 5 minutes, until the garlic begins to brown.

**2** Add the chicken and sauté until the chicken is pinkish-white in color, about 3 minutes.

**3** Add the broth and stir until well combined and the bottom of the pot is clear of any browned bits. Add the rice and *do not stir*, but rather just smooth it out on top.

**4** Secure the lid and move the valve to the sealing position. Hit Cancel followed by Manual or Pressure Cook on High Pressure for 3 minutes. When done cooking, allow a 10-minute natural release, followed by a quick release.

**5** In a food processor, combine the ginger and white parts of the scallions (reserving the very green tops for garnish) and pulse until very finely minced and slightly pureed. (NOTE: you can also finely chop the ginger and scallions with a knife but the food processor will make this so much easier.) Transfer the finely minced scallions and ginger to a bowl or salad dressing shaker and add the oil, soy sauce, and salt. Stir (or shake) until well combined.

**6** Once the lid is off the pot, stir the rice up. Enjoy in a bowl drizzled with the ginger-scallion oil to taste and the green portions of the scallions, if desired. Mix it all together and enjoy.

*lighter comforts* This dish is remarkably simple as is, but to make it even simpler (and vegetarian and dairy-free), skip the chicken, butter, and oil and begin at Step 3.

To add shrimp, toss it in the pot in Step 6 and the heat of the pot will cook it. Once curled and opaque (2–4 minutes), it's ready.

**JEFF'S TIP** The spectacular ginger-scallion oil doesn't have to be limited to just this dish. It goes beautifully on steamed veggies or any protein. I like to make a batch and keep it in a salad dressing shaker in my fridge for whenever I wish to give a serious flavor boost to basically anything.

## RISOTTO
# RANCHERO

Risotto is a super creamy, almost pasta-like rice, and when it's prepared in the Instant Pot it requires no babysitting and is consistently tender. Now I've always wanted to do a taco-inspired risotto dish because creamy rice and meat with a Mexican-style seasoning just go together like lovers...but I admittedly did this largely because I've never seen it done before. Folks, this creamy, cheesy taco party is going to absolutely knock your socks off. Goes great in taco shells or with my Chicken Mole (page 171).

| Prep Time | Sauté Time | Pressure Building Time | Pressure Cook Time | Total Time | Serves |
|---|---|---|---|---|---|
| 10 MIN | 10 MIN | 10-20 MIN | 6 MIN | 40 MIN | 4-6 |

1 tablespoon extra-virgin olive oil

2 tablespoons (¼ stick) salted butter

1 medium yellow onion, diced

1 pound ground beef or ground turkey

2 cups arborio rice

4 cups beef broth or chicken broth

1 (16-ounce) jar red salsa (use a thin one like Pace Picante sauce)

1 (1-ounce) packet taco seasoning

2 cups shredded Mexican cheese, plus more for serving, if desired

½ cup cotija cheese (or see Jeff's Tip)

**OPTIONAL MIX-INS**

10 ounces frozen corn

1 (7-ounce) can diced green chiles

¼ cup taco sauce

Sliced jalapeños

Black olives, pitted and sliced

**1** Add the olive oil and butter to the Instant Pot. Hit Sauté and Adjust to the More or High setting. Once the butter's melted, add the onion and sauté for 3 minutes, until softened and a bit translucent.

**2** Add the meat and break up with a spatula for 3 minutes, until it crumbles and lightly browns (but don't drain the juices—keep them for flavor).

**3** Stir in the rice and sauté for 1 minute.

**4** Add the broth, salsa, and taco seasoning. Stir well, giving the bottom of the pot a good scrape to make sure any browned bits come up.

**5** Secure the lid and move the valve to the sealing position. Hit Cancel followed by Manual or Pressure Cook on High Pressure for 6 minutes. Quick release when done. Stir the broth up with the risotto and you'll notice that it will thicken and absorb the remaining liquid very quickly.

**6** Add the cheeses as well as any of the optional mix-ins. Stir until well-combined, top with additional shredded cheese if you like, and serve.

**lighter comforts** I personally love the cheese in this dish since it really ties it all together, but to go a little lighter, leave it out or sub a low-fat or plant-based cheese.

**JEFF'S TIP** If you can't find cotija cheese, grated Parmesan is a comparable substitute.

# FRENCH ONION RISOTTO

GF

V + *(if using vegetable or onion broth and sugar-free steak sauce)*

I've always been a huge fan of everything "French onion"—in all its iterations. I've given you French Onion Soup (page 58), French Onion Chicken (in the orange book), and French Onion Pot Roast (in the blue book), and now I bring you French Onion Risotto. This one is quite decadent, to say the least, and serves up comfort and joy with each cheesy, oniony forkful.

| Prep Time | Sauté Time | Pressure Building Time | Pressure Cook Time | Total Time | Serves |
|---|---|---|---|---|---|
| 10 MIN | 20 MIN | 10–20 MIN | 6 MIN | 45 MIN | 4–6 |

- 4 tablespoons (½ stick) salted butter
- 2 large Vidalia (sweet) onions, sliced into strips
- 2 cups arborio rice
- 4 cups beef broth, vegetable broth, or onion broth (e.g., Sautéed Onion Better Than Bouillon)
- ½ cup dry red wine (like a cabernet)

- 2 teaspoons light brown sugar
- 1 teaspoon Worcestershire sauce or sugar-free steak sauce
- 1 teaspoon dried thyme
- 1 teaspoon kosher salt
- ½ teaspoon black pepper
- ¼ teaspoon garlic powder
- 1 bay leaf

- 1 (5.2-ounce) package Boursin herb cheese (any flavor) or 4 ounces brick cream cheese, cut into chunky cubes
- 1–2 cups shredded Swiss or Gruyère cheese (or any melty cheese of your choice), or more (see Step 5)
- Fried onions, for serving (optional, I use French's)

**1** Add the butter to the Instant Pot. Hit Sauté and Adjust to the More or High setting. Once the butter's melted, add the onions and sauté, stirring occasionally, for about 15 minutes, until they cook down, soften, and become a little brown in color.

**2** Add the rice and sauté, stirring well for about 1 minute.

**3** Add the broth, red wine, brown sugar, Worcestershire sauce, thyme, salt, pepper, and garlic powder. Stir well and deglaze (scrape the bottom of the pot with the mixing spoon to make sure no onion or rice have stuck to it). Top with the bay leaf.

**4** Secure the lid and move the valve to the sealing position. Hit Cancel followed by Manual or Pressure Cook on High Pressure for 6 minutes. Quick release when done. Discard the bay leaf.

**5** Stir the broth up with the risotto and you'll notice that the risotto will thicken and absorb the remaining liquid very quickly. Add the Boursin (or cream cheese) and Swiss cheese, starting with 1 cup, and then add more to your heart's content. Once the cheese is melded into the risotto, it's ready to serve. If desired, top with fried onions and some remaining cheese.

## GIVE IT A MELTY AU GRATIN TOP

Add another 1–2 cups shredded cheese and some fried onions to the top of the risotto just before serving in Step 5. Place the air fryer lid on top, hit Broil (400°F) for 3–5 minutes, and hit Start. Once the cheese is bubbly-brown to your liking, it's done.

*lighter comforts* Go easier on the sodium with a low-sodium broth. The brown sugar can also be omitted if you need to watch your intake there.

**JEFF'S TIP** Already made my amazing French Onion Soup (page 58) and have leftovers? You can just substitute those leftovers for the broth in Step 3! If you go this route, you can omit the red wine, brown sugar, Worcestershire sauce, thyme, salt, pepper, and garlic powder. Keep the onions as stated, though, as they will give the risotto more body and texture.

# MANCHEGO, MUSHROOM & MASCARPONE RISOTTO

Okay, the alliteration was too good to pass up here. Manchego (firm and nutty) and mascarpone (creamy and sweet) are two cheeses with very different flavors and textures. When paired with sautéed mushrooms, the flavors play off each other so nicely it's one for the books (and so, it had to be in one). These three very special M's are heroic on their own, but when combined with lush and decadent arborio rice, they become the Three Musketeers of the risotto world.

 GF

 V

| Prep Time | Sauté Time | Pressure Building Time | Pressure Cook Time | Total Time | Serves |
|---|---|---|---|---|---|
| 10 MIN | 10 MIN | 10–20 MIN | 6 MIN | 40 MIN | 4–6 |

- 1 tablespoon extra-virgin olive oil
- 4 tablespoons (½ stick) salted butter
- 2 large shallots, diced
- 1½ pounds baby bella mushrooms, sliced
- 3 cloves garlic, minced or pressed
- 2 cups arborio rice

- ½ cup dry white wine (like a chardonnay) or additional broth
- 4 cups mushroom broth or garlic broth (e.g., Mushroom or Garlic Better Than Bouillon)
- 1 teaspoon seasoned salt
- 1 teaspoon black pepper
- 1 teaspoon garlic powder

- 1 teaspoon Italian seasoning
- 8 ounces Manchego cheese, grated or chopped up
- ½ cup mascarpone cheese, plus more for serving
- White or black truffle oil, for serving (optional)
- Fig jam, for serving (optional)

**1** Add the oil and butter to the Instant Pot. Hit Sauté and Adjust to the More or High setting. Once the butter's melted, add the shallots and sauté for 2 minutes, until fragrant.

**2** Add the mushrooms and garlic and sauté for 5 minutes, until the mushrooms brown and cook down a bit. Add the rice and sauté for 1 minute.

**3** Add the wine (or ½ cup additional broth) and deglaze (scrape the bottom of the pot to dislodge any browned bits).

 **lighter comforts** While butter is great for sautéing mushrooms, you can sub ghee; or omit it and use ¼ cup olive oil.

**JEFF'S TIP** If mushrooms aren't for you, leave them out and use half the butter. Then cut the garlic sauté time in Step 2 to 1 minute instead of 5 minutes.

**4** Add the broth, seasoned salt, pepper, garlic powder, and Italian seasoning and stir.

**5** Secure the lid and move the valve to the sealing position. Hit Cancel followed by Manual or Pressure Cook on High Pressure for 6 minutes. Quick release when done. It may appear thick and soupy at this point and this is exactly what we want.

**6** Stir the broth up with the risotto and you'll notice that the risotto will begin to thicken very quickly. Add the Manchego and mascarpone cheeses and stir until melded and very creamy. If desired, upon serving drizzle with truffle oil and add additional mascarpone and a dollop of fig jam.

# CHICKEN CORDON BLEU RISOTTO

As well-known in America as in Switzerland, where it originated, chicken Cordon Bleu stuffs ham and Swiss cheese into a breaded chicken cutlet. In its original form, it's simply irresistible; my rendition takes it one step further as a risotto you'll never forget. I suggest this one on a wintry night after hitting the slopes (or shoveling your driveway). A Saint Bernard by your side while you eat is optional.

| Prep Time | Sauté Time | Pressure Building Time | Pressure Cook Time | Total Time | Serves |
|---|---|---|---|---|---|
| 10 MIN | 10 MIN | 10–20 MIN | 6 MIN | 40 MIN | 4–6 |

- 2 tablespoons (¼ stick) salted butter
- 1 large shallot, diced
- 1½ pounds boneless, skinless chicken breasts, sliced into ¼-inch-thick cutlets and then cut into bite-size pieces
- 3 cloves garlic, minced or pressed
- 2 cups arborio rice

- ½ cup dry white wine or additional chicken broth
- 4 cups chicken broth
- 1 teaspoon seasoned salt
- 1 teaspoon black pepper
- 1 teaspoon garlic powder
- 1 teaspoon mustard powder
- 2½ cups shredded Swiss or Gruyère cheese

- 1 (5.2-ounce) package Boursin herb cheese (any flavor), cut into chunky cubes
- 1 tablespoon Dijon mustard (optional)
- 1 pound ham (I use Virginia ham but any is fine), sliced deli-thin and diced, or sliced thick and cut into bite-size cubes
- Ritz crackers, crushed, for serving (optional)

**1** Add the butter to the Instant Pot. Hit Sauté and Adjust to the More or High setting. Once the butter's melted, add the shallot and sauté for 2 minutes, until fragrant.

**2** Add the chicken and garlic and sauté for about 3 minutes, until the chicken is pinkish-white in color. Add the rice and sauté for 1 minute.

**3** Add the wine (or broth) and deglaze (scrape the bottom of the pot to dislodge any browned bits).

**4** Add the broth, seasoned salt, pepper, garlic powder, and mustard powder and stir.

**5** Secure the lid and move the valve to the sealing position. Hit Cancel followed by Manual or Pressure Cook on High Pressure for 6 minutes. Quick release when done. It may appear thick and soupy at this point and this is exactly what we want.

**6** Stir the broth up with the risotto and you'll notice that it will begin to thicken very quickly as rice always continues to absorb the liquid. Add the shredded cheese and Boursin and stir until melded and very creamy.

**7** Add the Dijon (if using) and ham and stir until combined into the risotto. Serve and enjoy topped with crushed Ritz crackers, if desired.

*lighter comforts* Skip the Boursin and sub part-skim mozzarella for the Swiss cheese.

**JEFF'S TIPS** The deli section of your market will usually slice your ham for you as thick or thin as you want it. Ask them to slice the ham into ¼-inch-thick slices; 2 of these thick slices are about 1 pound.

Even if you're not a mustard lover, trust me on the mustard powder and Dijon—they blend in wonderfully once mixed in and are important to achieving those classic Cordon Bleu flavors.

# 5

# POULTRY

If there's one main ingredient that's the most popular and versatile, it's gotta be chicken. Cooking it in the Instant Pot ensures that it's tender, juicy, and delectable—and so this chapter pulls out all the stops. From my now famous Sour Cream & Onion Chicken to a classic Chicken Pot Pie, to my spin on Kung Pao Chicken, I wanted to reinvent old classics while drawing inspiration from cultural favorites. Buckle up for a culinary adventure around the globe because we're tackling some of the best dishes I've been inspired to create.

> Trying to impress, decades ago, I decided to make cherries jubilee. Had them all ready, poured on the booze, tried to light it. No go. Put more booze in. No go. Kept trying till finally it lit with a whoosh and started the drapes on fire.
>
> KIM • FORT WAYNE, INDIANA

 = AIR FRYER LID      = DAIRY-FREE

K = KETO     GF = GLUTEN-FREE

P = PALEO     V = VEGETARIAN

+ = COMPLIANT WITH MODIFICATIONS     VN = VEGAN

# CHAMPAGNE CHICKEN

It's time to pop the cork on a dish so popular, lush, and out-of-this-world, whoever you serve it to will raise a toast to you for making it (which is convenient because the champagne will already be open). But if you don't cook with alcohol, see my tip on how to make this simple and spectacular meal taste just as good. Serve the chicken on its own or over pasta, spaghetti squash, rice, and/or vegetables.

 K + *(see Lighter Comforts)*

 GF + *(see Lighter Comforts)*

| Prep Time | Sauté Time | Pressure Building Time | Pressure Cook Time | Total Time | Serves |
|---|---|---|---|---|---|
| 10 MIN | 12 MIN | 10–15 MIN | 5 MIN | 40 MIN | 4–6 |

1/3 cup all-purpose flour with a few shakes of salt, pepper, and garlic powder mixed in, for dredging

2 pounds boneless, skinless chicken breasts, sliced into 1/4-inch-thick cutlets

1/4 cup extra-virgin olive oil

2 tablespoons (1/4 stick) salted butter

2 large shallots, diced

3 cloves garlic, minced or pressed

1 pound baby bella mushrooms, sliced (optional)

1/2 cup dry champagne or prosecco (just make sure it's not sweet like a rosé, and see Jeff's Tips for a nonalcoholic alternative)

3/4 cup chicken broth

1 teaspoon Italian seasoning

1 teaspoon dried oregano

8–10 ounces cherry or grape tomatoes

5–8 ounces baby spinach

1 1/2 tablespoons cornstarch

1 1/2 tablespoons cold water

1 (5.2-ounce) package Boursin herb cheese (any flavor) or 4 ounces brick cream cheese, cut into chunky cubes

1/3 cup heavy cream or half-and-half

1 cup grated Parmesan cheese

2 teaspoons seasoned salt

**1** Put the flour mixture on a large plate. Dredge (coat) the chicken cutlets in the flour mixture on both sides so they're fully and lightly dusted.

**2** Add the olive oil to the Instant Pot, hit Sauté, and Adjust to the More or High setting. After 3 minutes of the oil heating, add the chicken in batches (2–3 at a time will fit) and lightly brown for 1 minute on each side. Transfer to a plate and repeat until all the chicken is lightly browned.

**3** Add the butter to the pot and scrape the bottom of any flour remnants. Add the shallots and garlic and sauté for 2 minutes. Add the mushrooms (if using) and sauté for another 2 minutes.

CONTINUES

**4** Add the champagne (or prosecco) and deglaze. Then add the broth, Italian seasoning, and oregano and stir well. Return the chicken to the pot. Top off with the cherry tomatoes and the spinach but *do not stir!* Just let it all rest on top. (NOTE: It will look like there's a lot of spinach but it cooks down to nothing.)

**5** Secure the lid and move the valve to the sealing position. Hit Cancel and then hit Manual or Pressure Cook on High Pressure for 5 minutes. Quick release when done.

**6** Meanwhile, make a slurry by mixing together the cornstarch and cold water in a small bowl until smooth.

**7** Using tongs, transfer the chicken to a serving dish. Hit Cancel and then hit Sauté and Adjust to the More or High setting to bring the pot to a bubble.

**8** While stirring, add the cornstarch slurry to the sauce. Let it bubble for 30 seconds while stirring constantly, then hit Cancel to turn the pot off.

**9** Add the Boursin (or cream cheese) and stir until well combined. Add the cream and stir in the grated Parmesan and seasoned salt. Ladle the sauce over the chicken in the serving dish and serve.

*lighter comforts* To make this dish gluten-free, use quinoa or coconut flour instead of all-purpose when dredging the chicken. Using coconut flour will also make it keto. Also, if you're following a very strict keto diet, omit the champagne and the cornstarch slurry, although the sauce will be slightly thinner.

 **JEFF'S TIPS** If you don't drink alcohol, simply leave the champagne out and add an additional ½ cup broth.

Have leftover sauce? Awesome! Serve it with a pasta dish or over rice the next day.

> My husband of forty years passed away three weeks ago; he was an excellent cook so I never learned how to cook myself. My autistic brother has lived with us so I've been having a rough time getting through the grief and not knowing how I would be able to feed him the way my Randy did. My niece Jenny has been teaching me how to "Instapot" and it's been very easy watching your videos and getting comfortable with cooking. I just wanted to let you know that you've been a huge help to me as I've been overwhelmed with grief and not sure how I was going to be the caretaker for my brother alone. Thank you. You have no idea how you've helped me, and I know Randy would be thanking you too!
>
> **JOHN · MOUNT PROSPECT, ILLINOIS**

# CHICKEN POT PIE

When I set out to make my version of a classic, American-style chicken pot pie, I knew it had to have a thick, hearty filling instead of a runny, watery one. My secret to really sending it home is to use a biscuit batter blended into the filling to make it thicker, richer, just right—and oh-so comforting.

| Prep Time | Sauté Time | Pressure Building Time | Pressure Cook Time | Baking Time | Total Time | Serves |
|---|---|---|---|---|---|---|
| 10 MIN | 10–15 MIN | 10–15 MIN | 5 MIN | 10–15 MIN | 45 MIN | 4–6 |

2 frozen puff pastry sheets (I use the 17.3-ounce package from Pepperidge Farm; or see Jeff's Tips for bread alternative)

2 tablespoons (¼ stick) salted butter

2 large shallots, diced

2 ribs celery, diced

2 pounds boneless, skinless chicken breasts, sliced into bite-size chunks

3 cloves garlic, minced or pressed

3 cups chicken broth

1 pound Idaho (russet) potatoes, peeled and cut into cubes

2 teaspoons poultry seasoning

2 teaspoons seasoned salt

1 teaspoon dried oregano

1 teaspoon dried thyme

1 teaspoon ground sage

½ teaspoon black pepper

1½ tablespoons cornstarch

1½ tablespoons cold water

1 cup Red Lobster Cheddar Bay Biscuit Mix (with garlic packet or not) or Bisquick

1 cup heavy cream or milk

⅓ cup shredded Cheddar cheese

1 (1-ounce) packet gravy mix

20 ounces mixed frozen vegetables (with corn, carrots, peas, and green beans)

1 large egg, beaten

## MAKE THE FILLING

**1** Take the pastry sheets out of the freezer and unwrap so they can thaw as you do everything else. (NOTE: Do *not* try to unfold them yet as they are frozen and will crack/break. Give them a solid 30 minutes.)

**2** Add the butter to the Instant Pot, hit Sauté, and Adjust so it's on the More or High setting. Once the butter's melted, add the shallots and celery and sauté for 3 minutes, until softened. Add the chicken and garlic and sauté for 3 minutes, until the chicken is pinkish-white.

**3** Add the broth, potatoes, poultry seasoning, seasoned salt, oregano, thyme, sage, and pepper and stir. Secure the lid and move the valve to the sealing position. Hit Cancel and then hit Manual or Pressure Cook on High Pressure for 5 minutes. Quick release when done.

CONTINUES

**4** As the chicken's cooking, make a slurry by mixing together the cornstarch and cold water in a small bowl until smooth. In a separate bowl, mix together the biscuit mix (with garlic packet if it has one—if not, no big deal), cream, and shredded cheese.

**5** When the lid comes off, hit Cancel and then hit Sauté and Adjust so it's on the More or High setting. When it begins to boil, add the slurry while stirring, followed by the gravy mix and frozen mixed vegetables. Stir for 2 minutes, until heated through and thickened.

**6** Stir in the biscuit batter and let simmer for 5 minutes, occasionally using the mixing spoon to scrape the bottom of the pot while the batter is cooking to keep any chicken or veggies from sticking.

---

### ASSEMBLE THE PIES

**7** Preheat the oven to 400°F (if not using the air fryer lid). By now, the puff pastry should be thawed (but still cool). Gently unfold the sheets. Position an 8- or 12-ounce oven-safe ramekin upside-down on top of the dough. Cut the pastry around the top of the ramekin, leaving an extra 1 inch to fold over the sides. Repeat to cut out four to six rounds. Place four to six ramekins on a foil-lined baking sheet and fill each to the brim with the pot pie filling. Seal the tops with the pastry rounds, with the excess folded over the sides. Brush with the egg.

**8** Pop in the oven for 10–15 minutes, until golden brown and flaky; oven temperatures can vary, so keep an eye on it. (You can also do this with the air fryer lid on broil [400°F] for 10 or so minutes, but you'll have to do it in batches of two pies.)

**JEFF'S TIPS** Instead of making pot pies with the puff pastry, you can save some time and place the filling in bread bowls from your favorite bakery, with the centers hollowed out.

You can also make one large pie: Place the filling in a standard pie dish and top with a larger sheet of the puff pastry cut around it, just like the instructions for the smaller ramekins. Brush with the egg as well. Baking time should be around the same but keep an eye on it until it's golden brown.

Regardless of the method you choose, you'll have plenty of leftover filling for future pies: It freezes well for up to 2 months.

*lighter comforts* This is obviously a pretty comforting dish, but in lieu of the cream or milk, feel free to sub a light cream, 2% milk, or unsweetened nondairy milk (such as almond, oat, or soy).

# CHICKEN TERIYAKI

Chicken teriyaki, originating from the Japanese immigrants who settled in Hawaii, is the star chicken dish at many Japanese restaurants—especially for those who aren't into sushi. And with that familiar, gleaming (that's what *teri* means), sweet and savory sauce, is it really any wonder kids and grown-ups alike love it so much? This recipe will bring my rendition of this dish to life in your very own kitchen. By the way, *yaki* means grilled, broiled, or pan-fried; with the popularity of Instant Potting, perhaps one day it will be amended to include "pressure cooked." Serve over my Fire Fried Rice (page 133).

 DF+ *(see Lighter Comforts)*

 GF+ *(see Lighter Comforts)*

| Prep Time | Sauté Time | Pressure Building Time | Pressure Cook Time | Total Time | Serves |
|---|---|---|---|---|---|
| 10 MIN | 6 MIN | 10–15 MIN | 4 MIN | 30 MIN | 4–6 |

- 1 tablespoon vegetable oil
- 1 tablespoon sesame oil (any kind)
- 1 tablespoon salted butter
- 3 pounds boneless, skinless chicken thighs or breasts, cut into bite-size pieces (lightly seasoned with a few pinches of seasoned salt, if desired)
- 3 cloves garlic, minced or pressed

- 1 tablespoon minced or grated ginger (I use squeeze ginger)
- 1/2 cup chicken broth
- 2 tablespoons rice vinegar or apple cider vinegar
- 1/4 cup low-sodium soy sauce, tamari, or coconut aminos
- 1/4 cup packed light or dark brown sugar
- 2 tablespoons cornstarch

- 2 tablespoons cold water
- 1/4 cup honey
- 2 tablespoons hoisin sauce
- 1 teaspoon Gravy Master or Kitchen Bouquet (optional)
- 1 bunch scallions, sliced (some reserved for topping)
- Sesame seeds, for serving (optional)

**1** Add the oils and butter to the pot and hit Sauté and Adjust so it's on the More or High setting. Once the butter's melted, add the chicken and sauté for 2 minutes, until pinkish-white in color (it should *not* be fully cooked in this stage). Add the garlic and ginger and sauté for 1 minute longer.

**2** Add the broth, vinegar, soy sauce, and brown sugar and stir well. Secure the lid and move the valve to the sealing position. Hit Cancel and then hit Pressure Cook or Manual on High Pressure for 4 minutes. Quick release when done.

**3** Meanwhile, combine the cornstarch and cold water in a small bowl until a smooth slurry is formed.

**4** Once the lid comes off, stir the honey and hoisin sauce into the pot until well combined.

**5** Hit Cancel and then hit Sauté and Adjust so it's on the More or High setting. Once the sauce begins to bubble, stir in the cornstarch slurry and allow it to bubble for 30 seconds while stirring; the sauce will have thickened up perfectly. Turn the pot off and stir in the Gravy Master or Kitchen Bouquet (if using) along with the scallions.

**6** Place in a serving bowl, top with sesame seeds, if desired, and additional scallions, and serve.

*lighter comforts* Make it dairy-free by omitting the butter.

Make it gluten-free with gluten-free hoisin sauce as well as tamari or coconut aminos instead of the soy sauce. Coconut aminos also make it soy-free.

**JEFF'S TIP** I personally think chicken thighs are the best cut of chicken for this dish since they're so juicy and tender. That said, if you prefer white meat and wish to use chicken breasts instead, the dish will be just as good!

# SOUR CREAM & ONION
## · CHICKEN ·

Every so often my brain explodes with a delicious idea to marry foods that deserve a wedding with a bang. With that, I'd like to extend an invitation to the joyful marriage ceremony of chicken and sour cream & onion. This recipe was an instant success when I originally shared it, and if you're a fan of the potato chips by the same name, you've just met one of your greatest culinary comforts. Serve the chicken over a bed of egg noodles or rice pilaf (page 140), and why not top it all with additional chives and crushed sour cream & onion potato chips?

 *(see Lighter Comforts)*

 *(see Lighter Comforts)*

| Prep Time<br>**10** MIN | Sauté Time<br>**25** MIN | Pressure Building<br>Time<br>**10–15** MIN | Pressure Cook<br>Time<br>**5** MIN | Total Time<br>**50** MIN | Serves<br>**4–6** |
|---|---|---|---|---|---|

**1/2 cup all-purpose flour with a few shakes of salt, black pepper, and garlic powder mixed in, for dredging**

**2 pounds boneless, skinless chicken breasts, sliced into 1/4-inch-thick cutlets**

**1/4 cup extra-virgin olive oil**

**2 tablespoons (1/4 stick) salted butter**

**1 large Vidalia (sweet) onion, sliced into thin strips**

**3 cloves garlic, minced or pressed**

**1 cup low-sodium chicken broth**

**1 (1-ounce) packet onion dip mix (any flavor)**

**1 cup sour cream**

**1 (5.2-ounce) package Boursin herb cheese (any flavor) or 4 ounces brick cream cheese, cut into chunky cubes (optional)**

**Bunch of chives, sliced into confetti-size pieces**

**1** Put the flour mixture on a large plate. Dredge (coat) the chicken cutlets in the flour mixture on both sides so they're fully and lightly dusted.

**2** Add the olive oil to the Instant Pot, hit Sauté, and Adjust to the More or High setting. After 3 minutes of heating, add the chicken in batches (two or three at a time will fit) and sear on each side for 1 minute, until lightly browned. Use tongs to transfer the seared chicken to a plate to rest. Repeat until all the chicken is seared.

**3** Add the butter to the pot. Once melted, add the onion and sauté, scraping the bottom of the pot, for 5–8 minutes, until softened like pasta, lightly browned, and just appearing a bit caramelized. (NOTE: The onions will release liquid so the browned bits on the bottom of the pot will come up as you lightly scrape.) Add the garlic and sauté for 1 minute longer.

**4** Add the broth and return the chicken to the pot, resting it on top of the onions and broth in a crisscross fashion. Secure the lid and move the valve to the sealing position. Hit Cancel and then hit Manual or Pressure Cook on High Pressure for 5 minutes. Quick release when done.

**5** Use tongs to transfer the chicken to a serving dish. Hit Cancel and then hit Sauté and Adjust so it's on the More or High setting. Stir the onion dip mix, sour cream, and Boursin or cream cheese (if using) into the sauce. Once the dairy is totally melded into the sauce, stir in the chives and hit Cancel to turn the pot off.

**6** Drape the sauce over the chicken in the serving dish (you'll likely have a good amount of sauce left over).

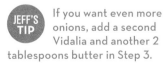**lighter comforts**   To make this dish gluten-free, use quinoa or coconut flour instead of all-purpose when dredging the chicken. Using coconut flour will also make it keto-friendly (if you're okay with using the onion dip mix).

Sub light or fat-free sour cream for regular. Greek yogurt works as well.

**JEFF'S TIP**  If you want even more onions, add a second Vidalia and another 2 tablespoons butter in Step 3.

# KUNG PAO CHICKEN

If you're a *Seinfeld* lover, you'll know George Costanza can't resist spicy kung pao chicken—and, like George, Jeffrey also likes his chicken spicy! This Chinese-American classic focuses on a spicy-sweet-savory sauce, peppers, and peanuts. It's a sure-fire hit every time. But don't worry, you can totally forego the spice if you wish. Serve over Fire Fried Rice (page 133).

 DF

 GF + *(see Lighter Comforts)*

| Prep Time | Sauté Time | Pressure Building Time | Pressure Cook Time | Total Time | Serves |
|---|---|---|---|---|---|
| **15** MIN | **10** MIN | **10–15** MIN | **7** MIN | **45** MIN | **4–6** |

- ¼ cup sesame oil (any kind)
- 1 medium white or yellow onion, sliced into 1-inch strips
- 1 green bell pepper, seeded and coarsely diced
- 1 red bell pepper, seeded and coarsely diced
- 1 bunch scallions, sliced, with crunchy white and light green bottoms separated from the softer dark green tops (reserve some for garnish if you like)
- 6 cloves garlic, minced or pressed

- 2 pounds boneless, skinless chicken breasts (about ½ inch thick), cut into 1-inch bite-size pieces
- 1 cup chicken broth
- ⅓ cup low-sodium soy sauce, tamari, or coconut aminos
- 2 tablespoons Chinese black vinegar (see Jeff's Tips)
- 2 tablespoons Shaoxing wine (see Jeff's Tips)
- 3 tablespoons cornstarch
- 3 tablespoons cold water
- ¼ cup hoisin sauce
- ¼ cup oyster sauce

- 2 tablespoons smooth peanut butter (optional, for a bit of a peanut kick to the sauce)
- ½–1 tablespoon chili-garlic sauce (optional, for lovely spice; add more or less to taste)
- 1 teaspoon crushed red pepper flakes (optional, if you want it very spicy; add more or less to taste)
- ½ cup roasted, salted, or dry-roasted peanuts, plus more for garnish
- Water chestnuts, diced (optional, for crunch)
- Dried red chile peppers (optional)

**1** Add the sesame oil to the Instant Pot, hit Sauté, and Adjust so it's on the More or High setting. Allow it to heat for 3 minutes, then add the onion, bell peppers, and dark green scallion tops and sauté for 3 minutes. Add the garlic and sauté for 1 minute.

**2** Add the chicken and sauté for another 3 minutes, stirring constantly, until pinkish-white in color (it shouldn't be fully cooked at this point).

**3** Add the broth and deglaze the bottom of the pot so anything that may have stuck comes up. Add the soy sauce, black vinegar, and Shaoxing wine. Give everything a good stir.

**4** Secure the lid and move the valve to the sealing position. Hit Cancel and then Manual or Pressure Cook on High Pressure for 7 minutes. Quick release when done.

**5** Meanwhile, make a slurry by mixing together the cornstarch and cold water in a small bowl until smooth.

**6** When the lid is off, it won't look gorgeous yet, but it's about to! Hit Cancel and then hit Sauté and Adjust so it's on the More or High setting again. As it comes to a bubble, add the hoisin sauce, oyster sauce, peanut butter (if using), chili-garlic sauce (if using), and red pepper flakes (if using). Stir well. When bubbling, stir in the cornstarch slurry, allow to bubble for 30 seconds, and then turn the pot off by hitting Cancel. Once the bubbles die down, the sauce will have become the perfect consistency—gravy-like and clinging to the tender chicken.

**7** Lastly, stir in the peanuts, water chestnuts (if using), and white and light green crunchy portions of the scallions. Transfer to a serving dish and top with more peanuts and dried red chile peppers if you desire.

 **JEFF'S TIPS** Chinese black vinegar is available at any international/Asian market and online. But you can sub Worcestershire sauce or balsamic vinegar if you wish. Shaoxing wine is also easily available at any international/Asian market and online. Or use sherry wine.

Want other vegetables in there, such as carrots, mushrooms, bamboo shoots, or baby corn? Add them while sautéing in Step 1.

*lighter comforts* Make it gluten-free by using gluten-free hoisin sauce and oyster sauce as well as tamari or coconut aminos in lieu of the soy sauce. Coconut aminos will keep it soy-free as well.

# SWEET & STICKY WINGS

DF

GF + *(if using tamari or coconut aminos)*

If a sticky, sweet, and smoky chicken wing is what you seek, stop right here at this recipe and give it a peek. The delectable mahogany sauce tastes as good as it looks with its deep, sweet, and savory flavors spread all over juicy chicken wings. I suggest crisping them at the end with the air fryer lid or in the oven for the best results.

| Prep Time | Pressure Building Time | Pressure Cook Time | Optional Crisping Time | Total Time | Serves |
|---|---|---|---|---|---|
| 5 MIN | 5–10 MIN | 8 MIN | 10–15 MIN | 20 MIN | 4–6 |

### THE WINGS
**1 tablespoon liquid smoke**

**3 pounds chicken wings, separated at the joint (in many markets you can find them already separated into flats and drumettes)**

### THE MAHOGANY GLAZE
**1/2 cup low-sodium soy sauce, tamari, or coconut aminos**

**1/2 cup honey**

**1/4 cup molasses**

**1 tablespoon minced or grated ginger (I use squeeze ginger)**

**3 cloves garlic, minced or pressed**

**2 teaspoons onion powder**

**1 teaspoon ground mustard powder (optional)**

**1** Lightly brush the liquid smoke all over the chicken wings.

**2** Place the trivet in the Instant Pot, pour in 1 cup water, coat the trivet with nonstick cooking spray, and place the wings on top. Secure the lid and move the valve to the sealing position. Hit Manual or Pressure Cook on High Pressure for 8 minutes. Quick release when done.

**3** While the wings are pressure cooking, stir together the mahogany glaze ingredients in a bowl until combined.

*lighter comforts* — Instead of molasses, use 1/4 cup pure maple syrup.

**4** Transfer the wings to a plate and drain the water from the pot.

**5** If you want to crisp up the wings (highly recommended!), you can use your oven (**see Jeff's Tip**) or the air fryer lid. (If you don't want to crisp the wings, just glaze them and serve.) **To air fry:** Add the trivet to the pot, coat with nonstick spray, and place as many wings as you can on it. Once one layer of wings fills up the trivet, brush the mahogany glaze on them, then add a second layer and glaze those. Repeat if necessary for a third layer.

**6** Add the air fryer lid, hit Broil (400°F) for 10–15 minutes, and hit Start to begin. Midway through the crisping process, flip the wings and glaze the other sides. (NOTE: The longer you go, the crispier the wings get, so be sure to check on them.)

**7** Transfer the wings to a serving dish and slather any remaining glaze on before serving!

**JEFF'S TIP** To crisp the wings in an oven, line a baking sheet with aluminum foil and coat with nonstick spray. Place the wings on the sheet, brush on the glaze, and broil for 5–10 minutes, flipping over midway through to glaze the other side, until fully crisped. (In order to reach the desired crispiness, keep an eye on it, as ovens vary.)

**JEFF'S TIP** If you want the sauce to have an even richer texture, beat 2 large eggs (or just the yolks for maximum richness) and whisk them into the sauce in Step 8, just after stirring in the slurry. The heat of the pot will fully cook the egg by the time the recipe is complete.

# CHICKEN DIVINE

 K <sup>+</sup> *(see Lighter Comforts)*

 P <sup>+</sup> *(see Lighter Comforts)*

 DF <sup>+</sup> *(see Lighter Comforts)*

 GF <sup>+</sup> *(see Lighter Comforts)*

The name here doesn't lie: It's a stunning and colorful dish featuring a bacon-infused lemon-butter sauce cascading over tender chicken cutlets. It's also adorned with sweet sun-dried tomatoes *and* the option to add tender artichoke hearts and savory capers or olives. What can I say? Like Bette Midler, it's simply divine. Serve on its own, or over angel hair pasta, spaghetti squash, rice, and/or vegetables.

| Prep Time | Sauté Time | Pressure Building Time | Pressure Cook Time | Total Time | Serves |
|---|---|---|---|---|---|
| 10 MIN | 12–20 MIN | 10–15 MIN | 5 MIN | 35 MIN | 4–6 |

- 1/2 cup all-purpose flour with a few pinches of garlic powder, Parmesan, black pepper, and seasoned salt mixed in, for dredging
- 2 pounds boneless, skinless chicken breasts, thinly sliced into 1/4-inch-thick cutlets
- 1/4 cup extra-virgin olive oil
- 3 tablespoons salted butter, divided
- 8 ounces pancetta or thick-cut bacon, diced (optional)

- 2 large shallots, diced
- 3 cloves garlic, thinly sliced
- 1/4 cup dry white wine (like a sauvignon blanc) or additional broth
- Juice of 2 lemons, rinds reserved with seeds discarded then sliced into thin disks
- 1 1/2 cups chicken broth
- 2 teaspoons dried basil
- 2 tablespoons cornstarch
- 2 tablespoons cold water

- 1/2 cup heavy cream or half-and-half
- 1/3 cup grated Parmesan cheese
- 1 (12-ounce) jar sun-dried tomatoes, roughly chopped, with 1 tablespoon of their oil
- 1 (14-ounce) can artichoke hearts, drained and ripped up by hand (optional)
- 1/4 cup capers or pitted kalamata olives, plus more for serving (optional)

**1** Put the flour mixture on a large plate. Dredge (coat) the chicken cutlets in the flour mixture on both sides so they're fully and lightly dusted. Set aside on a plate.

**2** Add the olive oil and 2 tablespoons of the butter to the Instant Pot, hit Sauté, and Adjust so it's on the More or High setting. After 3 minutes of heating, add the chicken in batches and lightly brown for about 90 seconds on each side. Transfer to a plate and set aside. Repeat until all cutlets are lightly browned.

**3** **Optional:** If using the pancetta, add it to the pot now and sauté for 8 minutes, until just beginning to crisp. Transfer with a slotted spoon to a paper towel–lined bowl and set aside.

CONTINUES

**4** Add the shallots and garlic to the pot and sauté for 3 minutes, until the garlic is browned. Add the wine (or broth) and lemon juice. Scrape and deglaze the bottom of the pot to free up any browned bits. Add the broth and basil, stirring well.

**5** Return the chicken to the pot, layering the cutlets in a crisscross fashion and topping with the lemon rinds. Secure the lid and move the valve to the sealing position. Hit Cancel and then hit Manual or Pressure Cook on High Pressure for 5 minutes. Quick release when done.

**6** Meanwhile, make a slurry by mixing together the cornstarch and cold water in a small bowl until smooth.

**7** Using tongs, transfer the chicken to a serving dish and place the lemon rinds in a bowl. Hit Cancel and then hit Sauté again so it's on the More or High setting.

**8** Add the remaining 1 tablespoon butter, the cream, and Parmesan and whisk well. Once bubbling, add the cornstarch slurry while stirring constantly. After 30 seconds of bubbling, hit Cancel to turn the pot off.

**9** Return the crisped pancetta to the pot (if using). Stir in the sun-dried tomatoes and their oil, the artichoke hearts (if using), and capers or olives (if using). Stir well. Let rest for 5 minutes to slightly cool, thicken, and come together.

**10** Spoon the sauce over the chicken in the serving dish and top with the reserved lemon rinds.

*lighter comforts*  To make this dish gluten-free, use quinoa or coconut flour instead of all-purpose when dredging the chicken. Using coconut flour will also make it keto-friendly (if you don't mind a slurry—otherwise, nix it).

To make it paleo, use coconut flour and sub ghee for the butter, a nondairy milk (such as almond) for the cream, and nutritional yeast for the Parmesan. And if you don't want a slurry, omit it.

To make it dairy-free, follow the paleo suggestions but leave out the butter/ghee.

# CHICKEN MOLE

Mole (pronounced MOH-lay), a dark, rich, and slightly bittersweet Mexican sauce, dates back to the Aztec Empire, where it was often an offering to the Gods—so you know it's gotta be good! One thing that makes it so special is that it contains chocolate! There are countless spins on this sauce and my take in the Instant Pot adds a few personal touches. Serve over Ruby Rice (page 38) or veggies.

| Prep Time | Sauté Time | Pressure Building Time | Pressure Cook Time | Total Time | Serves |
|---|---|---|---|---|---|
| 10 MIN | 12 MIN | 10–15 MIN | 7 MIN | 40 MIN | 4–6 |

- 2 tablespoons (¼ stick) salted butter
- 2 tablespoons vegetable oil
- 3 pounds skinless chicken thighs, kept whole (bone-in or -out is fine), seasoned with a pinch of kosher salt and black pepper
- 1 medium Spanish or yellow onion, diced
- 3 cloves garlic, minced or pressed

- 1½ teaspoons chili powder
- 1½ teaspoons ground cumin
- ½ teaspoon dried oregano
- ½ teaspoon ground cinnamon
- ¾ cup chicken broth
- 1 (10-ounce) can Ro-Tel diced tomatoes and chilies
- 1 (8-ounce) can tomato sauce
- 1 tablespoon cornstarch

- 1 tablespoon cold water
- ½ cup semisweet chocolate chips/ morsels
- 1 tablespoon smooth peanut butter (optional, see Lighter Comforts)
- Sesame seeds, for serving (optional)
- Cotija cheese, for serving (optional)

**1** Add the butter and oil to the Instant Pot, hit Sauté, and Adjust so it's on the More or High setting. Once the butter's melted, add the chicken in batches and sear for 30–60 seconds max on each side. (NOTE: The chicken may want to stick to the pot when flipped over, but just use some light force with the tongs to flip them.) Remove the chicken and repeat until all is seared.

**2** Add the onion to the pot and sauté for 3 minutes, until softened, scraping the bottom of the pot to get up any browned bits. Add the garlic and sauté for 1 minute.

**3** Add the chili powder, cumin, oregano, and cinnamon and stir constantly with the onions for 1 minute so the spices don't stick to the bottom of the pot.

CONTINUES

**4** Add the broth and really deglaze the bottom of the pot immediately. Everything will come up easily and nothing should be stuck to it. Add the Ro-Tel and tomato sauce. Stir well so everything is combined.

**5** Return the chicken to the pot (it doesn't need to be totally submerged in the sauce if some is above it). Secure the lid and move the valve to the sealing position. Hit Cancel and then hit Manual or Pressure Cook on High Pressure for 7 minutes. Quick release when done.

**6** Meanwhile, make a slurry by mixing together the cornstarch and cold water in a small bowl until smooth.

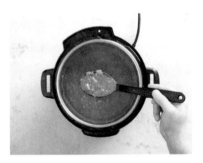

**7** Using tongs, transfer the chicken to a serving dish. Stir the chocolate chips and peanut butter (if using) into the sauce until totally melded. Hit Cancel and then hit Sauté and Adjust so it's on the More or High setting. Stir in the cornstarch slurry, allow it to bubble for 30 seconds, then hit Cancel to turn the pot off. The mole sauce will thicken up perfectly.

**8** Spoon the mole sauce over the chicken and top with some sesame seeds and crumbled cotija cheese if you like.

**lighter comforts** You don't need to add the peanut butter nor is it common in a mole sauce. It's also not dominant since we use just a little. I just think it elevates the flavor with a really nice subtle touch.

**JEFF'S TIPS** Prefer white meat over dark? Use 3 pounds of ½-inch-thick (but no thicker) boneless, skinless chicken breasts in place of the thighs. Same cook time.

Some people like their mole super smooth. If that's the case for you, simply take an immersion blender and puree the sauce at the end of Step 7, right before pouring over the chicken and serving.

My grandmother always bought all the grandkids the same peculiar present. One year she bought us all 4½-pound cans of instant mashed potatoes. I laughed so hard I had to leave the room.

SARAH • GERMANTOWN, WISCONSIN

# THAI CHICKEN SATAY

If you're familiar with Thai street food (or fabulous cocktail parties), you'll know what a delectable snack or meal chicken satay can be. Small pieces of chicken served on skewers with a smooth peanut-based sauce make satay sashay. The chicken is usually grilled, but under pressure we keep it soft and extra tender. It's wonderful over jasmine rice or alongside the Thai-Style Chicken Soup on page 88.

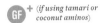

GF + *(if using tamari or coconut aminos)*

| Prep Time | Sauté Time | Pressure Building Time | Pressure Cook Time | Total Time | Serves |
|---|---|---|---|---|---|
| 5 MIN | 8 MIN | 10–15 MIN | 10 MIN | 35 MIN | 4–6 |

- 2 tablespoons (¼ stick) salted butter
- 2½ pounds chicken tenderloins
- 2 teaspoons low-sodium soy sauce, tamari, or coconut aminos
- 2 teaspoons Worcestershire sauce (trust me)

- 1 (14-ounce) can unsweetened coconut milk (it should be thin like water, not thick and lumpy)
- 4 ounces massaman curry paste (I use Maesri brand), divided
- Juice of 1 lime
- 3 tablespoons fish sauce
- 1 tablespoon apple cider vinegar
- 1 tablespoon minced or crushed ginger (I use squeeze ginger)

- ¼ cup fresh Thai basil or tarragon leaves
- 1 tablespoon light brown sugar
- 1 teaspoon ground cumin
- 2 tablespoons cornstarch
- 2 tablespoons cold water
- ½ cup smooth or chunky peanut butter

**1** Add the butter to the Instant Pot, hit Sauté, and Adjust so it's on the More or High setting. Once the butter's melted, add the chicken in batches and sear on each side for about 90 seconds, until lightly browned. Transfer to a plate, set aside, and repeat until all the tenderloins are lightly browned.

**2** Add the soy sauce and Worcestershire sauce to the pot and deglaze (scrape the bottom of the pot to free up any browned bits). Add the coconut milk, 2 tablespoons of the curry paste, the lime juice, fish sauce, vinegar, ginger, Thai basil (or tarragon), brown sugar, and cumin and stir.

**3** Return the chicken to the pot, placing the layers in a crisscross fashion. Secure the lid and move the valve to the sealing position. Hit Cancel and then hit Manual or Pressure Cook on High Pressure for 10 minutes. Quick release when done.

**4** Meanwhile, make a slurry by mixing together the cornstarch and cold water in a small bowl until smooth.

**5** Using tongs, transfer the chicken to a serving dish. (NOTE: To get fancy, skewer them lengthwise on wooden skewer sticks.)

**6** Hit Cancel followed by Sauté and Adjust to the More or High setting. Once bubbling, stir in the slurry and let bubble for 30 seconds. Hit Cancel to turn the pot off.

**7** Stir the remaining curry paste and the peanut butter into the sauce in the pot and let stand for 5 minutes. Slather the sauce over the chicken and serve.

*lighter comforts* For a slightly healthier option, use natural peanut butter, or sub sunflower butter, which is a great option for anyone with a peanut allergy.

**JEFF'S TIP** If you can't find massaman curry paste (I get mine online), you can use panang curry paste, or even red curry paste if you want it spicy.

# PIÑA COLADA CHICKEN

If you like piña coladas (go on, you can sing it if you like), you've just met a very creamy, sweet, and unique chicken dish. In some ways, it's similar to Sweet & Sour Chicken (page 42) but in lieu of a tangy honey sauce, this is as if a coconut and pineapple threw a party and then invited chicken to be the guest of honor. Serve over white rice or Pineapple Crab Fried Rice (page 232).

 *+ (see Lighter Comforts)*

| Prep Time | Pressure Building Time | Pressure Cook Time | Sauté Time | Total Time | Serves |
|---|---|---|---|---|---|
| 5 MIN | 10–15 MIN | 7 MIN | 3 MIN | 30 MIN | 4–6 |

**3 pounds boneless, skinless chicken thighs and breasts, cut into bite-size pieces**

**1 (14-ounce) can unsweetened coconut milk (it should be thin like water, not thick and lumpy)**

**1 tablespoon minced or grated ginger (I use squeeze ginger)**

**1 tablespoon rice vinegar or apple cider vinegar**

**Juice of 1 lime**

**3 tablespoons cornstarch**

**3 tablespoons cold water**

**1 (15-ounce) can full-fat sweetened coconut cream (this one should be thick and lumpy)**

**1 (14-ounce) can sweetened condensed milk**

**1 (20-ounce) can pineapple tidbits, drained**

**Toasted coconut flakes, for topping (optional)**

**1** Add the chicken, unsweetened coconut milk, ginger, vinegar, and lime juice to the Instant Pot. Stir well.

**2** Secure the lid and move the valve to the sealing position. Hit Cancel and then hit Manual or Pressure Cook on High Pressure for 7 minutes. Quick release when done.

 **JEFF'S TIP** Instead of a mix of chicken, you can use just breasts or just thighs.

**3** Meanwhile, make a slurry by mixing together the cornstarch and cold water in a small bowl until smooth.

**4** Once the lid comes off, hit Cancel and then hit Sauté so it's on the More or High setting. Once bubbling, add the cornstarch slurry while stirring constantly.

**5** After 30 seconds of bubbling, stir the sweetened coconut cream and condensed milk into the pot and continue to stir for 2 minutes.

**6** Hit Cancel to turn the pot off and stir in the pineapple. Let rest for 5 minutes to slightly cool, thicken, and come together. Top with toasted coconut flakes, if desired.

*lighter comforts* To make it dairy-free, sub sweetened condensed coconut milk for the condensed milk.

You can also use low-fat or fat-free condensed milk as well as unsweetened coconut flakes.

# CREAMY CREOLE CHICKEN

K <sup></sup> (see Lighter Comforts)

P <sup></sup> (see Lighter Comforts)

DF <sup></sup> (see Lighter Comforts)

GF <sup></sup> (see Lighter Comforts)

This is, without question, one of my all-time favorite chicken recipes. The zesty, creamy sauce screams flavor like a brass band marching down Bourbon Street, yet it's so incredibly simple to make. I am all about smothering this sauce over literally anything you desire (especially Rice Pilaf, page 140). Serve the chicken on its own or over pasta, Pineapple Crab Fried Rice (page 232), and/or vegetables.

| Prep Time | Sauté Time | Pressure Building Time | Pressure Cook Time | Total Time | Serves |
|---|---|---|---|---|---|
| 10 MIN | 12 MIN | 10–15 MIN | 5 MIN | 35 MIN | 4–6 |

½ cup all-purpose flour with a few pinches of garlic powder, Parmesan, black pepper, and seasoned salt mixed in, for dredging

2 pounds boneless, skinless chicken breasts, thinly sliced into ¼-inch-thick cutlets

¼ cup extra-virgin olive oil

1 tablespoon salted butter

1 bunch scallions, sliced

1 green bell pepper, seeded and diced

1 yellow or orange bell pepper, seeded and diced

3 cloves garlic, minced or pressed

1½ cups chicken broth

1 tablespoon Cajun/Creole/Louisiana seasoning (I use Tony Chachere's)

2 teaspoons dried parsley

½–1 teaspoon cayenne pepper (optional)

1 (14.5-ounce) can diced tomatoes, with their juices

2 tablespoons cornstarch

2 tablespoons cold water

⅓ cup heavy cream or half-and-half

1 (5.2-ounce) package Boursin herb cheese (any flavor) or 4 ounces brick cream cheese, cut into chunky cubes

⅓ cup grated Parmesan cheese

**1** Put the flour mixture on a large plate. Dredge (coat) the chicken in the flour mixture on both sides. Set aside on a plate.

**2** Add the olive oil and butter to the Instant Pot, hit Sauté, and Adjust so it's on the More or High setting. Once the butter's melted, add the chicken in batches and lightly brown for about 90 seconds on each side. Transfer to a plate, set aside, and repeat until all cutlets are lightly browned.

**3** Add the scallions and all the bell peppers to the pot and sauté for 5 minutes, until softened. Add the garlic and sauté 1 minute longer. Add the chicken broth, Creole seasoning, parsley, and cayenne (if using). Scrape and deglaze the bottom of the pot to free up any browned bits.

**4** Return the chicken to the pot, placing the layers in a crisscross fashion, then top with the diced tomatoes. Secure the lid and move the valve to the sealing position. Hit Cancel and then hit Manual or Pressure Cook on High Pressure for 5 minutes. Quick release when done.

**5** Meanwhile, make a slurry by mixing together the cornstarch and cold water in a small bowl until smooth.

**6** Using tongs, transfer the chicken to a serving dish. Hit Cancel and then hit Sauté again so it's on the More or High setting.

*lighter comforts* To make this dish gluten-free, use quinoa or coconut flour instead of all-purpose when dredging the chicken. Using coconut flour will also make it keto-friendly (if you don't mind a slurry).

To make it paleo, use coconut flour and also sub ghee for the butter, a nondairy milk (such as almond) for the cream, and nutritional yeast for the Parmesan. And if the slurry is an issue, omit it.

To make it dairy-free, follow the paleo suggestions but leave out the butter/ghee.

**7** Add the cream, Boursin or cream cheese, and Parmesan, and stir until combined. Once bubbling, add the cornstarch slurry while stirring constantly. After 30 seconds of bubbling, hit Cancel to turn the pot off. Let rest for 5 minutes to slightly cool, thicken, and come together.

**8** Spoon the sauce over the chicken in the serving dish.

**JEFF'S TIP** It's perfectly fine to make this as spicy as you wish. Adding more cayenne, 1 teaspoon crushed red pepper flakes, or even 1 teaspoon Zatarain's Concentrated Shrimp & Crab Boil will certainly do the trick.

# WICKED CHICKEN

Being an avid theatergoer, I pined for visiting my beloved Broadway during the year-and-a-half pandemic shutdown. And so listening to show tunes all day had to suffice. I don't think I need to tell you "witch" iconic character inspired this one, but it's safe to say that this smooth, pesto-kissed sauce adorned with greens may have you defying gravity once you try it. Serve it over a bed of pasta, zoodles, rice, veggies, or just on its own.

| Prep Time | Sauté Time | Pressure Building Time | Pressure Cook Time | Total Time | Serves |
|---|---|---|---|---|---|
| 10 MIN | 12 MIN | 10–15 MIN | 5 MIN | 40 MIN | 4–6 |

- 1/3 cup all-purpose flour, with a few dashes of salt, black pepper, and garlic powder whisked in
- 2 pounds boneless, skinless chicken breasts, thinly sliced into 1/4-inch-thick cutlets
- 1/4 cup extra-virgin olive oil

- 2 tablespoons (1/4 stick) salted butter
- 1 pound baby bella or white mushrooms, sliced
- 1 cup chicken broth
- 5–8 ounces baby spinach

- 1 (8-ounce) brick cream cheese, cut into 8 cubes (for easy melding)
- 1 cup pesto (see Jeff's Tips)
- 1/2 cup grated Parmesan cheese
- 10 ounces frozen peas (optional)
- Crumbled feta, for serving (optional)

**1** Put the flour mixture on a large plate. Dredge (coat) the chicken cutlets in the flour mixture on both sides so they're fully and lightly dusted.

**2** Add the olive oil to the Instant Pot, hit Sauté, and Adjust to the More or High setting. After 3 minutes of heating, add the chicken in batches and sear on each side for 1 minute, until lightly browned. Use tongs to transfer the seared chicken to a plate to rest. Repeat until all the chicken is seared.

**3** Add the butter to the pot. Once melted, add the mushrooms and sauté, stirring often, for about 3 minutes, until softened and cooked down.

**4** Add the broth and return the chicken to the pot, resting the cutlets on top of the mushrooms and broth in a crisscross fashion. Top with the spinach. Secure the lid and move the valve to the sealing position. Hit Cancel and then hit Pressure Cook or Manual on High Pressure for 5 minutes. Quick release when done.

**5** Use tongs to transfer the chicken to a serving dish. Hit Cancel and then hit Sauté and Adjust so it's on the More or High setting. Once it begins to bubble, stir in the cream cheese, pesto, Parmesan, and frozen peas (if using). Don't worry about them being frozen. The heat of the sauce will thaw them immediately. Once the cream cheese is melded into the sauce, hit Cancel to turn the pot off.

**6** Drape the sauce over the chicken in the serving dish and top with crumbled feta (if using).

 *lighter comforts* To make this dish gluten-free, use quinoa or coconut flour instead of all-purpose when dredging the chicken. Using coconut flour and omitting the peas will make it keto-friendly.

**JEFF'S TIPS** For a thicker sauce: Just after melding the cream cheese into the sauce in Step 5, mix together 2 tablespoons cornstarch with 2 tablespoons water in a small bowl to form a slurry. Add to the pot and immediately stir for 30 seconds, then hit Cancel to turn the pot off. The sauce will thicken nicely.

For the pesto, if you want to save time and use store-bought, Costco's Kirkland Signature brand pesto is by far my favorite. But if you want to make your own (like I love to do), add the following to a food processor and pulse until pureed:

- 1½ cups fresh basil leaves
- 3 cloves garlic, crushed
- ½ cup grated Parmesan
- ⅓ cup extra-virgin olive oil
- ¼ cup pine nuts

# JAMAICAN JERK CHICKEN

**P** **+** *(see Lighter Comforts and if you're okay with a slurry)*

**DF** **+** *(if using vegetable oil)*

**GF** **+** *(if using tamari or coconut aminos)*

Spicy lovers, rejoice! My take on the sweet and spicy Jamaican classic is going to make your mouth water—literally. It's a super vibrant chicken dish and quite simple to make (I wouldn't jerk you around when it comes to that). Just don't skip the marinating as it makes a big difference in the end result. Enjoy with Rice Pilaf (page 140).

| Prep Time | Marinating Time | Sauté Time | Pressure Building Time | Pressure Cook Time | Total Time | Serves |
|---|---|---|---|---|---|---|
| 10 MIN | 4–24 HRS | 10 MIN | 10–15 MIN | 10 MIN | 4 HRS 40 MIN | 4–6 |

## THE MARINADE

**1 Scotch bonnet, habanero, or Jamaican hot pepper, quartered with stem removed** (NOTE: These peppers are *extremely* spicy and will come across that way in the dish, but that's what jerk chicken's known for. If you want to cut down on some of the spice, remove and discard the inner ribs and seeds. For significantly less spice, use a jalapeño.) **WARNING:** *Do not rub your eyes directly after handling these peppers* or you'll be in for a rude awakening. After handling, rub your hands with a little vegetable oil and then wash with soapy water.

**1 (8-ounce) can pineapple rings or crushed pineapple (with their juices—try to get the 100% juice type instead of the heavy syrup)**

**1 small yellow onion, coarsely chopped**

**1 bunch scallions, coarsely chopped**

**3 cloves garlic, minced or pressed**

**Juice of 1 lime**

**¼ cup low-sodium soy sauce, tamari, or coconut aminos**

**1 tablespoon honey**

**1 tablespoon dark brown sugar**

**1 tablespoon Chinese five-spice (optional)**

**1 teaspoon ground allspice**

**1 teaspoon dried thyme**

**1 teaspoon ground ginger**

**1 teaspoon white pepper**

**1 teaspoon Cajun/Creole/Louisiana seasoning (I use Tony Chachere's)**

**½ teaspoon ground nutmeg**

## THE CHICKEN

**3 pounds boneless, skinless chicken thighs or 4 pounds bone-in, skin-on thighs (it's your choice)**

**3 tablespoons salted butter or vegetable oil**

**1 tablespoon cornstarch**

**1 tablespoon cold water**

**1 tablespoon barbecue sauce (I like Sweet Baby Ray's)**

**1 tablespoon hoisin sauce (optional)**

**1** Add the marinade ingredients to a blender/food processor and blend until the mixture has an applesauce consistency.

**JEFF'S TIP** Don't want any spice at all? Leave the chile pepper out—but then this dish will be nice instead of a jerk.

CONTINUES

**2** Lightly puncture each piece of chicken with a fork and place in a large plastic freezer bag. Pour half the marinade over the chicken; reserve the other half in an airtight container. Refrigerate both the marinated chicken and reserved marinade for 4 hours minimum, or up to 24 hours. (NOTE: Don't skip this step as it really gives the chicken the infused flavors this dish is known for.)

**3** When ready to cook, add the butter or oil to the Instant Pot, hit Sauté, and Adjust so it's on the More or High setting. Once the butter's melted, in batches, place the chicken in the pot and sear for about 90 seconds on each side. Transfer the chicken to a plate and repeat until all the chicken is lightly seared.

**4** Return the chicken to the pot, pour in the marinade from the bag along with the other half of the marinade reserved in the airtight container. Don't mix it in with the chicken, but rather just pour it over the chicken.

**5** Secure the lid and move the valve to the sealing position. Hit Cancel and then hit Manual or Pressure Cook on High Pressure for 10 minutes. Quick release when done.

**6** Meanwhile, make a slurry by mixing together the cornstarch and cold water in a small bowl until smooth.

**7** Once the lid comes off, transfer the chicken to a serving dish. Hit Cancel on the pot and then hit Sauté and Adjust so it's on the More or High setting. Once the sauce bubbles, stir in the cornstarch slurry and then immediately kill the heat by hitting Cancel. Once the bubbles die down a bit, the sauce will have thickened up to the perfect consistency.

**8** Add the barbecue sauce and hoisin sauce (if using) and give it a final stir. Drizzle the sauce over the chicken and serve.

 *lighter comforts* You can use 3 pounds of chicken breasts instead of thighs, just make sure they're no more than 1/2 inch thick.

You can make this dish paleo by using sugar-free barbecue sauce, using vegetable oil instead of butter, replacing the brown sugar with 1 tablespoon pure maple syrup, and omitting the hoisin sauce. This dish also requires a slurry, so it still won't follow the strictest of paleo guidelines, but will work for those following a slightly less-stringent paleo diet.

> I was raised by a single dad who loved cooking. When we were young, he would let us pick one new recipe a month. We always helped with meal prep. As an adult, using my knife skills and prepping vegetables for meals is very therapeutic for me. I love home-cooked meals, because I can control the ingredients. Sunday meal prep in the Instant Pot makes weekday meals so easy.
>
> DONNA • **ABINGTON, PENNSYLVANIA**

# CASSOULET

A quintessential winter dish, cassoulet is a French bean stew that is loaded with duck, chicken, and sausage. It is, without question, one of the most decadent, rich, and comforting things you'll ever eat, and will be sure to keep you extra warm in those frigid months. Traditionally, it's simmered all day on the stove in a Dutch oven, but using the Instant Pot will have it on your table in record time. The air fryer lid will also ensure a golden crusty top without your having to transfer it to a casserole dish for the oven. Serve with crusty French bread, of course.

 *(see Lighter Comforts)*

| Prep Time | Sauté Time | Pressure Building Time | Pressure Cook Time | Natural Release Time | Optional Crisping Time | Total Time | Serves |
|---|---|---|---|---|---|---|---|
| 10 MIN | 12 MIN | 15–20 MIN | 70 MIN | 20 MIN | 3–5 MIN | 2 HRS 15 MIN (see Jeff's Tips) | 4–6 |

- 1 tablespoon extra-virgin olive oil
- 4 tablespoons (½ stick) salted butter
- 1 pound duck legs confit or half bone-in duck breast (usually packaged pre-cooked, see Jeff's Tips)
- 1 pound skinless chicken thighs (either bone-in or -out is fine)

- 1 pound smoked sausage of your choice, cut into ¼-inch-thick disks (I use andouille; you can double this if you want a lot of sausage)
- 2 large shallots, diced
- 6 cloves garlic, sliced into slivers
- 5 cups chicken broth and/or ham broth (e.g., Ham Better Than Bouillon—I use 2½ cups of each)
- 1½ teaspoons dried thyme
- ¼ teaspoon ground nutmeg

- 1 ham hock (optional)
- 1 pound dried cannellini or great northern beans, rinsed (or use canned, see Jeff's Tips)
- 2 tablespoons tomato paste
- 2 bay leaves

**THE CRUST**
- 1 cup panko breadcrumbs
- ¼ cup grated Parmesan cheese
- 2 tablespoons olive oil
- 2 teaspoons dried parsley

**1** Add the olive oil and butter to the Instant Pot. Hit Sauté and Adjust so it's on the More or High setting. Once the butter's melted, add the duck and chicken and sear all over, 1–2 minutes on each side. Transfer with tongs to a plate when done.

**2** Add the sausage, shallots, and garlic to the pot and sauté for 3–5 minutes, until lightly browned. Scrape the bottom of the pot to get up any browned bits.

**3** Add the broth, thyme, and nutmeg to the pot and stir well, scraping the bottom of the pot. Add the ham hock (if using), chicken, duck, and beans but *do not stir*.

CONTINUES

**4** Top with the tomato paste and bay leaves.

**5** Secure the lid and move the valve to the sealing position. Hit Cancel and then hit Pressure Cook or Manual for 70 minutes on High Pressure. When done, allow a 20-minute natural release followed by a quick release.

**6** Just before the cassoulet is done releasing, mix the panko breadcrumbs with the Parmesan, olive oil, and parsley.

**7** After discarding the bay leaves, sprinkle the breadcrumb mixture on top of the finished cassoulet in the pot and add the air fryer lid. Hit Broil (400°F) for 3–5 minutes and hit Start. Or, to brown the crust in the oven, preheat the oven to 450°F. Transfer the cassoulet to a casserole dish and top with the breadcrumb mixture. Bake for 5–10 minutes, until you reach the desired crust (just keep an eye on it as oven temperatures can vary).

*lighter comforts* Use any chicken sausage for the smoked sausage. You can also skip the crust by leaving out those ingredients and skipping Steps 6 and 7.

Make it gluten-free by using gluten-free breadcrumbs for the crust.

 **JEFF'S TIPS** While I personally prefer the longer cook time with the dried beans, if you want a much quicker cook time, use two 15.5-ounce cans of canned cannellini beans (rinsed and drained) and pressure cook the cassoulet for 10 minutes on High Pressure with a quick release. The meat will have cooked just as well regardless of which time setting you use.

If you can't find duck legs, just add another pound of chicken thighs or skinless chicken legs/drumsticks.

I had just turned 60 when I decided it was time to learn how to cook. Prior to that, I had never used an oven and the stovetop was for canned soup only. After watching videos of the easiest recipes ever, I headed out to the grocery store. After confirming with the produce guy that what I was holding was indeed a shallot and being told no, I cannot buy a single carrot, I returned home. Prep was fun. I think my plasticware was sharper than my knives at the time. Dinner was edible. Spices were a bit off, but hey, I did this myself. I was impressed. Two points for self-esteem. Three years later, I actually look forward to preparing a meal, spiced to my preference, and plated immediately after being prepared. I'm a happier person for it.

JOSEPH • **RYE, NEW YORK**

# 6

# MEAT

If you're looking for a roast to gently slice up and eat with a fork, or your favorite activity is tearing into a meat-filled sandwich smothered in sauce and melty cheese, you've just found your favorite chapter. So pack your bags and your carnivorous appetite because we're making succulent stops 'round the world. From a tangy Mississippi Pot Roast to succulent Korean beef tacos to mouthwatering Jewish-style pastrami, I'm talking meat that's such a treat, that once you meet, prepare to eat.

I actually have a love-hate relationship with cooking. The drudgery of cooking every day sometimes gets to me. However, the thing that keeps me going and makes it all worth it is eating the good, nutritious food that I cooked with my family. My boys are now in their twenties...what started as the necessary daily task that I didn't like has turned into a daily labor of love for my family and a gift for my next generation to keep paying forward.

KRISTINA • JOPPA, MARYLAND

♨ = AIR FRYER LID   DF = DAIRY-FREE
K = KETO   GF = GLUTEN-FREE
P = PALEO   V = VEGETARIAN
+ = COMPLIANT WITH MODIFICATIONS   VN = VEGAN

# STEAK TIDBITS

## ON GARLIC BREAD

It's hard to put into words just how much I love this oversized open-faced sandwich of a meal, which was inspired by one from one of my favorite hometown restaurants. It features a bed of crusty garlic bread for tender flank steak that is smothered in a tangy homemade barbecue sauce and topped with a melty cheese blanket (hungry yet?). Eat it with a fork and knife, or devour it like a T-rex (guilty).

**GF** + *(see Lighter Comforts)*

| Prep Time | Sauté Time | Pressure Building Time | Pressure Cook Time | Natural Release Time | Oven Time | Total Time | Serves |
|---|---|---|---|---|---|---|---|
| 10 MIN | 8 MIN | 10–15 MIN | 12 MIN | 5 MIN | 5 MIN | 55 MIN | 4–6 |

### THE STEAK

1 cup ketchup

1 cup apple cider vinegar

1 cup packed light brown sugar

1/3 cup yellow mustard

1 tablespoon honey

1/2 teaspoon Worcestershire sauce

1 tablespoon onion powder

1 teaspoon garlic powder

1/2 teaspoon chili powder

1/4 teaspoon seasoned salt

3 pounds flank steak or boneless short ribs (Costco usually has both cuts)

Kosher salt, for rubbing

3 tablespoons salted butter

2 tablespoons cornstarch

2 tablespoons cold water

Muenster, mozzarella, or provolone cheese, sliced

### THE GARLIC BREAD

4 tablespoons (1/2 stick) salted or unsalted butter (I used salted for extra flavor)

2 teaspoons grated Parmesan cheese

1 teaspoon Italian seasoning

1/4 teaspoon Garlic Better Than Bouillon; or 2 cloves garlic, minced or pressed

1 wide loaf Italian bread

---

THE STEAK

---

**1** In a mixing bowl, combine the ketchup, vinegar, brown sugar, mustard, honey, Worcestershire sauce, onion powder, garlic powder, chili powder, and seasoned salt. Whisk until well combined, then set the sauce aside.

**2** Lightly rub the meat on both sides with the kosher salt. Slice against the grain into 1/2-inch-thick strips.

**3** Add the butter to the Instant Pot and hit Sauté and Adjust so it's on the More or High setting. Once the butter's melted, add the meat and lightly sear, stirring often, for 2 minutes. (NOTE: It will not look done, nor should it.)

CONTINUES

**lighter comforts** While the garlic bread clearly plays a key role in this recipe, you can forego it completely and serve the steak and sauce over rice, cauliflower rice, quinoa, and/or veggies (and skip Steps 6, 9, and 10). If you use sugar-free steak sauce in place of Worcestershire, it'll also be gluten-free.

**JEFF'S TIP** While this garlic bread rocks, if you prefer to use a pre-made garlic bread that comes in foil or frozen garlic bread from the supermarket, cook that according to the instructions on the package and skip Step 6 entirely (but still turn the oven to broil for creating the melty cheese top).

**4** Pour in the whisked sauce and stir so the steak is well coated. Allow to come to a bubble.

**5** Once the pot begins to bubble, secure the lid and move the valve to the sealing position. Hit Cancel and then hit Pressure Cook or Manual for 12 minutes on High Pressure. When done, allow a 5-minute natural release followed by a quick release.

THE GARLIC BREAD

**6** While the meat is cooking, prepare the garlic bread that the steak will rest on. Preheat the oven to 450°F. Place the butter in a bowl and microwave for about 30 seconds, until melted. Add the Parmesan, Italian seasoning, and Garlic Better Than Bouillon and mix until combined. Slice the bread lengthwise in half. Brush the garlic-butter on the cut sides of the bread. Place the bread on a foil-lined baking sheet and pop in the oven on the center rack. Bake for 5–10 minutes (I went for 10), until nicely browned and toasted. (NOTE: Keep an eye on it as oven temperatures can vary and you don't want to burn the bread!) Remove from the oven and turn the oven to broil.

THE SANDWICH

**7** Meanwhile, in a small bowl, make a slurry by mixing together the cornstarch and cold water until smooth.

**8** When the meat is done, use a slotted spoon to transfer it to a plate to rest for a few minutes. Then hit Cancel and Sauté and bring the sauce to a bubble. Add the cornstarch slurry while stirring and let bubble for 30 seconds. Hit Cancel to turn the heat off and let the sauce cool for a moment, until it stops bubbling.

**9** While the sauce is cooling, layer the meat onto the garlic bread, leaving some gaps. Pour some sauce over the meat (but don't douse it so the bread gets too soggy—you'll have plenty of sauce left for dipping), and then finish it off by layering the sliced cheese on top of everything.

**10** Pop the sandwich in the oven to broil for 3–5 minutes, until the cheese is melted and bubbled to your desire. (You can also do this with the air fryer lid on the Broil setting for 3–5 minutes, but I find the oven easier given the size of the sandwich.)

# MISSISSIPPI POT ROAST

When I served this pot roast to my partner Richard's family in Alabama, it was declared "rip-snortin'." I confess I had no clue what that meant but when heaping seconds were taken, I knew it had to be good. This newfound American classic takes a melt-in-your-mouth pot roast and gives the sauce a tangy twirl, making it irresistible. Even though we use pepperoncini as a key ingredient, it is not a spicy dish and you'll most likely lap up every last drop with some bread—it's also perfect when served over my Garlic Mashed Potatoes (page 258), Rice Pilaf (page 140), or Polenta Parmesan (page 250).

  (see Lighter Comforts)

 (see Lighter Comforts)

GF + (see Lighter Comforts)

| Prep Time | Sauté Time | Pressure Building Time | Pressure Cook Time | Natural Release Time | Total Time | Serves |
|-----------|-----------|------------------------|--------------------|-----------------------|------------|--------|
| 10 MIN | 15 MIN | 10–15 MIN | 65 MIN | 15 MIN | 2 HRS | 6 |

## THE ROAST

**¼ cup vegetable or canola oil**

**4 tablespoons (½ stick) salted butter**

**5 pounds chuck roast, cut into four even pieces**

**1 large yellow or Spanish onion, cut into ½-inch wedges**

**6 cloves garlic, minced or pressed**

**1 (16-ounce) jar pepperoncini or banana peppers, ½ cup of the juice reserved** (NOTE: If you fear spicy food, this won't actually make the dish spicy once it's cooked. The spice magically transforms into a rich flavor for the gravy—so make sure you add this!)

**1½ cups beef broth**

**2 (1-ounce) packets ranch dip mix (different from ranch dressing mix)**

**2 (1-ounce) packets au jus or beef gravy mix**

**2 tablespoons light or dark brown sugar**

## THE GRAVY POTION

**6 tablespoons (¾ stick) salted butter, semi-melted/ very softened (place in microwave for 10–15 seconds to speed this along)**

**⅓ cup all-purpose flour**

**¼ teaspoon Zatarain's Concentrated Crab & Shrimp Boil, optional** (NOTE: Only add if you want the gravy on the spicy side. And a little goes a *long* way: If you want more, taste the finished gravy first and then add a drop more.)

### THE ROAST

**1** Add the oil and butter to the Instant Pot, hit Sauté, and Adjust so it's on the More or High setting. After 3 minutes of heating up, in batches, sear each side of the roast pieces for about 2 minutes. (NOTE: Make sure you move the meat around for a few moments as soon as it touches the oil, otherwise it will want to stick to the bottom of the pot.) Once done searing, transfer the roast to a plate, keeping the remaining butter and oil in the pot.

*lighter comforts* If you wish to go lighter on the gravy potion, cut out the flour and butter. Instead, mix ¼ cup cornstarch or arrowroot powder together with ¼ cup cold water to form a slurry, then stir it into the pot along with the Zatarain's (if using) in Step 8. This also makes it gluten-free provided the gravy and dip packets used are as well.

If you want a richer gravy that is paleo, substitute 2 tablespoons pure maple syrup for the brown sugar, sub ghee for the butter, and use coconut flour instead of all-purpose flour. To make it keto, do the same except forego the brown sugar (and maple syrup), and you can still use regular butter. If you're not okay with a slurry, omit it for either lifestyle.

CONTINUES

**JEFF'S TIPS**

Look for a nice, marbled cut of chuck/pot roast with visible fat strands!

When you do the quick release, some of the sauce may slightly gush out. If that happens, either toss a dish rag over it or allow a full natural release to avoid any mess.

**2** Add the onion to the pot and, stirring constantly, sauté for about 3 minutes. It will release liquid and you will be able to dislodge any browned bits that are stuck. We want the bottom of the pot to be pretty much clear so that we have no issues when pressure cooking.

**3** Once the bottom of the pot is cleared and the onion is lightly translucent, add the garlic and sauté for another minute.

**4** Add the pepperoncini (I like to remove the stems before adding, and also reserve a few peppers for garnish at the end) and their juice, the broth, ranch dip mix, au jus/gravy mix, and brown sugar. Mix well.

**5** Return the seared meat to the pot, piling one piece on top of the other. Secure the lid and move the valve to the sealing position. Hit Cancel and then Manual or Pressure Cook on High Pressure for 65 minutes. When done, allow a 15-minute natural release followed by a quick release (see Jeff's Tips).

**6** When the lid comes off, use tongs to carefully transfer the meat to a serving dish (it will be *very* tender!). Hit Cancel, then hit Sauté and Adjust so it's on the More or High setting.

## THE GRAVY POTION

**7** As the sauce is coming to a bubble, in a separate bowl, mix together the gravy potion ingredients.

**8** Once the sauce is bubbling, whisk in the gravy potion and allow to bubble for 30 seconds. Turn the pot off by hitting Cancel. The sauce will have thickened perfectly.

**9** Ladle the gravy over the roast and, if desired, add a few of the reserved, uncooked pepperoncini for garnish and for some spice (as these will still have a kick).

# BLACK PEPPER BEEF

If I have a day that leaves me craving a plate of zesty red-meat comfort, my go-to is Chinese-American-style black pepper beef. The sauce, a triple-S blend of sweet, savory, and spicy, deserves to be paired with some butter-tender meat. This simple and spectacular version does the trick. Goes great over white or Fire Fried Rice (page 133).

**GF** + *(see Lighter Comforts)*

| Prep Time | Sauté Time | Pressure Building Time | Pressure Cook Time | Natural Release Time | Total Time | Serves |
|---|---|---|---|---|---|---|
| 10 MIN | 14 MIN | 10–15 MIN | 12 MIN | 5 MIN | 50 MIN | 4–6 |

- 2 tablespoons vegetable oil
- 1 tablespoon sesame oil (any kind)
- 1 white or yellow onion, cut into strips
- 2 green bell peppers, seeded and coarsely diced
- 6 cloves garlic, sliced into slivers

- 3 pounds flank steak, cut against the grain into ¼-inch-thick strips
- 1 cup beef broth
- ½ cup low-sodium soy sauce, tamari, or coconut aminos
- ¼ cup oyster sauce
- 2 tablespoons hoisin sauce

- 2 tablespoons black peppercorns, freshly cracked with a mortar and pestle (preferred) or freshly ground, plus more for serving
- ¼ teaspoon white pepper
- 3 tablespoons cornstarch
- 3 tablespoons cold water

**1** Add both oils to the Instant Pot and hit Sauté and Adjust so it's on the More or High setting. After 3 minutes of heating, add the onion, peppers, and garlic and sauté for 8 minutes, until the vegetables are softened and the garlic is browned. Transfer the veggies with a slotted spoon to a bowl and let rest.

**2** Add the beef and sauté for 3 minutes, until lightly browned on the edges. (NOTE: The beef will want to stick to the bottom, but just stir constantly as it will release its juices and will get slicker.)

**3** Add everything else *except* the reserved veggies, cornstarch, and water. Stir well and deglaze.

**4** Secure the lid and move the valve to the sealing position. Hit Cancel and then hit Pressure Cook or Manual for 12 minutes on High Pressure. When done, allow a 5-minute natural release followed by a quick release.

**5** Meanwhile, make a slurry by mixing together the cornstarch and cold water in a small bowl until smooth.

**6** Remove the beef with a slotted spoon and place in a serving bowl.

**7** Hit Cancel and then hit Sauté and Adjust so it's on the More or High setting. When the sauce bubbles, pour in the cornstarch slurry, stirring constantly, and let simmer for 30 seconds. Hit Cancel to turn the pot off.

**8** Return the sautéed veggies to the pot; as the bubbles die down the sauce will thicken up nicely. Grind in some additional black pepper, if desired.

**9** Spoon the sauce over the beef and toss until all the beef is covered. Top with additional cracked pepper, if desired.

*lighter comforts* This can be gluten-free if using gluten-free hoisin and oyster sauce, and tamari or coconut aminos instead of the soy sauce. By the way, using coconut aminos will also keep it soy-free.

**JEFF'S TIPS** Want it spicier? Add another 1–2 teaspoons crushed black peppercorns and another ¼ teaspoon white pepper.

Want it mild? Only use 1 teaspoon black peppercorns and omit the white pepper.

# PORK GYROS

I love Greek pork gyros, but we don't all have room for a giant spit at home. This rendition gives you that beloved flavor and texture by simply using pork ribs—which is perfect since the meat slides right off the bone! The final touches and spices are all it takes to make your very own spit-free pork gyro.

| Prep Time | Pressure Building Time | Pressure Cook Time | Natural Release Time | Crisping Time | Total Time | Serves |
|---|---|---|---|---|---|---|
| 10 MIN | 15–20 MIN | 25 MIN | 5 MIN | 10 MIN | 1 HR 5 MIN | 6 |

### THE PORK
- 2–4 pounds (up to 2 full racks) St. Louis or baby back ribs (pork loin back ribs), unseasoned
- 4 cups chicken broth or garlic broth (e.g., Garlic Better Than Bouillon)
- Juice of ½ lemon

### THE GYRO GLAZE (SEE JEFF'S TIPS)
- 3 tablespoons extra-virgin olive oil
- Juice of ½ lemon
- 1 teaspoon Greek seasoning (I like Cavender's) or seasoned salt
- 1 teaspoon ground coriander
- 1 teaspoon ground cumin
- 1 teaspoon garlic powder
- ½ teaspoon chili powder
- ½ teaspoon paprika
- ½ teaspoon dried oregano
- ½ teaspoon dried thyme
- ⅛ teaspoon ground cinnamon
- ½ teaspoon undiluted Garlic Better Than Bouillon (optional)

### OPTIONS FOR ASSEMBLING
- Pita or flatbread
- Tzatziki
- Hummus
- Red onion, diced or sliced into strips
- Tomato, diced
- Cucumber, diced

**1** Bend the racks of ribs into coils so they fit in the Instant Pot. Line them against the perimeter of the pot. (NOTE: If you wish to cut each rack in half before inserting for easier removal once cooked, feel free to do so.)

**2** Add the chicken broth and lemon juice to the pot. Secure the lid and move the valve to the sealing position. Hit Manual or Pressure Cook on High Pressure for 25 minutes. Allow a 5-minute natural release followed by a quick release.

**3** As the ribs are cooking, whisk together the glaze ingredients in a bowl and set aside.

 **JEFF'S TIPS** The glaze makes enough for one rack of ribs. Double the amounts if using two racks.

The meat is also really nice over a Greek salad!

**4** Transfer the ribs to a cutting board (they won't look pretty right now but that will soon change). It doesn't matter if they fall apart because we want them to. Allow the ribs to cool for 10 minutes as you discard the liquid they cooked in (or save by refrigerating or freezing for future use). Pat the liner pot dry with a paper towel and return it to the Instant Pot.

**5** Once the ribs are cool to the touch, pull all the bones from the meat (they should easily come out) and discard (or save for a bone broth). Lightly chop or shred up all the meat with two forks so you have nice, chunky pieces.

**6** **Crisp the Meat:** *With the air fryer lid:* Return the meat to the Instant Pot, pour the glaze on top, and stir well to coat all the meat. Add the air fryer lid, hit Broil (400°F) for 10 minutes, and hit Start. Carefully remove the lid and stir the meat once every 2½ minutes, until evenly crisped.

*With the oven:* Preheat the oven to broil. Transfer the meat to a baking sheet lined with nonstick foil. Brush all of the glaze over the meat. Pop it in the oven on the center rack and bake for 10 minutes, until the meat has a lovely, slightly crisp/slightly soft texture.

**7** Assemble your gyros by placing some meat on pita bread lined and topped with anything you wish!

*lighter comforts* Want chicken gyros? Sub boneless, skinless chicken thighs sliced into ¼-inch-thick strips instead! Use just 1 cup broth (instead of 4) and shorten the pressure cook time to 8 minutes with a quick release. All else remains the same.

# MONGOLIAN
## BEEF

One of the most delicious dishes you'll find is Mongolian beef, which actually originated in Taiwan in the twentieth century. There are countless ways to make it. Mine features a rich brown sauce that includes two magical ingredients that no kitchen should be without—hoisin and plum sauce: They both offer a wonderful sweet and savory punch. When the sauce is served with tender strips of flank steak, it's a dish the entire family will love. Serve over rice or noodles.

 *(see Jeff's Tip)*

 DF

 GF **+** *(see Lighter Comforts)*

| Prep Time | Sauté Time | Pressure Building Time | Pressure Cook Time | Natural Release Time | Total Time | Serves |
|-----------|-----------|-----------------------|-------------------|---------------------|-----------|--------|
| 10 MIN | 10 MIN | 10–15 MIN | 12 MIN | 5 MIN | 50 MIN | 4–6 |

**3 tablespoons sesame oil (any kind)**

**1 white or yellow onion, cut into strips**

**1 bunch scallions, sliced into 1-inch pieces, divided**

**6 cloves garlic, minced or pressed**

**3 pounds flank steak, cut against the grain into ¼-inch-thick strips**

**1 cup beef broth**

**¼ cup low-sodium soy sauce, tamari, or coconut aminos**

**¼ cup packed dark brown sugar**

**3 tablespoons cornstarch**

**3 tablespoons cold water**

**¼ cup hoisin sauce**

**¼ cup plum sauce (if you can't find this, just use another ¼ cup hoisin)**

**2 tablespoons molasses**

**Sesame seeds, for serving**

**1** Add the sesame oil to the Instant Pot and hit Sauté and Adjust so it's on the More or High setting. After 3 minutes of heating, add the onion and half the scallions and sauté for 3 minutes, until softened. Add the garlic and sauté 1 minute.

**2** Add the beef and sauté for 3 minutes, until lightly browned at the edges.

**3** Add the broth, soy sauce, and brown sugar and stir well. Secure the lid and move the valve to the sealing position. Hit Cancel and then hit Pressure Cook or Manual for 12 minutes on High Pressure. When done, allow a 5-minute natural release followed by a quick release.

**4** Meanwhile, make a slurry by mixing together the cornstarch and cold water in a small bowl until smooth.

**5** Hit Cancel and then hit Sauté and Adjust so it's on the More or High setting. When the sauce bubbles, add the cornstarch slurry while constantly stirring. Let simmer for 30 seconds, then hit Cancel to turn the pot off. The bubbles will die down and the sauce will thicken up nicely.

**6** Add the hoisin sauce, plum sauce, molasses, and most of the remaining scallions and stir until all is combined. Allow to rest for 5 minutes for the flavors to come together. Serve topped with the remaining scallions and sesame seeds, if desired.

**lighter comforts** If you want to make it gluten-free, be sure to use gluten-free hoisin sauce and plum sauce, and use tamari or coconut aminos in place of soy sauce. You can also omit the molasses if you want it a touch less sweet. And remember, coconut aminos are a soy-free alternative to soy sauce.

**JEFF'S TIP** Some like this crisped up a bit: After transferring all the beef and sauce to a serving dish, return however much beef you'd like to crisp back to the pot. Add the air fryer lid, hit Broil (400°F) for 10 minutes, and hit Start.

If someone needs to know they are appreciated, I bring them muffins or cookies. New baby? You get a casserole. Funeral? Casserole and cookies.

When I was growing up, my dad and I always baked together and those times are some of my happiest memories. Every week during college—all four years—I got a box of homemade cookies. It was how he showed his love.

RYAN • FAYETTEVILLE, NORTH CAROLINA

# SLOPPY JOES

In my lighter book, you met the lovely and popular Josephine, the herbivore sister of Sloppy Joe, but Joe called me and insisted on being in my next book for the carnivores. The perfect Sloppy Joe awaits you with open arms and lots of napkins.

  **DF**  **GF** + *(see Lighter Comforts)*

| Prep Time | Sauté Time | Pressure Building Time | Pressure Cook Time | Total Time | Serves |
|-----------|------------|------------------------|--------------------|------------|--------|
| 10 MIN | 15 MIN | 10–15 MIN | 6 MIN | 45 MIN | 4–6 |

2 tablespoons extra-virgin olive oil

1 yellow onion, diced

3 cloves garlic, minced or pressed

2 pounds ground beef (the less lean, the better)

1 (14.5-ounce) can diced tomatoes, with their juices

1/2 cup beef broth

2 tablespoons Worcestershire sauce

1 1/2 teaspoons seasoned salt

1 teaspoon liquid smoke (optional)

1/2 cup barbecue sauce

1/3 cup ketchup

2 tablespoons hoisin sauce

1 tablespoon Dijon mustard (optional, but adds wonderful flavor—even if you hate mustard)

2 (6-ounce) cans tomato paste
(NOTE: This may seem like a lot, but trust me—it's the perfect amount to not only cut the flavor evenly but to also provide the proper thickness to the Sloppy Joes.)

1/2 cup sweet relish (optional)

1–3 teaspoons undiluted Chili Better Than Bouillon (optional and to taste)

**TO SERVE**

Buns, tacos, or wraps, and any desired toppings (cheese, lettuce, jalapeños, black olives, etc.)

**1** Add the olive oil to the Instant Pot, hit Sauté, and Adjust so it's on the More or High setting. After 3 minutes of heating, add the onion and sauté for 3 minutes. Add the garlic and sauté for 1 minute.

**2** Add the ground beef and break it up so it begins to crumble. As this happens, it will release its juices. Use them to deglaze/scrape the bottom of the pot so it's totally free of any browned bits. Cook, scraping, until the beef is crumbled and beginning to brown, about 4 minutes. (NOTE: Do *not* drain the beef after browning—we want the juices in there for more flavor and to help bring the pot to pressure.)

**3** Add the diced tomatoes, beef broth, Worcestershire sauce, seasoned salt, and liquid smoke (if using). Stir well and let simmer for another 2–3 minutes.

**4** Secure the lid and move the valve to the sealing position. Hit Cancel and then hit Manual or Pressure Cook on High Pressure for 6 minutes. Quick release when done. (NOTE: When the lid comes off, it may look a bit liquidy—but have no fear as that's what we want! It'll thicken in the coming steps.)

**5** Give everything a stir and then add the barbecue sauce, ketchup, hoisin sauce, and mustard (if using). Stir until well combined.

**6** Finish by stirring in the tomato paste, relish (if using), and the Chili Better Than Bouillon (if using). Stir until fully melded into the Sloppy Joes. Let rest for 5–10 minutes and it will thicken nicely.

**7** Serve on buns; in tacos, tortillas, or lettuce wraps; over nachos, fries, or pasta; on hot dogs. Or simply in a bowl on its own! Feel free to top with shredded cheese or any other toppings of your choice.

*lighter comforts* To keep the sugar level down, feel free to halve the ketchup and barbecue sauce; and use no-salt-added tomato paste for less sodium.

Make it gluten-free with gluten-free hoisin sauce and barbecue sauce.

 **JEFF'S TIPS** Want it spicy? I like your style. Add either a diced jalapeño pepper while sautéing the onion and garlic in Step 1 or hot sauce while adding the other condiments in Step 5. Or both!

Want it thicker? Stir about ½ cup masa harina (corn flour) into the pot in Step 6.

# OSSO BUCO ALLA VODKA

One of the most succulent, fall-off-the-bone meats in the world is osso buco, which is typically veal shanks braised in a white wine and tomato sauce. My take gives it a creamy alla vodka flair and is truly succulent on every level. The shanks go beautifully with Polenta Parmesan (page 250) or over cooked spaghetti (see page 36).

 **K** + *(see Lighter Comforts)*

 **GF** + *(see Lighter Comforts)*

| Prep Time | Sauté Time | Pressure Building Time | Pressure Cook Time | Natural Release Time | Total Time | Serves |
|---|---|---|---|---|---|---|
| 10 MIN | 15 MIN | 10–15 MIN | 25 MIN | 10 MIN | 1 HR | 4–6 |

½ cup all-purpose flour with a few pinches of salt, black pepper, and garlic powder mixed in, for dredging

4–6 bone-in veal shanks, each cut about 1½ inches thick (many markets sell it this way, but if not, ask the butcher to do it)

¼ cup extra-virgin olive oil

2 tablespoons (¼ stick) salted butter

2 large shallots, diced

3 cloves garlic, minced or pressed

½ cup vodka (or additional ½ cup broth)

1 cup chicken broth

1½ cups marinara sauce of your choice (I like Victoria or Rao's), at room temperature

1 (14.5-ounce) can stewed tomatoes, roughly chopped, with their juices

¼ cup heavy cream or half-and-half

1 pound shredded mozzarella cheese

1 cup grated Parmesan cheese

1 (5.2-ounce) package Boursin herb cheese (any flavor) or 4 ounces brick cream cheese, cut into chunky cubes

⅓ cup fresh oregano leaves, plus more for serving

**1** Put the flour mixture on a large plate. Fully dredge the veal shanks in the flour mixture so all sides are fully coated.

*lighter comforts* Make it gluten-free by using quinoa or coconut flour instead of all-purpose when dredging the shanks. Using coconut flour will also make it keto-friendly.

**2** Add the olive oil to the Instant Pot, hit Sauté, and Adjust so it's on the More or High setting. After 3 minutes of heating, in batches, lightly brown the veal shanks for 1 minute on all sides (they should *not* be fully cooked at all—just a light sear). When done, transfer the shanks to a plate to rest.

**3** Add the butter to the pot. As it's melting, scrape the bottom of the pot so any flour remnants come up. Add the shallots and garlic and sauté for 3 minutes, until softened.

 **JEFF'S TIP** If veal isn't your cup of tea, try this with beef shanks or oxtail. Just as succulent and delicious.

**4** Add the vodka and let simmer for 1 minute, continuing to deglaze the bottom of the pot.

**5** Add the broth and the marinara sauce. Stir well. Return the veal shanks to the pot, layering them on top of one another. Top with the stewed tomatoes.

**6** Secure the lid and move the valve to the sealing position. Hit Cancel and then hit Manual or Pressure Cook on High Pressure for 25 minutes. When done cooking, allow a 10-minute natural release and then follow with a quick release.

**7** Remove the veal shanks with tongs and carefully place on a plate. (NOTE: They'll be super tender, so be gentle.) Add the cream, mozzarella, Parmesan, and Boursin or cream cheese to the pot. Stir until the dairy is fully combined into the sauce, then stir in the oregano. Let rest for 5 minutes.

**8** Spoon the sauce over the osso buco and serve topped with additional oregano, if desired.

**JEFF'S TIP** Before you discard the bone in each shank, know that a bonus of osso buco is the incredibly succulent marrow from the bone. You can easily suck it out, or spoon it onto a crispy piece of buttered bread! If you've never tried it before, now's the time! *Heaven.*

# KOREAN BEEF BULGOGI

## TACOS

Since I'm obsessed with tacos, I had to give bulgogi-style a whirl. Bulgogi is a traditional Korean grilled meat dish in which pears play a special role. Well, folks, my life has been forever changed as these magnificent beauties have quickly become my favorite. I like to wrap the meat up in a tortilla (corn or flour) with a little spicy mayo, sesame seeds, kimchi and—my own touch—wonton crisps for the ultimate experience. Goes nicely with Fire Fried Rice (page 133).

  DF

GF + *(if using corn tortillas and tamari or coconut aminos)*

| Prep Time | Optional Marinating Time | Pressure Building Time | Pressure Cook Time | Natural Release Time | Total Time | Serves |
|---|---|---|---|---|---|---|
| 10 MIN | 8–24 HRS | 10–15 MIN | 35 MIN | 10 MIN | 1 HR 5 MIN | 4–6 |

### THE MARINADE

1 (14- or 15-ounce) can pears, fully drained, *or* 2 Anjou pears, peeled and cored (NOTE: If using canned pears, try to get the ones with no sugar added or in lite syrup—although it doesn't matter much since we are draining them)

6 cloves garlic, smashed

1¼ ounces fresh ginger, peeled and cut into small chunks (you can also use 2–3 tablespoons minced ginger or squeeze ginger instead)

½ cup low-sodium soy sauce, tamari, or coconut aminos

¼ cup packed light or dark brown sugar

¼ cup honey

¼ cup hoisin sauce

2 teaspoons sesame oil (any kind)

1 teaspoon fish sauce (optional, and don't mind the pungent scent—it adds incredible flavor once combined with the other ingredients)

### THE BEEF

3 pounds chuck roast, cut into large chunks

### THE TACOS

Tortillas (corn or flour) or taco shells (any kind)

Spicy mayo (mix ¼ cup mayo with 1 tablespoon sriracha)

Kimchi

Sesame seeds

Wonton crisps (see Jeff's Tip in Naked Egg Rolls, page 46)

**1** Combine all the marinade ingredients in a food processor or blender and blend until pureed.

**2** Place the chunks of chuck meat in a gallon freezer bag and pour the marinade all over it. Squeeze the air out of the bag as you seal it. Place in the fridge to marinate for 8–24 hours if you can (see Jeff's Tip).

**3** When ready to cook, dump the beef and all the marinade into the Instant Pot. Hit Manual or Pressure Cook on High Pressure for 35 minutes. When done, allow a 10-minute natural release followed by a quick release.

**4** Using tongs, transfer the beef to a bowl and use two forks to shred it apart, which will happen with barely any effort since it will be so tender. Add ½–1 cup of the sauce to the shredded beef for additional flavor and to keep it moist.

**5** Assemble your tacos as you see fit and munch away!

 *lighter comforts* Forego the taco and serve the beef over a salad or in a lettuce wrap.

**JEFF'S TIP** Don't have time or forgot to marinate the meat? That's fine—you can forego the fridge time and skip the marinating in Step 2. However, while marinating the meat isn't a requirement for an absolutely amazing end result, if you have the time or are able to plan ahead, it adds more flavor to the beef and depth to the dish overall.

In 2017, my brother's wife passed away. She was born in Seoul and I knew her since I was 10 years old. Losing her hit me hard. One of my fondest memories is of her cooking.

So the year that we lost Young, we decided to have Korean food for most of the big holiday meals. It's our way to remember her and to honor her memory. It's also our very own tradition.

Of course my favorite is kalbi ribs. I now make kimchi all the time, too, and I make bulgogi and a few other things. My next try will be bibimbap.

TRACY • **MINNEAPOLIS, MINNESOTA**

# JEFFREY'S NEW YORK–STYLE PASTRAMI

 K + *(see Lighter Comforts)*

 P + *(see Lighter Comforts)*

 DF

 GF

Pastrami is something I can never, ever get enough of: But I'm not talking the cold, thin, supermarket cold-cut pastrami. I'm talking hot, thick-cut, tender, mouthwatering Jewish deli–style pastrami that can be transformed into the ultimate Reuben. My version doesn't require a smoker, is quicker than most, and is as New York as it gets.

| Prep Time | Pressure Building Time | Pressure Cook Time | Natural Release Time | Chilling Time | Oven Time | Total Time | Serves |
|---|---|---|---|---|---|---|---|
| 10 MIN | 10–15 MIN | 70 MIN | 15 MIN | 12–48 HRS | 1 HR | 15 HRS | 4–6 |

**1 (3- to 5-pound) corned beef brisket (make sure it's already corned and on the fattier side; these can be found pre-packaged in the meat section—see Jeff's Tips, page 211)**

**1 tablespoon liquid smoke**

**2 tablespoons ground coriander**

**1 tablespoon black pepper**

**1 tablespoon paprika**

**1 tablespoon dark brown sugar**

**1½ teaspoons garlic powder**

**1½ teaspoons onion powder**

**1 teaspoon ground sage**

**½ teaspoon ground mustard powder**

**1** Remove the corned beef brisket from the package. (If it came with a spice packet, discard or save it for something else as we won't be using it here.) Rinse the brisket under cold water for 1 minute (we want all of the brining agents removed as they're super salty). *Do not* cut any of the fat off the brisket. It is key to making a super tender, juicy, and flavorful pastrami! Brush the liquid smoke all over the brisket.

*lighter comforts* To make this keto or paleo, skip the brown sugar.

CONTINUES

**2** Place the trivet (handles facing up) and 1 cup of water in the Instant Pot. Rest the brisket on the trivet, fat side up (we do this so the fat seeps through the meat, providing extra wonderful flavor). Secure the lid and hit Manual or Pressure Cook on High Pressure for 70 minutes. When done, allow a 15-minute natural release followed by a quick release.

**3** Use the handles of the trivet and transfer the brisket to a plate. Let cool for 10 minutes. Dab the brisket with a paper towel to sop up excess liquid, but *leave the fat on it*—it's like butter now!

**4** Whisk together all the spices on a large plate until well-blended. Transform that corned beef into a pastrami by dredging it in all the spices on the plate so it's completely covered.

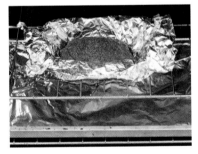

**5** Securely wrap in foil and place in fridge for at least 12 hours, or up to 2 days. This allows the corned beef to truly undergo a metamorphosis into a pastrami, without smoking it!

**6** When ready to serve, remove the pastrami from the fridge and, while still wrapped in foil, allow it to come to room temperature for 1 hour. (NOTE: This isn't mandatory, but is strongly suggested as it will make for an even more tender pastrami.)

**7** Preheat the oven to 275°F. Open the foil around the pastrami with the fatty side facing down (the top of the pastrami should be fully exposed and not covered with foil at this point), creating sort of a cradle/wall around the perimeter to try to keep any fat or seasonings from dripping while cooking. Once the oven is heated, place the cradled pastrami directly on the middle oven rack (not resting on a baking sheet) and place a baking sheet on the bottom oven rack to catch any fat drippings or spices that may fall off.

**8** Bake for 1 hour. Place the pastrami on a cutting board, discard the foil, and allow to cool for 5–10 minutes. Slice the pastrami into ¼-inch-thick slices and serve.

## MAKE REUBENS

- **Salted butter**
- **Rye bread or rye/pumpernickel swirl**
- **Russian or Thousand Island dressing**
- **Jeffrey's New York–Style Pastrami**
- **Swiss cheese**
- **Sauerkraut**

Butter each slice of bread on one side and place the slices butter side down in a frying pan over medium-high heat. On one slice of bread, schmear some dressing and top with a few strips of meat. On the other, lay a slice or two of cheese and some sauerkraut. After about 90 seconds–2 minutes (or when the bread looks golden brown), use a spatula to gently remove both pieces of bread to a plate. Then, place the cheese-and-sauerkraut slice face down on top of the meat slice, sandwiching it all together.

 **JEFF'S TIPS** When looking for a corned beef brisket you may find a flat or point cut. Here's the difference: A flat cut is less fatty and is easier to slice (that said, grab one that has some fat on it to ensure rich flavor and tenderness). A point cut is fattier and more marbled, will shrink more when cooked, and is better for making a hash or putting through a meat grinder. It's a matter of preference and either will work just fine—though I do prefer a point cut for a pastrami due to the extra fat.

If you wish to cure your own brisket, rub the following on a regular brisket in this order:

- **½ cup Morton Tender Quick Salt (it must be this exact salt)**
- **2 tablespoons dark brown sugar**
- **2 tablespoons black pepper**
- **1 tablespoon garlic powder**
- **1 tablespoon ground coriander**

Place the rubbed brisket in a ziplock bag large enough to hold it, get the air out, seal, and refrigerate for 6–7 days, turning the brisket over each day.

Take the brisket out of the bag and thoroughly rinse off the curing rub under cold water: It will be unpleasantly salty if you do not. Fill a large container with cold water and soak the brisket, completely submerged at room temperature, for 4 hours, changing the water every 30–45 minutes.

Once the above process is complete, dry the cured brisket thoroughly by dabbing with a paper towel. Brush the brisket all over with the liquid smoke, then continue the recipe at Step 2.

I was a young wife and mother making Thanksgiving dinner for my family and went into the kitchen to baste the turkey. But the house was old and a little crooked, so when I opened the oven door and pulled the pan out a little the oven rack tilted and the whole turkey came out of the pan and slid across my kitchen floor! I was screaming and had to jump over the hot bird headed my way. When it slammed into the refrigerator I burst into tears!

Then my husband came in (laughing so hard); he picked up the bird, put it back in the oven, gave me a big hug, and said, "It's all going to be alright." Good thing I had just mopped the floor!

LORI • **MARYSVILLE, WASHINGTON**

So, I don't cook. I don't really like cooking. I got my 6-quart Instant Pot in January 2020. My mom suggested your site and we used that. Then for my birthday I got book one, and I have been using the IP nonstop. I became the IP "expert" at my work and among my friends (I convinced three people to get their own). Now I'm gearing up to get a 3-quart for my sides. At this point, we are steadily becoming more and more debt-free and, aside from the house, we will be debt-free next year because we're not eating out all the time.

JESSICA • **NEWPORT NEWS, VIRGINIA**

# MEATBALLS MARINARA

When I think of melt-in-your-mouth meatballs, these come to mind. They will conjure up the best of an Italian nonna's Queens kitchen, no matter where you may make them. Whether you serve them on their own, pair them with spaghetti, or have them in the ultimate hero sandwich (page 214), I dare you to eat just one.

 **GF** + *(if using gluten-free breadcrumbs)*

 **V** + *(see Lighter Comforts)*

| Prep Time | Pressure Building Time | Pressure Cook Time | Natural Release Time | Total Time | Serves |
|-----------|------------------------|--------------------|----------------------|------------|--------|
| 10 MIN | 15–20 MIN | 20 MIN | 5 MIN | 50 MIN | 4–6 |

1 pound ground beef (the less lean, the better for meatballs!)

1/2 pound ground pork (or you can use 11/2 pounds ground beef total)

1/3 cup breadcrumbs

1/3 cup whole milk

1/2 cup grated Parmesan cheese, plus more for serving

6 cloves garlic, minced or pressed

2 tablespoons dried parsley

2 teaspoons seasoned salt

1 teaspoon black pepper

1 teaspoon dried oregano

1 large egg, slightly beaten

11/2 cups broth of your choice (I use Garlic Better Than Bouillon)

4 cups marinara sauce (I like Victoria or Rao's), at room temperature

Leaves from 1 bunch fresh basil, rinsed (optional)

**1** In a large mixing bowl, combine all the ingredients *except* the broth, marinara, and optional basil and mix together well by hand. Everything should form together into one giant meatball when done.

**2** Take some meat from the giant meatball and roll into an individual ball about 2 inches in diameter (a bit larger than a golf ball). Repeat to make about 12–15 meatballs.

**3** Add the broth to the Instant Pot, lay in the trivet (handles up), and spray the trivet with nonstick spray. Place each meatball (carefully, as they are uncooked and still impressionable) so they are resting on the trivet and then each other.

CONTINUES

**4** Secure the lid and move the valve to the sealing position. Hit Manual or Pressure Cook on High Pressure for 20 minutes. When done, allow a 5-minute natural release followed by a quick release.

**5** After removing the lid, the meatballs may look a bit fused together but don't worry, they aren't. Gently remove the trivet by taking one of the handles and allowing the meatballs to spill into the pot with the broth and drippings from the meat (**see Jeff's Tips**). Add the marinara sauce and basil (if using) to the pot. Hit Cancel followed by Sauté on the More or High setting. Once simmering, stir every so often for 5 minutes, then switch to the Keep Warm setting.

**6** Transfer the meatballs and sauce to a serving bowl and serve topped with some additional Parmesan and fresh basil, if desired.

## MAKE MEATBALL PARM HEROES

- **A few 6- to 8-inch hero rolls (like Italian bread or Portuguese rolls)**
- **Provolone cheese slices**
- **Shredded mozzarella**
- **A few sprinkles of grated Parmesan**

From the top, slice each hero roll lengthwise (so it looks similar to a top-sliced hot dog bun). Be careful not to cut all the way through so you can leave one end intact to support the cheese and meatballs and allow for easy resting once under the broiler. Line each roll with two slices of provolone and three meatballs with sauce spooned over them, and finish with as much shredded mozzarella and grated Parmesan as you desire. Pop into the toaster oven (or regular oven) and set to broil for 2–3 minutes; then keep an eye on them so they don't burn (oven temperatures can vary, after all). They're done when the cheese is all melted/slightly browned and the bread is slightly toasted. Let cool for a minute or two before tearing into them.

*lighter comforts* You can use 1½ pounds of any kind of ground meat for these meatballs, be it chicken, turkey, or bison.

If you're a vegetarian (and okay with eggs to bind your "meat"balls), use a plant-based meat that suits you, such as Beyond or Impossible meat.

**JEFF'S TIPS** I prefer to keep the broth in the pot just before adding the marinara sauce in Step 5. It gives it a really nice consistency and the meat drippings add such rich flavor. If you wish to have a thicker sauce, discard some or all of the broth. Then return the meatballs followed by the marinara. The reason we don't pressure cook with the sauce to begin with is because 4 cups of chunky, pureed tomatoes may cause a burn notice.

These meatballs would work perfectly in The Best Spaghetti & Meatballs (page 95). Just make sure they're the size of Ping-Pong balls as opposed to larger than golf balls to avoid any clogging, since we're cooking with pasta.

# CARIBBEAN SHORT RIBS

K + (see Lighter Comforts)

P + (see Lighter Comforts)

DF + (see Lighter Comforts)

GF + (if using tamari or coconut aminos)

It's been a while since I was able to travel to Caribbean sands and enjoy the spectacular cuisine that goes along with them. So I took a cue from a classic Jamaican oxtail stew (see Jeff's Tips) and swapped the oxtail for short ribs, making something so outrageous that just a taste would transport me back to my tropical happy place. No airfare required. Serve over Rice Pilaf (page 140) or Polenta Parmesan (page 250).

| Prep Time | Sauté Time | Pressure Building Time | Pressure Cook Time | Natural Release Time | Total Time | Serves |
|---|---|---|---|---|---|---|
| 10 MIN | 15 MIN | 10–15 MIN | 45 MIN | 15 MIN | 1 HR 35 MIN | 4–6 |

### THE RUB

¼ cup packed light or dark brown sugar

1 tablespoon kosher salt

1 teaspoon garlic powder

1 teaspoon onion powder

1 teaspoon allspice

1 teaspoon dried thyme

1 teaspoon paprika

1 teaspoon curry powder (optional)

### THE SHORT RIBS

3 pounds short ribs

¼ cup vegetable oil

4 tablespoons (½ stick) salted butter, divided

1 tablespoon Worcestershire sauce

1 large Spanish or yellow onion, diced

1 bunch scallions, sliced

2 medium carrots, peeled and sliced into ¼-inch-thick disks

1 tablespoon low-sodium soy sauce, tamari, or coconut aminos

3 cloves garlic, minced or pressed

1 cup beef broth

¼ cup ketchup

2 tablespoons cornstarch

2 tablespoons cold water

2 tablespoons tomato paste

1 teaspoon Gravy Master or Kitchen Bouquet (optional)

1 (16-ounce) can butter beans, drained and rinsed

**1** On a large plate, whisk together the rub ingredients. Dredge the short ribs in the rub, coating them all over.

**2** Add the oil and 2 tablespoons of the butter to the Instant Pot, hit Sauté, and Adjust so it's on the More or High setting. After 3 minutes of heating, in batches, add the coated short ribs and sear for 45–60 seconds on each side, until just slightly seared. Remove with tongs when done and let sit on a plate to rest.

**3** Add the Worcestershire sauce and deglaze (scrape the bottom of the pot to dislodge any bits stuck to it). Add the remaining 2 tablespoons butter and stir it around to make it melt quickly.

CONTINUES

**4** Add the onion, scallions, and carrots and sauté for 2 minutes. Add the soy sauce and continue to sauté for another 3 minutes. Add the garlic and sauté for 1 minute longer.

**5** Add the broth and ketchup and stir until everything is well combined. Return the seared short ribs to the pot (it's fine to rest them on top of each other). Secure the lid and move the valve to the sealing position. Hit Cancel and then hit Manual or Pressure Cook on High Pressure for 45 minutes. When done, allow a 15-minute natural release followed by a quick release.

**6** Meanwhile, make a slurry by mixing together the cornstarch and cold water in a small bowl until smooth.

**7** When the lid comes off, use tongs to carefully transfer the short ribs to a large serving dish to rest (they will be fall-off-the-bone tender). Hit Cancel and then hit Sauté and Adjust to the More or High setting. Once bubbling, stir in the cornstarch slurry. After 30 seconds of bubbling, hit Cancel to turn the pot off. Stir in the tomato paste until melded and then add the Gravy Master (if using) and beans and allow everything to rest for 3–5 minutes so the beans are heated and the gravy thickens nicely.

**8** When ready to serve, stir the gravy and ladle it over the ribs on the serving dish.

*lighter comforts* To keep the sugar level down, omit the brown sugar and ketchup. If you do so and replace the Worcestershire with sugar-free steak sauce and omit the butter beans, this dish will be keto (so long as you don't mind a little cornstarch slurry). Using ghee in place of the butter will make it paleo, and omitting the butter will make it dairy-free.

**JEFF'S TIPS** If you want this dish to have a kick, dice a seeded and ribbed Scotch bonnet/habanero/Jamaican hot pepper (*super spicy*) or jalapeño pepper (medium spicy) and add to the pot with the other veggies in Step 4.

You can make this a more classic Jamaican oxtail stew by subbing 3 pounds of oxtails for the short ribs. They're just as succulent. Everything else in the recipe remains the same.

# ASIAGO BEEF FLORENTINE PUFFS

K + *(see Lighter Comforts)*

GF + *(see Lighter Comforts)*

This new dish I've dreamed up combines my love of two very different cuisines. Inspired by Britain's own classic beef Wellington, with its tender meat, mushrooms, and puff pastry, and Tuscany's sauces featuring spinach, cream, and cheese (I chose Asiago), I give you a dish so outrageous, you won't have time for a fork—luckily, the puffs are made to be eaten with your hands. Not only is it a wonderful dinner, it also makes for amazing hors d'oeuvres when entertaining. The filling also goes perfectly with my Garlic Mashed Potatoes (page 258) or Polenta Parmesan (page 250), and is glorious over pasta, rice, and veggies.

| Prep Time | Sauté Time | Pressure Building Time | Pressure Cook Time | Natural Release Time | Oven Time | Total Time | Serves |
|---|---|---|---|---|---|---|---|
| 10 MIN | 15 MIN | 10–15 MIN | 30 MIN | 10 MIN | 20 MIN | 1 HR 20 MIN | 6–8 |

- 3 tablespoons extra-virgin olive oil
- 1 (2½- to 3-pound) chuck roast (I love Costco's), cut into smaller bite-size chunks
- ½ cup dry white wine (like a sauvignon blanc), divided
- 4 tablespoons (½ stick) salted butter
- 1 pound baby bella mushrooms, sliced (optional, see Jeff's Tips)
- 2 large shallots, diced
- 6 cloves garlic, minced or pressed

- 1 cup garlic broth (e.g., Garlic Better Than Bouillon) or beef broth
- 1 teaspoon dried thyme
- 1 teaspoon garlic salt
- 1 teaspoon garlic powder
- 1 teaspoon Italian seasoning
- 8–10 ounces baby spinach
- 6–12 Pepperidge Farm puff pastry shells, kept frozen; or 2 sheets Pepperidge Farm puff pastry, fully thawed and unfolded (see Jeff's Tips)

- 2 tablespoons cornstarch
- 2 tablespoons cold water
- ½ cup heavy cream
- 1 cup shredded Asiago (or grated Parmesan) cheese
- 1 (5.2-ounce) package Boursin herb cheese (any flavor) or 4 ounces brick cream cheese, cut into small chunks
- 1 tablespoon Dijon mustard (optional)
- 2 teaspoons dried parsley

**1** Add the olive oil to the Instant Pot, hit Sauté, and Adjust so it's on the More or High setting. After 3 minutes of heating, add the meat and sauté, stirring often for 2–3 minutes, until just lightly browned on all sides. Transfer to a plate and set aside.

**2** Add ¼ cup of the wine to the pot and deglaze (scrape the bottom to dislodge any browned bits). Add the butter; once melted, add the sliced mushrooms, shallots, and garlic. Sauté for 5 minutes, until the mushrooms are lightly browned.

**3** Return the meat to the pot and add the remaining ¼ cup wine, the broth, thyme, garlic salt, garlic powder, and Italian seasoning and stir, making sure the bottom of the pot is smooth and cleared of any browned bits. Top with the spinach but *do not stir.*

**4** Secure the lid and move the valve to the sealing position. Hit Cancel followed by Manual or Pressure Cook on High Pressure for 30 minutes. When done, allow a 10-minute natural release followed by a quick release.

**5** While the meat is pressure cooking, preheat the oven to 400–425°F. Bake the frozen puff pastry shells or thawed puff pastry rounds according to package instructions (keep an eye on them as oven temperatures can vary).

**6** Make a slurry in a small bowl by mixing together the cornstarch and cold water until smooth. Hit Cancel and then hit Sauté and Adjust so it's on the More or High setting. Once bubbling, add the slurry while constantly stirring. After 30 seconds of bubbling, add the cream, Asiago (or Parmesan), Boursin, Dijon (if using), and parsley. Stir until fully melded before hitting Cancel to turn the pot off. Let the filling rest for 5 minutes.

**7** Gently ladle the filling into the puff pastry shells and serve.

*lighter comforts* Sub almond milk for the cream and skip the Boursin. It'll be a bit less decadent this way, but still quite satisfying.

If you want to skip the puff pastry, you've just made it gluten-free and keto.

**JEFF'S TIPS** If using pastry sheets instead of shells, use a mini muffin tray. Cut the pastry sheets into rounds large enough to press into the muffin cups so a bowl-like shape forms (similar to pastry shells). Bake according to package instructions, keeping an eye on them so they don't burn.

If you're not into mushrooms, leave them out, skip the butter, and just sauté the shallots and garlic for 2–3 minutes instead of 5.

You will have at least enough filling for 12 (or more) puff pastry shells and can freeze any leftovers for a month or so.

# PORK PAPRIKASH

Paprikash is a staple Hungarian dish often made with chicken or veal. But I wanted a special pork recipe in this book and let me tell you something, you're gonna get it with this one. This is my take on a truly wonderful dish that features a lush, velvety, creamy tomato sauce infused with a key ingredient that gives the dish its name: paprika! Spoon over egg noodles or French Onion Risotto (page 146).

 *(if you don't mind a slurry)*

 GF

| Prep Time | Sauté Time | Pressure Building Time | Pressure Cook Time | Natural Release Time | Total Time | Serves |
|---|---|---|---|---|---|---|
| 10 MIN | 10 MIN | 10–15 MIN | 30 MIN | 10 MIN | 1 HR 10 MIN | 4–6 |

- 2 tablespoons (¼ stick) salted butter
- 1 large yellow onion, diced
- 2 yellow or orange bell peppers, seeded and diced
- 3 cloves garlic, minced or pressed
- 1 cup garlic broth (e.g., Garlic Better Than Bouillon) or chicken broth

- 1 (28-ounce) can crushed tomatoes
- 2 tablespoons paprika (Hungarian paprika is traditional, but regular or smoked will do)
- 1 teaspoon garlic powder
- 1 teaspoon onion powder
- 3 pounds pork tenderloin, sliced into bite-size pieces
- 2 tablespoons cornstarch

- 2 tablespoons cold water
- 1 tablespoon seasoned salt
- ½ cup sour cream
- ¼ cup heavy cream or half-and-half
- 1 (5.2-ounce) package Boursin herb cheese (any flavor) or 4 ounces brick cream cheese, cut into small chunks

**1** Add the butter to the Instant Pot, hit Sauté, and Adjust so it's on the More or High setting. Once melted, add the onion and peppers and sauté for 5 minutes. Add the garlic and sauté for 1 minute longer.

**2** Add the broth, crushed tomatoes, paprika, garlic powder, and onion powder to the pot. Stir well and then nestle in the pork. Secure the lid and move the valve to the sealing position. Hit Cancel followed by Manual or Pressure Cook on High Pressure for 30 minutes. When done, allow a 10-minute natural release followed by a quick release.

**3** Meanwhile, make a slurry in a small bowl by mixing together the cornstarch and cold water until smooth.

**4** Hit Cancel and then hit Sauté and Adjust to the More or High setting. Once bubbling, stir in the cornstarch slurry. After 30 seconds of bubbling, hit Cancel to turn the pot off. Stir in the seasoned salt, sour cream, cream, and Boursin or cream cheese until melded into the sauce. Let rest for 5 minutes before serving. Sprinkle additional paprika, if desired.

*lighter comforts* You can sub Greek yogurt for the sour cream, fat-free half-and-half for the cream, and just leave out the Boursin.

**JEFF'S TIP** Obviously, Boursin isn't common in a classic Hungarian paprikash, but then again, I'm known for putting some simple (and tasty) spins on classics. I love the flavor it adds but you can definitely leave it out.

# 7

# SEAFOOD

The ocean brings some of the tastiest and most exciting meals to the table. I personally love how quickly the Instant Pot cooks shellfish and fish fillets under pressure while also allowing some serious creativity to flow and keep things current (see what I did there?).

Seafood offers comfort from high tide to low, but it's even more wonderful when it's prepared in the most foolproof manner possible, with the push of a button under pressure.

My home and everything in it was lost to wildfires. My partner and I moved into the lower level of his parents' house. Cooking is my love language, so I created a "kitchen" in a family room that is built around my 8-quart Duo Crisp. With it, I have been able to spend the past six months cooking homemade food and bringing comfort to us as we heal from such a catastrophic loss.

Watching your YouTube channel and discovering delicious recipes to cook for us has kept us sane during this difficult time.

Our new house will be ready in another month but even though I will have a beautiful new oven, my Instant Pot will always have a place of honor in my kitchen!

RACHEL • OTIS, OREGON

= AIR FRYER LID    DF = DAIRY-FREE

K = KETO    GF = GLUTEN-FREE

P = PALEO    V = VEGETARIAN

+ = COMPLIANT WITH MODIFICATIONS    VN = VEGAN

# GUMBO

The Louisiana legend known as gumbo is just one of those things that, unless it's made the exact way your Gran Gran did it, could cause some controversy amongst even the closest of friends. My favorite gumbo includes okra (which, in many languages of West Africa, is the word for *gumbo*), andouille, and shrimp, built on a base of a roux (butter and flour paste) and the Cajun Holy Trinity of onion, pepper, and celery. This dish does have the most ingredients of any recipe in this book, but they're all easy-to-find and most are likely already in your pantry. Gran Gran never even needs to know about my controversial secret ingredient that's made this gumbo receive many a rave review.

 *(see Lighter Comforts)*

| Prep Time | Sauté Time | Pressure Building Time | Pressure Cook Time | Natural Release Time | Total Time | Serves |
|-----------|------------|------------------------|--------------------|----------------------|------------|--------|
| 15 MIN | 30 MIN | 15–25 MIN | 10 MIN | 5 MIN | 1 HR 15 MIN | 6–8 |

- 4 tablespoons (½ stick) salted butter
- 1 medium yellow onion, finely diced
- 1 green bell pepper, seeded and finely diced
- 3 ribs celery, finely diced, with leafy tops reserved
- 1 bunch scallions, sliced and divided in half (crunchy white bottoms separate from softer green tops)
- 1 pound boneless, skinless chicken thighs, cut into bite-size pieces
- 1 pound andouille sausage (or any smoked Cajun-style sausage you wish to use), diced or cut into ¼-inch-thick disks
- 6 cloves garlic, minced or pressed
- ½ cup vegetable oil
- ½ cup all-purpose flour

- 2 tablespoons Cajun/Creole/Louisiana seasoning (I use Tony Chachere's), divided
- ¼ teaspoon Gravy Master or Kitchen Bouquet (optional)
- Juice of ½ lemon
- 2 teaspoons Worcestershire sauce
- 1 teaspoon Zatarain's Concentrated Shrimp & Crab Boil (optional, for spice)
- 8 cups chicken broth or ham broth (e.g., Ham Better Than Bouillon) or a mix of both
- 2 (14.5-ounce) cans diced tomatoes, with their juices (optional, see Jeff's Tips)
- 2 teaspoons light brown sugar
- 2 teaspoons black pepper
- 2 teaspoons paprika
- 2 teaspoons dried thyme

- 1 teaspoon ground cumin
- 1 teaspoon cayenne pepper (optional, and more or less to taste)
- ¼ teaspoon white pepper (optional)
- 3 tablespoons cornstarch
- 3 tablespoons cold water
- 10 ounces frozen cut okra, thawed and rinsed
- ⅓ cup ketchup (yes, you read that right—and trust me)
- 1½ pounds raw large shrimp (thawed if frozen), peeled and deveined (tail on or off)
- Cooked white or brown rice, for serving
- Oyster crackers, for serving

**1** Add the butter to the Instant Pot, hit Sauté, and Adjust so it's on the More or High setting. Once the butter's melted, add the onion, bell pepper, celery, and white parts of the scallions. Sauté for 5 minutes, until softened.

**2** Add the chicken, sausage, and garlic and sauté for another 3–5 minutes, until the sausage is lightly cooked and the chicken is pinkish-white (it shouldn't be fully cooked). When done, remove the liner pot and dump the veggies, chicken, and sausage into a large bowl and set aside (it's okay if a few stragglers remain in the pot).

**3** Next, create the Cajun roux by adding the vegetable oil, flour, and 1½ teaspoons of the Cajun seasoning to the pot. Whisk/stir often for a solid 5 minutes, scraping the bottom of the pot often with a wooden spatula or spoon, until it becomes a nicely browned roux (the color should look like peanut butter). (NOTE: Make sure you whisk and scrape constantly or the roux may burn onto the pot.)

**4** After about 5 minutes, once the roux is beginning to darken, add the Gravy Master or Kitchen Bouquet (if using), lemon juice, Worcestershire sauce, and Zatarain's (if using). The roux will immediately puff up.

**5** Add the broth and diced tomatoes (if using). Deglaze the bottom of the pot to make sure none of the roux is sticking. Add the remaining 1½ tablespoons Cajun seasoning, the brown sugar, black pepper, paprika, dried thyme, cumin, cayenne pepper (if using), and white pepper (if using). Stir well and return the chicken, sausage, and veggies to the pot.

**6** Secure the lid and move the valve to the sealing position. Hit Cancel and hit Manual or Pressure Cook on High Pressure for 10 minutes. When done cooking, allow a 5-minute natural release followed by a quick release.

**7** Meanwhile, make a slurry by mixing together the cornstarch and cold water in a small bowl until smooth.

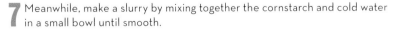

CONTINUES

**8** When the lid comes off, hit Cancel and then hit Sauté and Adjust so it's on the More or High setting. Stir in the okra, leafy celery tops, and the softer green parts of the scallions. Once bubbling, stir in the cornstarch slurry and ketchup (my controversial secret ingredient) and let bubble for 30 seconds, stirring constantly.

**9** Add the shrimp to the pot and allow to bubble for 1–3 minutes, stirring occasionally and checking on the shrimp so they don't overcook (they cook fast!). They should be opaque and curled up when ready. Hit Cancel to turn the pot off.

**10** Ladle into bowls with rice and top with some crackers, if desired.

**lighter comforts** Don't care for shrimp or sausage? Leave 'em out! If you do, you'll have chicken gumbo. To make a vegetarian gumbo, use a plant-based sausage and vegetable, onion, or garlic broth (all available in Better Than Bouillon).

**JEFF'S TIPS** Don't let the ketchup throw you off—it's my secret ingredient and adds such a wonderful and subtle undertone of flavor.

Skip the canned tomatoes if you like your gumbo tomato-free (Cajun-style) rather than tomato-filled (Creole-style).

# SHRIMP & CHEESE GRITS

It's hard to tell whether it was my Southern-born partner Richard or *My Cousin Vinny* that inspired me to make this cheesy, creamy Southern comfort, but it's as easy and tasty as it gets. Be sure to use old-fashioned, stone ground or hominy grits and *not* instant or quick "5-minute" ones. As the film will tell you, they're sacrilegious to many a Southerner, plus they tend to not play nicely in the Instant Pot—they'll end up overcooked.

DF + *(see Lighter Comforts)*
GF
V + *(see Lighter Comforts)*

| Prep Time | Pressure Building Time | Pressure Cook Time | Natural Release Time | Sauté Time | Total Time | Serves |
|-----------|------------------------|--------------------|--------------------|-----------|-----------|--------|
| 10 MIN | 15–20 MIN | 10 MIN | 5 MIN | 3 MIN | 45 MIN | 4–6 |

3 cups water

3 cups garlic broth (e.g., Garlic Better Than Bouillon) or vegetable broth

2 tablespoons extra-virgin olive oil

1½ cups old-fashioned, stone ground or hominy white grits (NOTE: It must be these and *not* instant or 5-minute grits. And avoid yellow grits—those are for polenta, page 250.)

½ cup heavy cream or half-and-half (optional, see Jeff's Tips)

2–4 tablespoons (¼–½ stick) salted butter (see Jeff's Tips)

1 (5.2-ounce) package Boursin herb cheese (any flavor) or 4 ounces brick cream cheese (optional)

1½–2 pounds raw large or jumbo shrimp (thawed if frozen), peeled and deveined (tail on or off)

2 cups shredded cheese of your choice (Cheddar or Gouda works great)

2–3 teaspoons freshly cracked black pepper, to taste (optional)

A few dashes of hot sauce, to taste, plus more for serving (optional)

Sliced chives, for garnish (optional)

**1** Add the water, broth, olive oil, and grits to the Instant Pot (see Jeff's Tips). Stir well. Secure the lid and move the valve to the sealing position. Hit Manual or Pressure Cook on High Pressure for 10 minutes. When done cooking, allow a 5-minute natural release followed by a quick release.

**2** Once the lid's off, give everything a good stir so the grits are smoothed out and blended with the remaining liquid. Add the cream (if using), butter, and Boursin or cream cheese (if using) and stir until melded into the grits.

**3** Hit Cancel and then hit Sauté and Adjust so it's on the More or High setting. Once bubbling, add the shrimp and sauté for 2–3 minutes, stirring frequently and scraping the bottom of the pot. As soon as they begin to curl and appear opaque, hit Cancel to turn the pot off and then hit Keep Warm.

CONTINUES

**4** Fold in the cheese (if you know, you know). Then, add the pepper (if using) and hot sauce (if using) and stir until melded into the grits. Then let rest for 3–5 minutes to slightly thicken. Serve topped with chives, additional pepper, and hot sauce, if desired.

 *lighter comforts* Should you wish to go lighter on the dairy, skip the butter and cream. You'll have slightly thicker grits, but some prefer them that way. You can also use an unsweetened nondairy milk (like almond) in place of the cream and omit the shredded cheese and try dairy-free Boursin to make it dairy-free.

Not into seafood but craving the grits? Skip the shrimp and Step 3 entirely.

**JEFF'S TIPS** This recipe is best made in a 6-quart Instant Pot due to the pot's circumference and the grits having a slight tendency to stick to the bottom of the pot—they should cook perfectly as written but may leave a little layer for you to scrub off when done. However, if you want to make it in an 8-quart, add an additional 2 cups water; to make it in a 3-quart, halve the recipe. The cook time is universal for all three sizes.

If you want thicker grits, leave out the cream but be mindful that, like pasta and grains, grits always continue to absorb liquid and thicken as they rest.

How buttery you want your grits is up to you. Start with 2 tablespoons, then you can always add more!

My hubby died a couple of years ago. After six months, I bought an Instant Pot. Two months later, Covid hit, and the rest is history. I found you, Jeffrey, and never looked back. I've been cooking for family and friends ever since. A fun learning curve! I have gifted your book to a *lot* of people, some who didn't even have an Instant Pot. My latest share was your cute music video singing the Chicago tune, and it didn't even involve cooking. Love you, Kiddo, and hope you keep up your good work for a long, long time.

DONNA • **BURLINGTON, WISCONSIN**

I never thought that I'd be much of a cook. Then, one day, I asked my mom for her recipe for macaroni and cheese and I discovered something magical when I started making it; as I whisked the sauce, tasting and making sure it was just right, my kitchen smelled like *home*.

Making family recipes brings memories and people back, and that is a powerful thing. It's the same reason I use my grandma's old and battered colander. It's a reminder of her and keeps her present in my life.

ADRIENNE • **COCONUT CREEK, FLORIDA**

I'm from Alabama, and live in Mississippi. Food down here is how we show our love, how we remember, and how we make memories. When I fry chicken, I think of my grandmothers. Making cornbread dressing with chicken reminds me of my dad. There is nothing like seeing your loved ones enjoy what you have prepared with love for them. It's amazing how much cooking can do for the soul.

ELAINE • **GULFPORT, MISSISSIPPI**

# THE ULTIMATE TUNA CASSEROLE

Prepare yourself for my take on one of the most classic and comforting Americana dishes you've ever known, made with little effort whatsoever. Even if the thought of tuna under pressure makes you scratch your head, trust me on this one—it tastes like a chicken pot pie casserole (**Fun Fact:** This is just my famous Cockadoodle Noodles repurposed as tuna casserole). Check out Jeff's Tips to make this buffalo style. That one is pure joy.

| Prep Time | Sauté Time | Pressure Building Time | Pressure Cook Time | Natural Release Time | Total Time | Serves |
|---|---|---|---|---|---|---|
| 10 MIN | 8 MIN | 5–10 MIN | 2 MIN | 7–10 MIN | 35 MIN | 4–6 |

- 4 tablespoons (½ stick) salted butter
- 1 pound baby bella mushrooms, sliced (optional)
- 1 tablespoon Worcestershire sauce
- 3½ cups garlic broth (e.g., Garlic Better Than Bouillon) or chicken broth
- 1½ teaspoons dried basil
- 1 teaspoon garlic powder
- 1 teaspoon onion powder

- 1 teaspoon black pepper
- 1 (12-ounce) bag egg noodles (I use wide ribbons)
- 4 (5-ounce) cans albacore tuna (see Jeff's Tips), drained
- 20 ounces frozen veggie mix (corn, carrots, peas, and green beans)
- 1 cup heavy cream or half-and-half
- ¼ cup ranch dressing (not the mix, but actual dressing)

- 2 cups shredded cheese blend of your choice (I like Colby Jack)
- ½ cup grated Parmesan cheese
- 1 (5.2-ounce) package Boursin herb cheese (any flavor) or 4 ounces brick cream cheese, cut into small chunks (optional)
- 1–2 tablespoons hot sauce (optional)
- 1–2 teaspoons seasoned salt (optional)

**1** Add the butter to the Instant Pot. Hit Sauté and Adjust so it's on the More or High setting. Once melted and bubbling, add the mushrooms and sauté for 5 minutes, until softened and browned.

**2** Add the Worcestershire sauce and deglaze (scrape the bottom of the pot to dislodge any browned bits of mushroom).

**3** Add the broth, basil, garlic powder, onion powder, and black pepper to the pot and stir well.

**4** Layer the following ingredients in this order, evenly smoothing each layer with a wooden spatula, *but without ever stirring between each layer:* the noodles, tuna, and frozen veggies.

**5** Secure the lid and move the valve to the sealing position. Hit Cancel and then hit Manual or Pressure Cook on High Pressure for 2 minutes. Allow a 7-minute natural release for firmer noodles and a 10-minute release for softer. Follow with a quick release.

**6** Add the cream, ranch dressing, shredded cheese, Parmesan, Boursin or cream cheese (if using), and hot sauce (if using). Stir until fully melded. If you wish to add the optional seasoned salt, start with 1 teaspoon and add to taste. Serve.

## ADD A RITZY CRUST

- **1 sleeve Ritz Crackers, smashed and crumbled**
- **4 tablespoons (½ stick) salted butter, melted**
- **¼ cup bacon crumbles (optional)**

Mix the crumbled Ritz crackers with the melted butter and bacon crumbles (if using). Evenly sprinkle on top of the finished tuna casserole. Add the air fryer lid, hit Broil (400°F) for 5–10 minutes, and hit Start. You can also do this in the oven in a casserole dish at 425°F (keep an eye on it as oven temperatures can vary). Once the crust is golden brown, serve.

 **JEFF'S TIPS** Not into tuna? Use canned chicken instead—just drain it like you would canned tuna.

To make this buffalo style, sub ¼–½ cup buffalo wing sauce for the 1–2 tablespoons hot sauce in Step 6. You can also make it barbecue style by using ⅓ cup of your favorite barbecue sauce instead.

*lighter comforts* Leave out the Boursin, and use low-fat Cheddar and fat-free half-and-half.

# PINEAPPLE CRAB

**FRIED RICE**

Every one of my three absolute favorite dishes at my local Thai restaurant is fried rice: Thai basil (in my orange book), pineapple, and crab. But sometimes I don't feel like choosing between the three, and that's where this fried rice comes in. If you don't have Thai basil in your local market, tarragon contributes a similar note of flavor.

 **DF**

**GF** + *(see Lighter Comforts)*

| Prep Time | Pressure Building Time | Pressure Cook Time | Natural Release Time | Sauté Time | Total Time | Serves |
|---|---|---|---|---|---|---|
| 15 MIN | 5–15 MIN | 3 MIN | 10 MIN | 15 MIN | 50 MIN | 4–6 |

- 2 cups jasmine rice, rinsed for 90 seconds and drained
- 2 cups water or fish broth (e.g., Fish Better Than Bouillon)
- 1/3 cup chopped fresh cilantro, plus more for garnish (optional)
- 1/2 cup vegetable oil
- 1 large white or yellow onion, diced
- 1 large red bell pepper, seeded and sliced into matchsticks

- 5 ounces kale, chopped
- 1 bunch scallions, sliced, some reserved for serving
- 2 cups fresh Thai basil or tarragon leaves, plus more for garnish
- 6 cloves garlic, sliced into slivers
- 4 large eggs, lightly beaten
- 1 pound lump crabmeat, drained

- 1/4 cup low-sodium soy sauce, tamari, or coconut aminos
- 1/4 cup oyster sauce
- 2 tablespoons fish sauce
- 2 tablespoons hoisin sauce
- 1 (20-ounce) can crushed pineapple, pineapple tidbits, or pineapple chunks (see Jeff's Tips), drained
- Sesame seeds, for garnish

**1** Add the rinsed rice to the Instant Pot along with the broth and cilantro (if using) and stir. Secure the lid and move the valve to the sealing position. Hit Manual or Pressure Cook on High Pressure for 3 minutes. When done, allow a 10-minute natural release followed by a quick release. Fluff the rice with a fork.

**2** Hit Cancel and transfer the rice to a bowl. You can either rinse the liner pot and return it to the Instant Pot (just make sure it's totally dry before returning) or leave as is (it will be more prone to things getting stuck to the bottom in the next step, but not a big deal).

**3** Add the oil to the pot and hit Sauté and Adjust to the High or More setting. After 3 minutes of heating, add the onion, bell pepper, kale, scallions, basil, and garlic and sauté for 5 minutes, until softened.

**4** Move the veggies to one side of the pot. Pour the eggs on the other side and add the crab. Stir constantly to scramble the eggs and heat the crab. Once scrambled, mix with the veggies. Turn off the pot by hitting Cancel.

**5** Return the rice to the pot and top with the soy sauce, oyster sauce, fish sauce, hoisin sauce, and pineapple. Stir until everything is fully tossed and coated. Serve topped with cilantro, scallions, basil, and sesame seeds, if desired.

*lighter comforts* To make this dish gluten-free, use tamari or coconut aminos (instead of soy sauce) and gluten-free hoisin and oyster sauce. To keep it soy-free, use coconut aminos.

**JEFF'S TIPS** Select the kind of canned pineapple based on how chunky you want it to be: Crushed will almost dissolve into the rice; tidbits will be a medium presence; and chunks will be exactly that. All that said, although it's pineapple fried rice, you can leave it out if you're not a fan.

This dish isn't designed to be spicy, but if you want it that way, add up to 1 teaspoon Zatarain's Concentrated Shrimp & Crab Boil and/or up to 1 teaspoon crushed red pepper flakes while the vegetables are sautéing in Step 3.

I got my Instant Pot three years ago at Christmas. I'd just gotten out of the hospital after three months and four major operations. I did not have the strength nor the energy to prepare regular meals. The Instant Pot was a lifesaver. I managed to feed my husband and make meals that I could eat and that would help me get my strength back. I didn't have to lift heavy pans or pots nor did I have to babysit the pot if I was not feeling well...my husband could even use it. It is my favorite appliance today and I still use it almost every day. Thank you and your wonderful recipes.

HEIDI • GREENFIELD PARK, QUEBEC, CANADA

# LOBSTERINO MAC & CHEESE

You've seen it at fancy steakhouses and upscale pubs: Now, make it at home in all its simple, comforting glory. This dish is a sophisticated, grown-up version of the super popular mac & cheese recipe from my orange book. If you're looking to be more budget-conscious but still want to feel like you're eating lobster, you can use tender langostino meat instead. Be warned: Keeping your claws off the whole pot may be a challenge.

| Prep Time | Sauté Time | Pressure Building Time | Pressure Cook Time | Optional Crisping Time | Total Time | Serves |
|---|---|---|---|---|---|---|
| 10 MIN | 10 MIN | 10–20 MIN | 6 MIN | 5–10 MIN | 40 MIN | 4–6 |

- 4 tablespoons (½ stick) salted butter, divided
- 1½–2 pounds thawed lobster tail, shelled and meat chopped into small chunks; or 1–2 pounds langostino meat (Costco sells this in their fresh seafood section)
- ¼ cup dry white wine (like a sauvignon blanc)
- 4 cups lobster broth (e.g., Lobster Better Than Bouillon) or garlic broth

- 1 pound medium shells (or any short-form pasta such as cavatappi)
- 1 pound shredded sharp Cheddar cheese (white or yellow)
- ¼ cup grated Parmesan cheese
- 1 tablespoon Dijon mustard (optional)
- 1 tablespoon hot sauce (optional)
- White or black truffle oil, for serving (optional)

**OPTIONAL CRUST**
- 1 sleeve Ritz Crackers, smashed and crumbled
- 4 tablespoons (½ stick) salted butter, melted

**OPTIONAL LOBSTER MAC ROLLS**
- Top-sliced hot dog buns (I like brioche or pretzel buns)

**1** Add 2 tablespoons of the butter to the Instant Pot. Hit Sauté and Adjust so it's on the More or High setting. Once melted and bubbling, add the lobster meat and sauté for 3–5 minutes, adding the wine after a minute to deglaze the bottom of the pot. Sauté until the meat is mostly cooked and opaque (it's fine if some is still pink). Transfer to a bowl with a slotted spoon and set aside to rest.

**2** Add the broth and pasta to the pot and stir well (one of the rare cases we stir in pasta). Top with the remaining 2 tablespoons butter.

**3** Secure the lid and move the valve to the sealing position. Hit Cancel and hit Manual or Pressure Cook on High Pressure for 6 minutes. Quick release when done.

**4** When the lid comes off, it will look soupy. This is a good thing as it's the base for the sauce. Add the Cheddar, Parmesan, Dijon (if using), and hot sauce (if using) and stir until the cheese melds into the sauce and becomes creamy and dreamy.

**5** Return the lobster meat to the pot and stir until it's fully cooked (no pink should remain). Serve with some truffle oil drizzled on top, if desired.

**6** **For a crust:** Mix the crumbled Ritz crackers with the melted butter. Evenly sprinkle on top of the finished mac and cheese. Secure the air fryer lid, hit Broil (400°F) for 5–10 minutes and hit Start. Once the crust is golden brown, serve. You can also do this in a casserole dish in a 425°F oven (keep an eye on it as oven temperatures can vary).

**7** **For rolls:** Alternatively, serve it in hot dog buns for lobster mac rolls!

*lighter comforts* For a lighter option, forego the crust and sub a low-fat cheese for the Cheddar.

**JEFF'S TIPS** If the sauce is a bit thick for your liking after it sets, add a few splashes of milk or cream while reheating and stir. Adding milk or cream is also a great way to revive any leftovers when microwaving.

Wanna be as happy as a clam? Separate two (6-ounce) cans of chopped clams from their juices. Add the clam juice in Step 2 and reduce the broth to 3⅔ cups. Then, add the clams in Step 5 along with the lobster/langostino meat. Incredible.

# PAELLA

For me, the holy grail of seafood dishes is the Spanish crown jewel known as paella. From shellfish to chorizo, this saffron-infused rice dish has it all. Traditionally, it is made in a very large pan over an open fire to give it that classic *socarrat*, or crispy bottom layer of rice. I like the texture with a touch of creaminess, which the Instant Pot will take care of, but in this case we can also give the top layer of the rice that sought-after finishing crisp with the air fryer lid.

DF⁺ (see Lighter Comforts)

GF

| Prep Time | Sauté Time | Pressure Building Time | Pressure Cook Time | Optional Crisping Time | Total Time | Serves |
|---|---|---|---|---|---|---|
| 15 MIN | 15 MIN | 10–15 MIN | 10 MIN | 5–10 MIN | 50 MIN | 4–6 |

¼ cup vegetable oil

2 tablespoons (¼ stick) salted butter

1 large Spanish or yellow onion, chopped

1 green bell pepper, seeded and diced

1 red bell pepper, seeded and diced

1 pound Spanish chorizo, sliced into ¼-inch-thick disks (optional, you could also use crumbled-style Mexican chorizo)

3 cloves garlic, minced or pressed

Grated zest of 1 lemon

1 teaspoon saffron

3½ cups fish broth (e.g., Fish Better Than Bouillon) or garlic broth

½ cup dry white wine (like a chardonnay)

1 (14.5-ounce) can diced tomatoes, with their juices

1 teaspoon turmeric

1 (14-ounce) box yellow rice (arroz amarillo)

1 pound raw large shrimp (thawed if frozen), deveined (shell on or off depending on how you like it)

1 pound raw scallops (thawed if frozen)

1 pound raw calamari rings (thawed if frozen)

10 ounces frozen peas (optional)

Chopped fresh Italian (flat-leaf) parsley, for garnish (optional)

**1** Add the oil and butter to the Instant Pot and hit Sauté and Adjust so it's on the More or High setting. Once the butter's melted, add the onion and bell peppers and sauté for 2–3 minutes, until slightly softened.

**2** Add the chorizo (if using) and sauté for 2 minutes. Then add the garlic, lemon zest, and saffron and sauté for 1 minute longer.

**3** Add the broth, white wine, diced tomatoes, turmeric, and rice and stir well. Secure the lid and move the valve to the sealing position. Hit Cancel and hit Manual or Pressure Cook on High Pressure for 10 minutes. Quick release when done.

**4** Give everything a good stir. There will be some extra broth and we will use that to cook our shrimp, scallops, and calamari as the excess broth continues to be absorbed by the rice.

**5** Hit Cancel and then hit Sauté and Adjust so it's on the More or High setting. Add the shrimp, scallops, calamari, and peas (if using). Stir it all into the rice and cook for about 5 minutes, scraping the bottom of the pot to keep the rice from sticking. Once the shrimp are curled and opaque and scallops are of the proper white/light pink color, you're done (just cut a scallop open if you aren't sure to see if it's cooked).

**6** Transport the paella to a serving dish or large cast-iron skillet, sprinkle on parsley (if using), and serve!

 **JEFF'S TIP** Use whatever proteins you prefer! I like to add up to a pound of boneless, skinless chicken breasts or thighs sliced into bite-size pieces in Step 2 along with the chorizo.

**7** **For a crispy top:** Just before serving, secure the air fryer lid. Hit Broil (400°F), for 5–10 minutes, and hit Start. Check on it every 5 minutes or so and feel free to stir so the rice crisps. Just don't overdo it because we don't want the seafood to dry out. You can also bake the paella in a cast-iron skillet in the oven at 450°F for 5–10 minutes, until the top layer of rice is crispy (but keep an eye on it as oven temperatures can vary).

 *lighter comforts* To make it dairy-free, omit the butter and add another 2 tablespoons vegetable oil.

# LOADED LOBSTER BISQUE

K + *(if you're okay with wine)*

P + *(see Lighter Comforts)*

GF

If you're craving a silky, creamy, tomatoey lobster bisque worthy of a five-star gourmet experience with minimal work, this is the one. Every single bisque lover I've known has raved about this one—and then chastised me because it wasn't yet published in a book. So here it is!

| Prep Time | Sauté Time | Pressure Building Time | Pressure Cook Time | Total Time | Serves |
|---|---|---|---|---|---|
| 10 MIN | 10 MIN | 5–10 MIN | 2 MIN | 30 MIN | 4 |

- 4 tablespoons (½ stick) salted butter
- 1–2 pounds thawed lobster tail, shelled, meat chopped into small chunks (see Jeff's Tip)
- 1 large shallot, diced
- 3 scallions (whiter, crunchier parts), sliced
- 3 cloves garlic, minced or pressed
- ¼ cup dry white wine (like a sauvignon blanc)

- ⅓ cup sherry wine
- 1 cup lobster broth (e.g., Lobster Better Than Bouillon)
- 2 teaspoons Worcestershire sauce
- ½–2 teaspoons Tabasco sauce (optional, use less for less zest and more for a little more intensity)
- 1 teaspoon dried thyme
- 1 teaspoon paprika

- 1 teaspoon Old Bay seasoning (optional)
- 2 bay leaves
- 2 cups heavy cream or half-and-half
- 2–4 tablespoons tomato paste (start with 2 and add more to taste)
- Oyster crackers, for serving (optional)

**1** Add the butter to the Instant Pot. Hit Sauté and Adjust so it's on the More or High setting. Once melted and bubbling, add the lobster meat and sauté for 3–5 minutes, until cooked and opaque. Transfer to a bowl with a slotted spoon and set aside to rest.

**2** Add the shallot, scallions, and garlic to the pot and sauté in the butter for 3 minutes.

**JEFF'S TIP** You can use langostino meat in place of lobster. Costco usually sells it in their seafood section, where it's already crumbled. Although it's technically in the crab family, the flavor and texture greatly resemble lobster.

**3** Add the white wine and sherry and deglaze the bottom of the pot with a wooden spoon/spatula to remove any remnants that may have stuck to it.

*lighter comforts* To make it paleo, sub ghee for the butter and an unsweetened nondairy milk such as almond or cashew for the cream.

**4** When the wine bubbles (which will be quickly), add the broth, Worcestershire sauce, Tabasco (if using), thyme, paprika, and Old Bay (if using). Do a final scraping of the bottom of the pot with a wooden spoon/spatula and once it bubbles, add the bay leaves.

**5** Secure the lid and move the valve to the sealing position. Hit Cancel and then hit Manual or Pressure Cook on High Pressure for 2 minutes. Quick release when done.

**6** Discard the bay leaves. Hit Cancel and then Sauté and Adjust so it's on the More or High setting. Add the cream and 2 tablespoons tomato paste and stir until it's all blended together.

**7** Take an immersion blender and blend until pureed. This is when you can decide if you want to add more tomato paste. Hit Cancel to turn the pot off.

**8** As the bubbles die down, add the cooked lobster meat to the bisque and stir for 1 minute. Ladle into bowls and top with some oyster crackers, if desired.

# UMAMI FISH FILLETS

**P** + *(see Lighter Comforts)*

**DF**

**GF** + *(if using tamari or coconut aminos)*

Fish is one of the easiest things you can make in the Instant Pot as it's quick, won't heat up (or smell up) your kitchen, and is totally hassle-free. This sweet and savory honey-garlic sauce will complement any fillet you choose, the Instant Pot will prepare a fish that cuts like butter, and the end result is a total win for fish lovers. It's great any time of year and goes well with my Polenta Parmesan (page 250), Sesame Peanut Noodles (page 97), and Rice Pilaf (page 140).

| Prep Time | Pressure Building Time | Pressure Cook Time | Sauté Time | Total Time | Serves |
|---|---|---|---|---|---|
| 10 MIN | 5–10 MIN | 4 MIN | 3 MIN | 25 MIN | 4–6 |

- 1 cup garlic broth (e.g., Garlic Better Than Bouillon) or vegetable broth
- 2 tablespoons sesame oil (any kind)
- 2 tablespoons balsamic vinegar
- 2 tablespoons light or dark brown sugar

- 6 cloves garlic, minced or pressed
- 1 tablespoon minced or grated ginger (I use squeeze ginger)
- 1½ teaspoons Chinese five-spice powder
- 4–6 fish fillets of your choice (see Jeff's Tip), fully thawed and about ¼ to ½ inch thick

- 2 tablespoons low-sodium soy sauce, tamari, or coconut aminos
- 1½ tablespoons cornstarch
- 1½ tablespoons cold water
- ⅓ cup honey
- 1 tablespoon hoisin sauce (optional)

**1** Add the broth, sesame oil, vinegar, brown sugar, garlic, ginger, and Chinese five-spice to the Instant Pot. Whisk until combined.

**2** Lay the trivet, handle side up, in the pot. Place a parchment round on top of the trivet. Lay the fillets on the parchment round, brushing the soy sauce on the top of each as you stack them on top of each other in a crisscross fashion. Pour any leftover soy sauce into the pot.

**3** Secure the lid and move the valve to the sealing position. Hit Cancel and then hit Manual or Pressure Cook on High Pressure for 4 minutes. Quick release when done.

**4** Stir together the cornstarch and cold water in a small bowl to form a slurry.

 *lighter comforts* If you sub pure maple syrup for the brown sugar and are okay with a slurry, this will make it paleo. By the way, you can always omit the slurry—the sauce will just be thinner.

 **JEFF'S TIP** I designed this recipe to be used with any kind of popular fish. I suggest salmon, tilapia, cod, or mahi-mahi. Whichever you choose, just make sure it is sliced into fillets about ¼ to ½ inch thick.

**5** Carefully remove the trivet with the fillets and transfer the fillets to a plate. Hit Cancel and then Sauté and Adjust so it's on the More or High setting. Add the slurry while stirring constantly for 30 seconds; the sauce will thicken. Hit Cancel to turn the pot off.

**6** Stir in the honey and hoisin sauce (if using). Spoon the sauce over the fish and serve.

# 8

# VEGETABLES & SIDES

You're about to discover a chapter full of comforting dishes that focus on veggies and sides perfect for any table. I'll take you on a journey, with main dishes such as the lighter Moo Shu Mushroom Wraps and the more decadent cheesy Chiles Rellenos Enchilada Casserole. And then there are the wonderful sides that complement so many other meat and poultry recipes, like some serious Garlic Mashed Potatoes and Creamed Spinach.

Whatever you choose, it's a garden of eatin'.

The pandemic has been horrible, as we all know. I was afraid to go into stores to shop for food. I was literally having panic attacks. Reading through your recipes made me go out to get the ingredients because the pictures looked beautiful and I had to try them. You have turned me into a fabulous, confident cook. My husband even gets into the act. Thank you for helping me get through the pandemic with the love of cooking and the excitement of trying new recipes.

CATHY • NORTH OLMSTED, OHIO

♨ = AIR FRYER LID     DF = DAIRY-FREE

K = KETO     GF = GLUTEN-FREE

P = PALEO     V = VEGETARIAN

✚ = COMPLIANT WITH MODIFICATIONS     VN = VEGAN

# · CHILES RELLENOS ·
# ENCHILADA CASSEROLE

 K<sup>+</sup> *(see Lighter Comforts)*

 GF<sup>+</sup> *(see Lighter Comforts)*

V

If I'm in a vegetarian mood when going out for Mexican, I'll be on a mission for chiles rellenos. These are typically mild poblano peppers stuffed with ooey-gooey melty Monterey Jack cheese and then fried in a batter. Here, we're simplifying the process and turning them into an enchilada-style casserole that even the kids will go nuts for. Serve with Ruby Rice (page 38).

| Prep Time | Sauté Time | Pressure Building Time | Pressure Cook Time | Optional Baking Time | Total Time | Serves |
|---|---|---|---|---|---|---|
| 10 MIN | 10 MIN | 10–15 MIN | 3 MIN | 20 MIN | 35 MIN | 4–6 |

4 tablespoons (½ stick) salted butter

1 large Spanish or yellow onion, diced

¼ cup all-purpose flour

2 cups garlic broth (e.g., Garlic Better Than Bouillon) or vegetable broth

6 poblano peppers (see Jeff's Tips), sliced into ¼-inch-wide strips

¼ cup salsa verde (you can also use red salsa, but I prefer green for this), plus more to taste (see Jeff's Tips)

2 cups shredded Monterey Jack or pepper Jack cheese

10–12 small flour or corn tortillas (fajita size is best for this)

1 cup sour cream

1 (7-ounce) can diced green chiles (these are mild), with their juices

½ cup crumbled cotija cheese (use grated Parmesan if you can't find cotija)

1½ tablespoons cornstarch

1½ tablespoons cold water

2 cups shredded Mexican cheese blend

**1** Add the butter to the Instant Pot, hit Sauté, and Adjust so it's on the Less or Low setting. (NOTE: This is the only recipe in the book we Sauté on Less/Low due to the combining of flour with only butter and onion in Step 2.) Once the butter's melted, add the onion and sauté for 3 minutes, until softened.

**2** Whisk in the flour constantly until just lightly browned, about 1 minute.

 **JEFF'S TIPS** If your market doesn't carry poblano peppers, you can sub green bell peppers.

Start with ¼ cup salsa, then if you feel the filling is too thick, add more to your liking.

**3** Add the broth and scrape the bottom of the pot so it's clear of any browned bits. Nestle the pepper strips into the pot, but *do not stir.* Secure the lid and move the valve to the sealing position. Hit Cancel and then hit Manual or Pressure Cook on High Pressure for 3 minutes. Quick release when done.

CONTINUES

**4** Using a slotted spoon, transfer the peppers to a mixing bowl (it's okay if some of the onions come along with it). Add the salsa and Jack cheese, and mix together until combined.

**5** Spray a 9x13-inch casserole dish with nonstick spray. Using a ⅓-cup measuring cup, scoop the pepper-cheese mixture onto the tortillas. Roll each up, leaving the ends open, and arrange in the casserole dish, seam side down.

**6** Add the sour cream to the Instant Pot and whisk until combined. Add the diced green chiles and cotija cheese and stir.

**7** Meanwhile, make a slurry by mixing together the cornstarch and cold water in a small bowl until smooth.

**8** Hit Cancel and then Sauté and Adjust so it's on the More or High setting. Once bubbling, add the slurry while stirring constantly for 30 seconds and the sauce will thicken. Hit Cancel to turn the pot off.

**9** Generously pour the sauce over the enchiladas and top with the shredded Mexican cheese.

**10** **For a baked finish (suggested):** Bake in the oven at 350°F, uncovered, for 20 minutes, or until the cheese is lightly browned.

*lighter comforts* To make it keto, use keto-friendly tortillas and sub coconut flour for the all-purpose. You can also leave out the cornstarch slurry unless you're okay with it (although the sauce will be thinner).

To make it gluten-free, sub quinoa flour or coconut flour for the all-purpose and use corn or other gluten-free tortillas.

# THE ULTIMATE STUFFED MUSHROOMS

 **DF** ⁺ *(see Lighter Comforts)*

**V**

If I see stuffed mushrooms on a menu, chances are they're getting ordered. Making them in your Instant Pot will ensure your mushrooms won't dry out and will remain juicy with each bite. The caps are stuffed with a magical breadcrumb filling (use panko) and then drizzled with a Parmesan marsala-infused sauce to send them over the top. This recipe offers an optional—yet strongly suggested—oven-roast or air-fry finish—but the mushrooms are still irresistible without that touch.

| Prep Time | Pressure Building Time | Pressure Cook Time | Optional Roasting Time | Total Time | Serves |
|---|---|---|---|---|---|
| 15 MIN | 5–10 MIN | 5 MIN | 5–10 MIN | 30 MIN | 4–6 |

## THE FILLING
¾ cup panko breadcrumbs
¼ cup extra-virgin olive oil
¼ cup grated Parmesan cheese
3 cloves garlic, minced or pressed
2 tablespoons sliced fresh chives
1 teaspoon Italian seasoning

1 teaspoon dried parsley
½ teaspoon seasoned salt

## THE MUSHROOMS AND SAUCE
1½ pounds baby bella or white button mushrooms, stemmed, caps hollowed out for filling
¾ cup mushroom broth (e.g., Mushroom Better Than Bouillon) or vegetable broth

¼ cup marsala wine
1½ tablespoons cornstarch
1½ tablespoons cold water
¼ cup grated Parmesan cheese
1 teaspoon Italian seasoning
1 tablespoon tomato paste

**1** Add the filling ingredients to a bowl and mix with a fork until combined.

**2** Using a spoon, stuff each mushroom cap with the filling.

**3** Add the broth and marsala to the Instant Pot. Gently place the mushrooms in a steamer basket, resting on top of each other with the filling facing up. Lower the basket into the pot. Secure the lid and move the valve to the sealing position. Hit Cancel and then hit Manual or Pressure Cook on High Pressure for 5 minutes. Quick release when done.

CONTINUES

**4** Meanwhile, make a slurry by mixing together the cornstarch and cold water in a small bowl until smooth.

**5** Remove the steamer basket and use tongs to carefully transfer the mushrooms to a platter.

**6** Hit Cancel followed by Sauté and Adjust so it's on the More or High setting. Add the Parmesan, Italian seasoning, and tomato paste to the liquid in the pot and stir until blended from the heat of the pot. Stir in the cornstarch slurry and let bubble for 30 seconds. Hit Cancel to turn the pot off.

*lighter comforts*  Sub nutritional yeast for the Parmesan.

**7** **For the optional (suggested) roasted finish in the oven:** Preheat the oven to 425°F. Place the mushrooms in a cast-iron skillet or on a parchment-lined baking sheet. Roast on the top rack for 5–10 minutes, until the tops have browned and become slightly crispy.

**For the optional (suggested) roasted finish with the air fryer lid:** Transfer the sauce from the pot to a bowl to rest. Place the air fryer basket with the metal divider in the empty pot and lay in as many mushrooms as possible in one layer (you'll likely need to do this in a few batches). Secure the air fryer lid, hit Broil (400°F) for 5 minutes, and hit Start. They should be browned and a bit crispy on the edges when done. If you feel it needs more time, add another 5 minutes (but check on them to make sure they don't burn).

**8** Drizzle the sauce over the roasted mushrooms and serve.

**JEFF'S TIP**  To give these 'shrooms a land and/or sea touch, add about ¼ cup bacon crumbles and/or a 6-ounce can of lump crab meat (drained) to the filling ingredients.

# POLENTA
## PARMESAN

Polenta, a dish steeped in Italian tradition, is in many ways similar to what we in the States know as grits. The main difference is that polenta is cornmeal made from yellow corn whereas grits is cornmeal made from white corn (like hominy). As with risotto, the Instant Pot changed the game of how easy polenta can be to make. This recipe creates polenta so outrageously comforting, it'll feel like taking a nap on the fluffiest of polenta clouds.

**GF**

**V**  *(if you're okay with eggs)*

| Prep Time | Pressure Building Time | Pressure Cook Time | Total Time | Serves |
|---|---|---|---|---|
| 5 MIN | 5–10 MIN | 10 MIN | 25 MIN | 4–6 |

- 1½ cups polenta (these are yellow grits; I use Bob's Red Mill)
- 2 teaspoons seasoned salt, divided
- 2 teaspoons black pepper, divided, plus more for serving
- 1 teaspoon dried sweet basil

- 6 cups garlic broth (e.g., Garlic Better Than Bouillon) or vegetable broth
- 2 tablespoons (¼ stick) salted butter, cut into small pieces
- 2 large eggs (see Jeff's Tip)

- ½ cup grated Parmesan cheese, plus more for serving
- 1 teaspoon dried parsley
- White or black truffle oil, for serving (optional)

**1** Add the polenta, 1 teaspoon of the seasoned salt, 1 teaspoon of the pepper, the basil, broth, and butter to the Instant Pot. Stir well.

**2** Secure the lid and move the valve to the sealing position. Hit Cancel and then hit Manual or Pressure Cook on High Pressure for 10 minutes. Quick release when done.

**3** Meanwhile, in a bowl, whisk together the eggs, Parmesan, parsley, the remaining 1 teaspoon seasoned salt, and the remaining 1 teaspoon pepper.

**4** When the lid comes off the pot, add the egg mixture to the polenta and stir for 2 minutes, *really* scraping the bottom of the pot until the egg is cooked into the polenta. Let rest for 5 minutes. Top with additional black pepper, Parmesan, and a drizzle of truffle oil, if desired, and serve.

 *lighter comforts* Cut the Parmesan down to ¼ cup.

 **JEFF'S TIP** If you're not into eggs, simply leave them out and add the rest of the ingredients mentioned in Step 3 directly to the pot in Step 4.

# SESAME GINGER BRUSSELS SPROUTS

K + *(see Lighter Comforts)*

P + *(see Lighter Comforts)*

DF

GF + *(see Lighter Comforts)*

V

This dish pairs the goodness of Brussels sprouts with the sweet, savory, and slightly sour touch of one of my favorite sauces: the ginger garlic sauce served at Japanese steakhouses. If you don't love Brussels sprouts but you love that sauce—which is based on soy sauce, tamari, or coconut aminos and loaded with minced ginger, garlic, and lemon—you're about to cross over to the green side.

| Prep Time | Pressure Building Time | Pressure Cook Time | Optional Roasting Time | Total Time | Serves |
|---|---|---|---|---|---|
| 10 MIN | 5–10 MIN | 1 MIN | 5–15 MIN | 25 MIN | 4–6 |

½ cup low-sodium soy sauce, tamari, or coconut aminos

¼ cup sesame oil (any kind)

¼ cup minced or grated ginger (I use squeeze ginger)

Juice of 1 lemon

3 cloves garlic, minced or pressed

1 tablespoon onion powder

2 teaspoons white sugar

½ teaspoon rice or white vinegar

2–3 pounds Brussels sprouts, stems trimmed, halved

1 bunch scallions, sliced, some reserved for serving

1 tablespoon sesame seeds, for serving

**1** Add all the ingredients except the Brussels sprouts, scallions, and sesame seeds to the Instant Pot. Stir until combined.

**2** Add the Brussels sprouts and scallions and toss in the sauce.

**3** Secure the lid and move the valve to the sealing position. Hit Cancel and then hit Manual or Pressure Cook on High Pressure for 1 minute. Quick release when done.

**lighter comforts** To make it keto, paleo, and soy-free, use coconut aminos for the soy sauce and omit the sugar.

To make it gluten-free, use tamari or coconut aminos in place of the soy sauce.

**JEFF'S TIP** Halving the Brussels sprouts is key because it allows the sauce to seep directly into their layers. Some markets already sell them halved to save a little prep time.

**4** **To crisp the sprouts (optional):** Secure the air fryer lid, hit Broil (400°F) for 5–10 minutes, and hit Start. Air fry to your desired crispness. You can also do this in the oven on a foil-lined baking sheet at 400°F for 10–15 minutes (keep an eye on it as oven temperatures can vary).

**5** Toss the Brussels sprouts with additional scallions and transfer to a serving dish. Sprinkle with sesame seeds just before serving.

# MOO SHU MUSHROOM WRAPS

 K <sup>+</sup> *(see Lighter Comforts)*

 P <sup>+</sup> *(see Lighter Comforts)*

DF

GF <sup>+</sup> *(see Lighter Comforts)*

V

This hearty Chinese-inspired dish generally features a protein embedded in a delicious cabbage-based filling that is laced with hoisin and plum sauce, rolled in a paper-thin pancake, and served as a wrap. In my spin, we forego meat with the steak of the veggie world: portobello mushrooms. I also use simple tortillas for the wrapping. These vegetarian wraps are completely addicting and great with Wonton Soup (page 75). The filling by itself is also wonderful over rice.

| Prep Time | Sauté Time | Pressure Building Time | Pressure Cook Time | Total Time | Serves |
|---|---|---|---|---|---|
| 10 MIN | 10 MIN | 5–10 MIN | 3 MIN | 30 MIN | 4–6 |

- ¼ cup sesame oil (any kind)
- 1 pound portobello mushrooms, sliced into ¼-inch-thick strips
- 1 large white or yellow onion, sliced into ¼-inch wedges
- 1 bunch scallions, sliced ¼ inch thick

- 3 cloves garlic, minced or pressed
- 1 (12- to 14-ounce) bag shredded cabbage/coleslaw mix
- ½ cup vegetable broth
- ¼ cup low-sodium soy sauce, tamari, or coconut aminos
- 1½ tablespoons cornstarch

- 1½ tablespoons cold water
- ¼ cup hoisin sauce, plus more for serving if you like
- 2 tablespoons plum or duck sauce (if you can't find, just add an additional 2 tablespoons hoisin)
- 1 bag fajita-size flour or corn tortillas

**1** Add the sesame oil to the Instant Pot, hit Sauté, and Adjust so it's on the More or High setting. After 3 minutes of heating, add the mushrooms, onion, and scallions and sauté for 5 minutes, until the mushrooms are softened and browned. Add the garlic and sauté 1 minute longer.

 **JEFF'S TIPS** If mushrooms aren't your thing, feel free to sub literally any veggie you wish in place of them. Bell peppers, asparagus, green beans—the sky's the limit. Same cook time for all.

If you want more cabbage (and a crunchier texture), add up to another 14-ounce bag in Step 5 after stirring in the hoisin and plum sauces. It will heat up during the 5-minute resting period,

**2** Add the shredded cabbage, broth, and soy sauce. Mix together very well.

**3** Secure the lid and move the valve to the sealing position. Hit Cancel, and then hit Manual or Pressure Cook on High Pressure for 3 minutes. Quick release when done.

**4** Meanwhile, make a slurry by mixing together the cornstarch and cold water in a small bowl until smooth.

**5** Hit Cancel and then hit Sauté and Adjust so it's on the More or High setting. Once bubbling, add the slurry while stirring constantly and let bubble about 30 seconds. Hit Cancel to turn the pot off. Stir in the hoisin and plum sauces until blended in. Let rest for 5 minutes to thicken.

**6** Warm the tortillas in the microwave for 15 seconds. Spoon the moo shu onto the tortillas, top with additional hoisin sauce, if desired, and roll up.

 *lighter comforts* To make it keto and paleo (and if you're okay with a slurry), use Bibb lettuce to wrap instead of tortillas.

To make it gluten-free, use corn tortillas and gluten-free hoisin sauce and sub tamari or coconut aminos for the soy sauce. Using coconut aminos will also make it soy-free.

# BUNDT STUFFING

If you're a fellow carb lover like me, stuffing is what you crave most at the Thanksgiving table. But I'm a firm believer that it doesn't have to be Turkey Day to enjoy stuffing, and you deserve better than the stuff from a box. We're going to literally *ring* in the best with this sliceable recipe—Bundt-style. Serve the slices of stuffing with my Champagne Chicken (page 154) or Mississippi Pot Roast (page 193)—or, of course, turkey and gravy.

| Prep Time | Toasting Time | Sauté Time | Pressure Building Time | Pressure Cook Time | Crisping Time | Total Time | Serves |
|---|---|---|---|---|---|---|---|
| 10 MIN | 10 MIN | 11 MIN | 5–10 MIN | 15 MIN | 5–10 MIN | 1 HR | 4–6 |

1 loaf white bread, sliced and cubed

6 tablespoons (¾ stick) salted butter

3 ribs celery, diced

1 medium yellow onion, diced

1¼ cups turkey broth (e.g., Turkey Better Than Bouillon), chicken broth, or vegetable broth

1 teaspoon seasoned salt

1 teaspoon ground sage

1 teaspoon dried thyme

½ teaspoon poultry seasoning

½ teaspoon celery salt

½ teaspoon black pepper

**1** To toast the bread, preheat the oven to 400°F. (Or **see Jeff's Tips** for air fryer toasting.) Place the cubed bread on a large baking sheet and toast on the top rack of the oven for 10 minutes, flipping the bread halfway through. When done, the cubes should be lightly browned in color and on the firmer, toastier side. Place the toasted bread chunks in a large mixing bowl and set aside. Reduce the oven to 350° and keep the oven on for Step 6.

**2** While the bread's toasting in the oven, add the butter to the Instant Pot, hit Sauté, and Adjust to the More or High setting. Once the butter's melted, add the celery and onion and sauté for 3 minutes. Add the broth, seasoned salt, sage, thyme, poultry seasoning, celery salt, and pepper and stir. Hit Cancel to turn the pot off.

**JEFF'S TIPS** Although the oven is probably the best method for Steps 1 and 6, you can absolutely use the air fryer lid instead. To toast the bread in Step 1, place the bread cubes in the Instant Pot (no fryer basket needed). Secure the air fryer lid, hit Broil (400°F) for 10–15 minutes, and hit Start. Then, prior to Step 6, make sure the pot is drained of the water. Rest the carefully de-panned stuffing on the trivet, secure the air fryer lid, hit Broil (400°F) for 5–10 minutes and hit Start.

If you have leftover stuffing, chop into crouton-size pieces, bake again until crispy, and use in my Big Easy Corn Chowder (page 90).

**3** Pour the pot's contents over the toasted bread chunks and mix together well so all the bread is coated (it will soften a bit).

**4** Spray a 6-cup Bundt pan with nonstick cooking spray. Take all of that coated bread and stuff it into the Bundt—really pack it all in. Cover with foil, poking a hole in the middle to allow the steam to go through the open center of the pan.

**5** Add the liner pot back to the Instant Pot (no need to rinse), place the trivet with the handles facing up in the pot, and add 1½ cups water. Carefully place the Bundt pan on the trivet. Secure the lid and move the valve to the sealing position. Hit Manual or Pressure Cook on High Pressure for 15 minutes. Quick release when done.

**6** Using the handles of the trivet, carefully remove the Bundt pan and flip it onto a foil-lined baking sheet. Tap the Bundt with a spoon to release the stuffing. Place in the 350°F oven on the center rack and bake for 5–10 minutes to slightly crisp up the stuffing (keep an eye on it so it doesn't get overdone as oven temperatures can vary). Cut into slices to serve.

*lighter comforts* Use a multigrain or lighter bread in place of white. Using a gluten-free or keto-friendly bread will also make it compliant for those lifestyles.

# · GARLIC · MASHED POTATOES

If there's a classic and reliable side that goes with just about any dish, it's mashed potatoes. I prefer to keep the skins on so they create texture to play off the garlicky, cream-cheesy goodness I load the potatoes up with. If you give these a shot, you just might never make your mashed potatoes any other way again. Pure decadence.

K + *(see Lighter Comforts)*

GF

V

| Prep Time | Pressure Building Time | Pressure Cook Time | Total Time | Serves |
|-----------|------------------------|--------------------|------------|--------|
| 5 MIN | 5–15 MIN | 15 MIN | 30 MIN | 4–6 |

**5 pounds baby white and/or baby red potatoes (I use 2½ pounds of each), whole and skins-on, rinsed** (NOTE: Yukon Gold or red bliss potatoes work great too—just cut them into quarters with the skins on.)

**1½–2½ cups garlic broth (e.g., Garlic Better Than Bouillon) or chicken broth** (see Jeff's Tips)

**8 cloves garlic, peeled**

**8 tablespoons (1 stick) salted butter, cut into quarters**

**2 (5.2-ounce) packages Boursin herb cheese (any flavor) or 8 ounces brick cream cheese**

**1 bunch fresh chives, sliced**

**1 tablespoon garlic salt**

**1½ teaspoons black pepper**

**¼–½ cup grated Parmesan cheese (optional)**

**A few splashes heavy cream, half-and-half, or milk (optional)**

**1** Add the potatoes, broth, and garlic (in that order) to the Instant Pot and hit Manual or Pressure Cook on High Pressure for 15 minutes. Quick release when done.

**2** Using a potato masher, mash the potatoes up in the pot. It may appear soupy at first, but once fully mashed, the potatoes will absorb all the broth.

**3** Add the butter, Boursin or cream cheese, chives, garlic salt, pepper, and Parmesan cheese (if using). Stir until well combined. If you want it creamier, add a few splashes of cream and stir to your desired consistency.

*lighter comforts*   Sub 2 large heads of chopped-up cauliflower (stalks removed) for the potatoes and it'll be keto.

**JEFF'S TIPS**   Using 2½ cups broth will make for a very creamy, yet thinner mashed potato—almost like a fancy puree. If you want it thicker, only use 2 cups broth. If you want it very thick, use only 1½ cups. Remember, you can always make it thinner by adding more broth and cream in Step 3, but you can't go in reverse once mashed!

Leftovers will thicken in the fridge due to the Boursin or cream cheese. Simply place in the microwave or on the stove, add a little cream to loosen it up, and blend.

# CREAMED SPINACH

If you wanted to know what really made Popeye strong enough to lift a house, it's this creamed spinach. A wonderful complement to any protein (especially those that contain olive oil—wink wink), this will be one of the first dishes to disappear at the table. Goes great with Chicken Divine (page 169) or Osso Buco alla Vodka (page 204). Check out Jeff's Tips for some special touches.

| Prep Time | Sauté Time | Pressure Building Time | Pressure Cook Time | Total Time | Serves |
|---|---|---|---|---|---|
| 5 MIN | 7 MIN | 5-10 MIN | 5 MIN | 25 MIN | 4-6 |

- 2 tablespoons (¼ stick) salted butter
- 1 yellow onion, diced
- 3 cloves garlic, minced or pressed
- 1½ cups garlic broth (e.g., Garlic Better Than Bouillon) or vegetable broth

- 1 teaspoon garlic powder
- 1 teaspoon onion powder
- 1 teaspoon seasoned salt
- ½ teaspoon black pepper
- 1 pound baby spinach
- 2 tablespoons cornstarch
- 2 tablespoons cold water

- ½ cup heavy cream or half-and-half
- 1 (5.2-ounce) package Boursin herb cheese (any flavor) or 4 ounces brick cream cheese
- ½ cup grated Parmesan cheese
- 2 cups shredded mozzarella cheese

**1** Add the butter to the Instant Pot, hit Sauté, and Adjust to the More or High setting. Once the butter's melted, add the onion and sauté for 3 minutes, until slightly softened. Add the garlic and sauté for 1 minute.

**2** Add the broth, garlic powder, onion powder, seasoned salt, and black pepper. Stir well.

**3** Top with the baby spinach. Secure the lid and move the valve to the sealing position. Hit Manual or Pressure Cook on High Pressure for 5 minutes. Quick release when done.

**4** Meanwhile, make a slurry by mixing together the cornstarch and cold water in a small bowl until smooth.

**5** Hit Cancel followed by Sauté and Adjust so it's on the More or High Setting. Add the cream, Boursin or cream cheese, and Parmesan. Stir until fully combined.

**6** As the pot bubbles, stir in the mozzarella until combined, followed by the cornstarch slurry. After 30 seconds, hit Cancel to turn the pot off and let rest, stirring occasionally and scraping the bottom of the pot, for 5 minutes, before serving.

*lighter comforts* You can ditch the cream for unsweetened nondairy milk (such as almond). You can also give dairy-free Boursin a shot instead of regular.

**JEFF'S TIPS** To add some artichokes to the mix, add in 1–2 14.5-ounce cans of artichoke hearts (drained and ripped up by hand) in Step 6 after adding the slurry. This will evoke a supreme spinach and artichoke dip (so a bag of chips may come in handy too).

The cornstarch slurry is responsible for giving this creamed spinach a nice, thick consistency. If you want it thinner, go for 1 tablespoon cornstarch and 1 tablespoon water.

To reheat any leftovers (be it in the Instant Pot on Sauté or in the microwave), add a little more cream to thin it out.

# RICHARD'S BLACK-EYED PEAS

My Southern partner Richard introduced me to the tradition of having smoky black-eyed peas on New Year's Day. He tells me that you're supposed to toss a shiny penny into the pot when it cooks—whoever finds it in their bowl has an extra prosperous year. I don't include that step in this recipe, but it still makes for a prosperous and superb side for basically any dish.

| Prep Time | Pressure Building Time | Pressure Cook Time | Natural Release Time | Total Time | Serves |
|---|---|---|---|---|---|
| 5 MIN | 10–20 MIN | 30 MIN | 30 MIN | 1 HR 15 MIN | 4–6 |

**1 smoked ham hock (optional)**

**3 cups chicken broth or vegetable broth**

**3 cups ham broth (e.g., Ham Better Than Bouillon; if you don't have it, just use 6 cups chicken or vegetable broth)**

**1 (1-pound) bag dried black-eyed peas**

**1 yellow onion, diced**

**OPTIONAL FIXIN'S**

**Sweet or hot chow chow (this is basically Southern-style relish)**

**Mayonnaise (Richard loves Duke's)**

**1** Add the ham hock (if using), broths, black-eyed peas, and onion to the Instant Pot. Stir well.

**2** Secure the lid and move the valve to the sealing position. Hit Manual or Pressure Cook on High Pressure for 30 minutes. When done, allow a 30-minute natural release followed by a quick release.

**3** Using tongs, remove the ham hock, then feel free to rip any meat off the bone and return to the pot.

**4** Stir everything and let cool for 10 minutes (it will thicken up when really cooled down). Plate and mix in some chow chow and mayo, if desired.

*lighter comforts* Want it vegan? Skip the ham hock and use 6 cups vegetable broth.

RICHARD'S TIP Since this is a classic Southern New Year's dish, if you have it, use 1/2–1 pound leftover holiday ham (diced) in place of the ham hock.

My fondest memories of time shared with loved ones center largely on the kitchen. As a transplant to NYC from a region with limited access to authentic Italian food, I enjoy even hearing someone speak of their Nonna's methods for eggplant parmesan and am captivated when I can watch them cook. I likewise enjoy sharing tips like how to preheat oil in a skillet for the perfect crust on my made-from-scratch cornbread or replace a store-bought graham-cracker pie crust with a complementary breakfast cereal. A bustling kitchen full of friends preparing a potluck of personal specialties together can simultaneously introduce new family traditions and inspire nostalgia for your own.

RICHARD • JACKSON, ALABAMA

# ISRAELI (PEARL) COUSCOUS

DF<sup>+</sup> *(if using olive oil)*

GF<sup>+</sup> *(see Lighter Comforts)*

V

VN<sup>+</sup> *(if using olive oil)*

Israeli couscous, pearl-shaped and larger than North African couscous, is a wonderfully fun and tasty grain. It makes for a quick and simple side that is packed with comfort and goes great with just about anything. What's more, it tastes great hot or cold.

| Prep Time | Sauté Time | Pressure Building Time | Pressure Cook Time | Total Time | Serves |
|---|---|---|---|---|---|
| 5 MIN | 8 MIN | 5-10 MIN | 6 MIN | 25 MIN | 4-6 |

- 2 tablespoons (¼ stick) salted butter or extra-virgin olive oil
- 2 cups Israeli (pearl) couscous (regular or tri-color)
- 1 yellow bell pepper, seeded and diced

- 1 red bell pepper, seeded and diced
- 2½ cups vegetable broth or onion broth (e.g., Sautéed Onion Better Than Bouillon)
- 1 teaspoon seasoned salt

- ½ teaspoon black pepper
- Red wine vinaigrette dressing (or a sauce from any chicken or beef dish—see Jeff's Tip), to drizzle

**1** Add the butter to the Instant Pot, hit Sauté, and Adjust so it's on the More or High setting. Once it's melted, add the couscous and sauté for about 2 minutes, until lightly toasted. Add the bell peppers and sauté for 3 minutes longer, until lightly softened.

**2** Add the broth, seasoned salt, and black pepper and stir well. Secure the lid and move the valve to the sealing position. Hit Cancel and hit Manual or Pressure Cook on High Pressure for 6 minutes. Quick release when done.

**3** Fluff the couscous with a fork, transfer to a serving bowl, and add a splash of vinaigrette dressing or sauce.

*lighter comforts* Use gluten-free Israeli couscous to make it gluten-free.

 **JEFF'S TIP** Since the chicken and meat dishes in this book are designed to give you extra sauce, this dish is a perfect example of where to put those leftovers. In place of the dressing, drizzle some sauce from my Chicken Divine (page 169) or Pork Paprikash (page 220) over the couscous.

# 9

# DESSERT

The only thing sweeter than a plate of dessert is how easy it can be to make. I've always been intimidated by the idea of baking, but these recipes will allow even the novice baker to turn out some serious confection perfection. I can't think of a more comforting chapter to close out this book with.

A 7x3-inch springform pan and 6-cup Bundt pan are important (and affordable) accessories to have on hand.

Before I met my husband his diet consisted of a lot of frozen meals and fast food. I come from a large Jewish family where we learn early that food equals love and that eating is one of the greatest pleasures we have. Through the years we have been together we have shared a lot of loss, heartache, and scary medical problems but we still sit next to each other every night when we eat and I always sneak a look at the smile he brings to our table.

WILLIAM · **HOLLYWOOD, FLORIDA**

My future mother-in-law and I were getting dinner ready. She had just gotten through telling me no one helps her anymore. As we were working, she put the potatoes in the bowl of her stand mixer but didn't secure it properly and it shifted through partway, sending the bowl with the mashed potatoes in it flying out all over the floor. She looked at me, shrugged, and scooped them back in the bowl to finish them up. Neither of us ate the potatoes. I always helped in the kitchen.

KIMBER · **RAINIER, OREGON**

I am an empty nester who used to *love* cooking. Our son is all grown up, married, and moved away…and my husband and I work all of the time. I lost my joy for cooking! I found your page about a year ago and have been watching your love for blessing people with yummy food. It warmed my heart and brought me *so much* joy! I tried your recipe for beef Stroganoff tonight and WOW!!! WOW!!! How can anything be so easy and yummy? You renewed my joy in taking care of others and I am so thankful!

TARA · **HARKER HEIGHTS, TEXAS**

| | | | |
|---|---|---|---|
| ♨ = AIR FRYER LID | | DF = DAIRY-FREE | |
| K = KETO | | GF = GLUTEN-FREE | |
| P = PALEO | | V = VEGETARIAN | |
| ✚ = COMPLIANT WITH MODIFICATIONS | | VN = VEGAN | |

JEFF'S
TIPS

Always be mindful of how much dough you're using as you want to make sure you have enough to properly assemble the cake. If you find you have too little dough left when sealing the top of the cake, you can thin out the remaining dough by patting it between your hands. It's far more important the bottom and sides have enough dough than the top, as they need to support all the filling.

Store any leftovers in an airtight container for up to 5 days. Microwaving leftovers for 10–15 seconds will restore them to the ooey-gooey s'mores style we all love!

# STUFFED S'MORES CAKE

V + *(if you're okay with eggs)*

When I released this decadent dessert on my blog, everyone went absolutely bonkers. Picture everything you love about s'mores, and then picture stuffing that into a cake. Once you slice into it, ooey-gooey chocolate and marshmallow lava spills from the dense and moist graham cracker crust. It's a sure-(camp)fire hit. Goes great with a scoop of ice cream.

| Prep Time | Pressure Building Time | Pressure Cook Time | Total Time | Serves |
|---|---|---|---|---|
| 20 MIN | 5–10 MIN | 40 MIN | 1 HR 5 MIN (1 HR 20 MIN with cooling time) | 6–8 |

**THE DRY**

1 cup graham cracker crumbs

1 cup all-purpose flour

¼ teaspoon baking soda (*not* baking powder)

¼ teaspoon kosher salt

**THE WET**

8 tablespoons (1 stick) salted butter, softened (either leave it out on the counter for 2 hours or zap in microwave for 10–15 seconds, until soft but not melted), plus more for greasing the pan

½ cup tightly packed light brown sugar

¼ cup white sugar

1 large egg

1 tablespoon pure maple syrup

1½ teaspoons vanilla extract

**THE FILLING**

2 XL-size (about 4.4 ounces each) Hershey bars (it *must* be Hershey's for the best s'mores experience!)

1 (7½-ounce) jar Marshmallow Fluff (*do not* use regular marshmallows as they will expand into a mess)

**1** Combine the dry ingredients in a large mixing bowl and whisk together until fully combined. Set aside.

**2** Now let's focus on the wet ingredients: In a stand mixer with the paddle attachment (or another large mixing bowl if using an electric hand mixer), combine the softened butter and brown and white sugars. Start on a low speed and work your way to a 4-speed or medium speed, until the butter and sugar are creamed, about 30 seconds. Add the egg, syrup, and vanilla. Mix for about 15 seconds, until combined.

**3** Add the dry ingredients and start on a low speed (flour likes to go all over the place so always start on a low speed). Once the dry and wet ingredients are combined, up it one speed higher and let mix for about 30 seconds, until a thick batter-like dough has formed. Set aside.

*lighter comforts* This is a joke, right? If you make this one, the calories don't count!

CONTINUES

**4** Take a 7x3-inch springform pan and generously grease the bottom and sides with additional butter. Fit in a 7-inch parchment round and butter the top of that too. Take about one-third of the dough and press it into the bottom of the pan, giving it a supple bottom that is about ½ inch thick, not too thin. Take another third of the dough and line it along the sides of the pan, attaching it to the dough on the bottom of the pan. It should come up to about ¼ inch below the lip of the pan. Like using a pottery wheel, work your way around the pan to make sure the dough is evenly distributed. This ensures we'll have outer edges of the cake and it will keep the s'mores filling secure inside. Layer in one of the Hershey bars (break it up to lay it in properly) and then use a silicone or rubber spatula to smooth the Marshmallow Fluff on top (you can use up to the whole jar if you desire). Then top it off with the remaining Hershey bar. Lay the remaining dough over the top Hershey bar layer so it's totally covered and connected to the dough lining the sides. The top layer of dough should come up to just slightly under the lip of the pan. Cover the top of the pan with foil, making sure you don't press the foil directly onto the top layer of dough, but rather have it somewhat loose on the pan.

**5** Add the trivet and 2 cups water to the Instant Pot. Rest the springform pan on the trivet, secure the lid, and move the valve to the sealing position. Hit Manual or Pressure Cook on High Pressure for 40 minutes. Quick release when done. Using the trivet's handles with oven mitts or a dish towel, carefully transport the cake to the counter, remove the foil, and let rest for 15 minutes to slightly cool. Take a paring knife and carefully get in between the inside of the pan and the edge of the cake and loosen it up. Unlatch the pan so the cake is freed.

**6** Serve it immediately, when the center will be super ooey-gooey like a giant lava cake. Or, let it fully cool for 3–4 hours and it will become like a s'mores cookie bar! Slice into wedges when serving. **See Jeff's Tips** for storing and reheating leftovers.

# · PEANUT BUTTER–BANANA ·
# CHEESECAKE

My favorite desserts include chocolate, banana, and peanut butter—I can't be alone in that. So I felt it necessary to make a cheesecake that celebrates this decadent combination. The result is everything you could have hoped for in a dessert. In fact, it's so easy and indulgent, it was featured on a special Halloween-themed *Rachael Ray* episode. See Jeff's Tips on how to make it more candy-focused.

 **GF** + *(see Lighter Comforts)*

 **V** + *(if you're okay with eggs)*

| Prep Time | Pressure Building Time | Pressure Cook Time | Natural Release Time | Total Time | Serves |
|---|---|---|---|---|---|
| 25 MIN | 5–10 MIN | 60 MIN | 30 MIN | 2 HRS (8 HRS with refrigeration and resting time) | 6–8 |

- 1 cup graham cracker crumbs
- ¼ cup crushed peanuts (best to pulse the peanuts in a food processor or wrap in paper towels and pound with a mallet)
- 4 tablespoons (½ stick) salted butter, melted, plus more for greasing the pan

- 2 (8-ounce) bricks cream cheese, at room temperature (this is important—have them sit out for at least 3 hours)
- ½ cup smooth peanut butter
- ¾ cup white sugar
- 1 tablespoon all-purpose flour
- 1 (3.4-ounce) package banana Jell-O instant pudding mix (it *must* be instant)

- ½ teaspoon vanilla extract
- 2 large eggs, at room temperature (as important as the cream cheese to be room temp)
- 12 Reese's peanut butter cups
- Chocolate spread of your choice (I use Nutella, but you could also try Dulce de Leche, page 47, for a different flavor profile)

 **1** Grease a 7x3-inch springform pan very well with butter (bottom and sides). Line with a 7-inch parchment round and butter the top of the parchment paper as well.

**2** Mix together the graham cracker crumbs, crushed peanuts, and melted butter and transfer to the greased pan. Use the bottom of a drinking glass to flatten the crumbs so they make an even crust on the bottom that climbs halfway up the sides of the pan. Pop in the freezer for 15 minutes.

*lighter comforts* To make this dish gluten-free, use gluten-free graham crackers and sub cornstarch for the flour.

CONTINUES

**3** Using a stand mixer with the paddle attached or a strong hand mixer (don't bother trying this by hand, folks), make the batter by mixing together the cream cheese and peanut butter on low speed until no lumps remain. While the mixer is running, add in this order: the sugar, flour, pudding mix, vanilla, and eggs (one at a time). Keep mixing on low speed until no lumps remain and it's a super thick, yet smooth, frosting-like consistency, about 1 minute.

**4** Remove the pan from the freezer. Use a silicone spatula to scrape half the batter into the crust so the bottom is totally covered. Add six of the peanut butter cups, arranging them in a circle with one in the middle. Scrape the remaining batter on top (it's okay if you have some left over) and smooth with a spatula. Cover the pan with aluminum foil and place on the trivet.

**5** Add 2 cups water to the Instant Pot. Carefully lower the trivet with the pan resting on it into the pot. Secure the lid and move the valve to the sealing position. Hit Manual or Pressure Cook on High Pressure for 60 minutes. When done, allow a full natural release (which will take about 30 minutes).

**6** Carefully remove the pan from the Instant Pot and remove the foil (the cake should be slightly jiggly when it comes out). Let rest on the counter to cool for 30 minutes. (NOTE: *Do not* skip the cooling by popping it right into the fridge. It *must* cool for 30 minutes at room temperature as the heat is still cooking and firming up the inside). Then refrigerate, still in the pan, for *at least* 5–8 hours.

**7** When ready to serve, take a sharp knife and *carefully* glide it in between the inside of the pan and the edge of the cheesecake, then slowly open the latch of the springform pan to release it.

**8** Gently frost the entire top of the cheesecake with the spread. Cut the remaining peanut butter cups in half and place on top for decoration. Let rest at room temperature for 1 hour before serving. Keep any leftovers refrigerated.

**JEFF'S TIPS** If banana isn't your thing, feel free to use vanilla or chocolate or any flavor Jell-O pudding mix you enjoy. Just make sure it's instant, and don't leave it out of the recipe as it keeps the cheesecake firm.

This cheesecake is also a great excuse to use up leftover Halloween candy (or "borrow" some from your kids). Instead of just the peanut butter cups in Step 4, use ½–1 cup of a mix of chocolate candies such as M&Ms and chopped-up pieces of your favorite candy bars (Twix, Snickers, etc.). Then, in Step 8, use more to top the frosted cheesecake.

# APPLE SPICE CAKE

 DF+ *(see Lighter Comforts)*

GF+ *(see Lighter Comforts)*

V+ *(if you're okay with eggs)*

This is a wonderful cake for fall when apple picking goes into full swing. It's a simple yet moist and dense cake that uses box mix with a few added goodies. As it turns out, sugar and (apple) spice do make everything nice.

| Prep Time | Pressure Building Time | Pressure Cook Time | Total Time | Serves |
|---|---|---|---|---|
| 10 MIN | 5–10 MIN | 50 MIN | 1 HR 5 MIN (1 HR 35 MIN with cooling time) | 6–8 |

## THE CAKE

1 (15.25-ounce) box spice cake mix

1/3 cup vegetable oil

3 large eggs

1 cup apple cider (preferred) or apple juice

1 large Granny Smith apple, peeled, cored, and diced

## THE APPLE CIDER GLAZE

1 cup confectioners' (powdered) sugar

2 tablespoons (1/4 stick) salted butter

2–3 tablespoons apple cider (preferred) or apple juice, warmed or lukewarm (not cold)

1/2 teaspoon vanilla extract

1/2 teaspoon ground cinnamon

### THE CAKE

**2** Generously spray the entire inside of a 6-cup Bundt pan (which will fit your 6- or 8-quart Instant Pot) with nonstick cooking spray. Pour in the batter, making sure not to overfill.

**3** Cover the pan with aluminum foil and puncture a hole down the center of the Bundt opening for steam to pass through.

**1** Combine the cake mix, oil, eggs, and cider in a large mixing bowl. Beat with a hand (or stand) mixer until no lumps remain. Stir in the apple.

**4** Add 2 cups water to the Instant Pot followed by the trivet. Rest the Bundt pan on the trivet, secure the lid, and move the valve to the sealing position. Hit Manual or Pressure Cook on High Pressure for 50 minutes. Quick release when done. Remove the pan and trivet from the pot, remove the foil, and allow the cake to cool for 30 minutes sitting on the trivet on the counter.

**5** About 30 minutes before you're ready to serve, make the apple cider glaze. Sift the sugar into a large mixing bowl. Separately microwave the butter for 20–30 seconds, until melted. Add the melted butter, the warmed cider (use 2 tablespoons for a thicker glaze and 3 for a thinner one), vanilla, and cinnamon to the bowl and whisk/beat until totally smooth, forming an icing-glaze consistency.

**6** When ready to serve, use a knife to make sure the cake is detached from the walls of the pan. Place a plate on top of the Bundt pan, do a quick and careful flip, then gently tap the pan so the cake slides out. Drizzle the glaze over and serve.

 *lighter comforts* Use a gluten-free cake mix to make it gluten-free and skip the glaze to make it dairy-free.

**JEFF'S TIP** If you'd rather a spice-free cake, use a yellow cake mix.

I have an elderly neighbor who lives across the street. Her husband of over 65 years lives in an assisted living facility that doesn't allow any visitors! She is so lonely! I visit and take her a variety of soups at least weekly, all made in the Instant Pot. She just beams and tells me they are absolutely fabulous. Happy to bring her joy and IP nourishment because I love my Instant Pot and your wonderful recipes!

CAROL • **ST. GEORGE, UTAH**

# RADICAL RICE PUDDING

DF <sup>+</sup> *(see Lighter Comforts)*

GF

V <sup>+</sup> *(if you're okay with eggs)*

Not only is rice pudding one of the easiest and tastiest treats your Instant Pot will serve up, it's also one of the most customizable, making it a go-to to satisfy your sweet cravings any time of day, night, and everything in between.

| Prep Time | Pressure Building Time | Pressure Cook Time | Natural Release Time | Sauté Time | Total Time | Serves |
|---|---|---|---|---|---|---|
| 5 MIN | 5–10 MIN | 3 MIN | 10 MIN | 5 MIN | 30 MIN (4 HRS with cooling and refrigeration time) | 4 |

1 cup arborio rice (the same rice used for risotto)

1½ cups water

½ teaspoon ground cinnamon

¼ teaspoon kosher salt

⅛ teaspoon ground nutmeg

2 large eggs

2 cups heavy cream, divided

1 teaspoon vanilla extract

¾ cup white sugar

2 tablespoons pure maple syrup

**OPTIONAL MIX-INS AND TOPPINGS**

Chocolate or peanut butter chips

Caramel topping, butterscotch topping, or chocolate syrup

Mini marshmallows or Marshmallow Fluff

Cinnamon Toast Crunch or Frosted Flakes cereal

Nuts

Fruit

Eggnog, RumChata rum cream, or Bailey's Irish Cream

**1** Add the rice, water, cinnamon, salt, and nutmeg to the Instant Pot and stir. Secure the lid and move the valve to the sealing position. Hit Manual or Pressure Cook on High Pressure for 3 minutes. When done, allow a 10-minute natural release followed by a quick release.

**2** While the rice is cooking, prepare the egg custard by placing the eggs, ½ cup of the cream, and the vanilla extract in a mixing bowl. Whisk together until beaten and combined. Set aside.

**3** Once the lid comes off the Instant Pot, hit the Cancel button and then hit Sauté and Adjust so it's on the More or High setting. Stir in the remaining 1½ cups cream, the sugar, and maple syrup.

**4** Now, place a fine-mesh strainer that you can rest on the lip of the pot over the pot. Pour the egg custard through it into the pudding. (We use a strainer so it catches the excess gooey parts of the egg that would compromise this amazing rice pudding's texture.)

**5** As soon as you pour in the egg mixture, stir constantly for 3–5 minutes (remember, dairy likes to stick to stainless steel pots!). As you do this, everything will gradually begin to thicken. Once it really begins to boil, hit Cancel to turn the pot off. Immediately remove the inner pot and set on a burn-resistant surface (like a cutting board).

**6** Let the pot cool for 30 minutes, then transfer the pudding to a serving bowl. Cover with a lid and pop in the fridge for a good 3–5 hours so that the rice pudding becomes nice and chilled.

**7** When ready to serve, mix any toppings or dairy of your choice into the pudding.

*lighter comforts* Make it dairy-free by subbing a sweetened or unsweetened nondairy milk for the whole milk.

**JEFF'S TIPS** Rice is one of those things that never stops absorbing the liquid that engulfs it. That means if you have this in your fridge for a bit, it may get *super* thick (which is just the way I like it). If you'd rather have a thinner rice pudding, just mix in a little more milk (or dairy cordials) of your choice right before serving!

This recipe can be doubled. Same cook time.

# BERRY BRÛLÉE  TART

This scrumptious dessert brings together the tastiest and simplest crème brûlée, a stunning tart, and berries to blow not only *your* mind, but those you serve it to as well. Simply spectacular on every level—especially with that glistening, solid sugar–topped crust protecting the custard-like filling.

**V** + *(if you're okay with eggs)*

| Prep Time | Pressure Building Time | Pressure Cook Time | Natural Release Time | Total Time | Serves |
|---|---|---|---|---|---|
| 5 MIN | 5–10 MIN | 45 MIN | 10 MIN | 1 HR 5 MIN (7 HRS with refrigeration time) | 6–8 |

## THE TART

**1½ cups graham cracker crumbs**

**6 tablespoons (¾ stick) salted butter, melted, plus more for greasing the pan**

**2 cups heavy cream**

**6 egg yolks (just the yolks)**

**6 tablespoons white sugar**

**1½ teaspoons vanilla extract**

**⅛ teaspoon ground cinnamon**

**1 tablespoon all-purpose flour**

**1 (3.4-ounce) package vanilla (or any flavor) Jell-O instant pudding mix (it *must* be instant)**

**1 cup berries of your choice**

## THE SUGARY CRUST

**¼ cup white or raw sugar**

**1** Grease a 7x3-inch springform pan very well with butter. Line the pan with a 7-inch parchment round and butter the top of the parchment paper as well.

**2** Mix together the graham cracker crumbs and melted butter and place in the greased pan. Use the bottom of a drinking glass to flatten the crumbs so they make an even crust on the bottom that climbs totally up the sides of the pan, reaching just under the lip. Pop in the freezer for 15 minutes to firm up.

**3** Microwave the cream in a 4-cup Pyrex or medium microwave-safe bowl for 60 seconds. Whisk the egg yolks, sugar, vanilla, cinnamon, flour, and pudding mix into the warmed cream until no lumps remain.

*lighter comforts* Skip the sugary crust to cut down a bit on the indulgence and top with some fat-free whipped topping and additional berries instead. You can also sub monk fruit sweetener for the white sugar.

 **JEFF'S TIP** Because of the required chilling phase in Step 6, it's always wise to start this recipe either first thing in the morning for dessert that evening, or 24 hours in advance so it can set overnight.

**4** Remove the pan from the freezer. Pour the filling into the crust (NOTE: You may not use it all—be mindful not to let it overflow) and gently add the berries. Smooth with a spatula, cover with aluminum foil, and place the pan on the trivet.

**5** Add 1½ cups water to the Instant Pot. Carefully lower the trivet with the pan resting on it into the pot. Secure the lid and move the valve to the sealing position. Hit Manual or Pressure Cook on High Pressure for 45 minutes. When done, allow a 10-minute natural release followed by a quick release.

**6** Carefully remove the pan from the Instant Pot and remove the foil (the filling should be slightly jiggly when it comes out). Let sit on the counter to cool for 1 hour, then refrigerate for *at least* 6 hours.

**7** When ready to serve, take a sharp knife and *carefully* glide it in between the inside of the pan and the edge of the tart and loosen it up, then slowly open the latch of the springform pan to release it.

**8** **For the sugary crust,** evenly sprinkle the sugar on top of the tart and, very carefully, in circular motions, use a culinary torch to caramelize the top to the hue of your liking. After 5 minutes of torching, serve. Keep any leftovers refrigerated.

# ACKNOWLEDGMENTS

I always wait until the very last second my publisher gives me to write this section because it's so important I don't forget anyone (and I still do).

I have to start this one off by giving eternal gratitude to the thousands who took the time to share their hilarious, emotional, tear-jerking, and beautiful stories with me. You've made me experience rolling hills of emotions that would put Coney Island's Cyclone to shame. I want you to know I read every last one. I truly wish I could have included all of them in this book, but then I wouldn't have room for any of the recipes for you to make so you could then read the stories while enjoying that Stuffed S'Mores Cake. You've made this book so special and I thank you to infinity.

To Mom & Dad. Without either of you, I wouldn't believe in myself and I wouldn't have been able to set off on this newfound path (much less write three books). There aren't enough "thank-yous" and "I love yous" to both of you. And when I go into hermit mode once I'm working on a book, thank you for continuously ignoring my requests for privacy to remind me I also have loving parents to talk to.

To Richard, my Butch Biscuit (check out his stuff). What can be said at this point? You've dealt with this madness three times now and still you're somehow beside me. Your patience is to be envied as much as your wit. Thank you for letting me immortalize your black-eyed peas recipe in the book and for walking Banjo in the mornings. Your impressive garden also came in quite handy for whenever I needed a beautiful pepper or some fresh oregano (it's a good thing I dislike raw tomatoes, though, or your beloved heirlooms would have been devoured by yours truly). I love you dearly. Always will.

Oh, Banjo, the Norwich terrier from Queens, New Yawk! You sat in a blanket curled up by my feet for what felt like every word I typed (in fact, you're there now).

And as I typed each recipe I recalled how every time you'd *beg* for a sample (and sometimes, you'd get one). You're the best furry companion a neurotic Jewish boy and collected Southern gentleman could ask for and I love you more than you love cheese (which is, like, a *lot*). And you can't even read this so I must be going slightly mad.

To Amanda, David, Levi, Stevie, and now, Mack! In the last book I couldn't even properly name Mack because Amanda was pregnant with him and about to give birth and *of course* that happened *one* week *after* my final edits were due before the book went to print. But you're here now and Uncle Jeffrey cannot *wait* to take you, Levi, and Stevie to Disney (finally) and watch you all smile (or scream) when we ride "it's a small world," the Haunted Mansion, and maybe even Space Mountain! (Well, maybe when Mack's a little older). Think of it as my "thank-you" for all the "video testimonials" you've given me to share with my audience (even though you prefer chicken nuggets and pizza). I cherish every second of our time together. But please stop growing up so fast, okay?

To my literary agent, Nicole Tourtelot. You know how to get your clients what they deserve and though I'm not in on your discussions as I sit back and let you do all the dirty work, this book was definitely a product of your strong will and determination. Thank you for the trilogy.

To my editor, Michael Szczerban, for the extraordinary opportunity to make a third book happen and trusting me to share my edible ideas with the world. You really let your authors *be* authors and that is a very special gift. Thanks for providing me with such robust and professional guidance. You are the heart of Voracious and the team you've assembled is no less than top-of-the-line.

To my associate editor, Thea Diklich-Newell, for helping shape the early stages of the manuscript into the book it is today. Your tips and queries are appreciated and have taught me a thing or two.

To my trusted production editor, Pat Jalbert-Levine, who has been the most organized, amazing, and wonderful person to work with (and how lucky I am to have gotten her to do it three times)! Not many can do what you do and there is no way these books would look the way they do without your brilliance and unmatched attention to detail. Thank you.

To Deri Reed, who copyedited the book—a job that is one of the most crucial and complex in this book-writing process. I am so thankful for your incredibly thorough notes and for all the blips you caught that would have made me seem more foolish than I already am.

To Nyamekye Waliyaya, the book's production and manufacturing manager. I'm not sure we've ever communicated directly with one another, but the fact that you navigated the publication of my books through a pandemic, on time, and into the homes of hundreds of thousands, well, you're clearly a prodigy. Thank you.

To Jess Chun and Katherine Akey in marketing and Lauren Ortiz in publicity—thank you for all your efforts on behalf of this book.

To Laura Palese, who is one of the greatest designers on the face of this earth. Not only did you make my vision come to life in a way that surpassed my expectations, but you had a *new* challenge with this book by squeezing in the stories. I couldn't love it more, and any author lucky enough to have you transform their manuscript from a boring document to a work of art should jump for joy and do a cartwheel while giving you freshly baked Levain cookies.

To Lexi Zozulya, who has done it yet again. Perfectly (even with some scares). Folks, every delicious photo you see in this book was captured by him and him alone and I want to devour every single one of them (and I guess I did). You are tenacious, wise, detailed, and without a doubt the greatest troubleshooter and most prepared person I've ever encountered. It's not easy to be in such close quarters for a 17-day shoot with another strongheaded fella (aka me) but in the end, it is always, *always* worth it. Thank you, my trusted friend.

To Carol J. Lee, for not only being my lightning-fast, super creative, and spectacular food stylist for the second time, but also for showing me how to properly fold wontons for the book. The day will soon come when I take one of your revered dumpling classes because they're pretty much my favorite food ever. It's also rare to meet someone who can juggle as much as you do at once and not flinch while sporting a constant "can-do" attitude to boot. I'll have what you're having.

To Rachael Ray, for being one of the most inspirational, legendary, down-to-earth, and just FUN people I have had the extreme good fortune not only to have met a few times, but to have done a few demos alongside (spilled soup and all). Your wise words of encouragement and kindness are something I will carry with me for the rest of my life. I will always be your fan.

To Erin Fitzpatrick Rose, for being the archetypal senior producer of a major daytime television talk show. Not only am I forever grateful for the opportunities you've given me to share my schtick with Rachael and the nation, but I am also in awe of how on top of things you always are. You're a true star.

To Denise Silverman, because I stupidly forgot to thank you in the blue book for all your health tips. And I don't need to tell you again how your self-starting story inspires me (but I just did anyway). Love to you, Mike, and Jesse.

To Amy, April, Alex, Sandy, Marcelo, Zak, Jamie, Kevin, Kelly, Dan, Michael, Daila, Andy, Laura, Bryan, Michele, Sarah, James, Eric, Steven, Josh, and Wayne, for being some of my nearest and dearest. I love you all.

And now to you, my reader, for once again trying, trusting, and sharing my recipes. Sometimes our own little worlds can be a bit of a drab and gray place. But whenever I see one of my recipes shared by one of you, or a kind note from one of you or if you've stopped me on the street to say hi—it provides enough sunshine to feel I'm walking on it (cue the song). *You* are why I've been on this wild ride and I'll never forget it.

Of course I must be forgetting someone so I'll just end with a thank-you to each and every one of you. We can never tell the future, and so even if this is my final book, it has been a beautiful, rewarding ride. If not, I'll see you next time. 😶‍🌫️

# INDEX

# ABOUT THE AUTHOR

Jeffrey Eisner is the author of two #1 national bestsellers, *The Step-by-Step Instant Pot Cookbook* and *The Lighter Step-by-Step Instant Pot Cookbook*. He is the creator of *Pressure Luck Cooking*, an acclaimed, easy-to-follow Instant Pot recipe video blog and website. Featured on the Food Network, *Good Morning America*, and *Rachael Ray*, Jeff creates his famously flavorful recipes at home—both rurally and in Queens, New York.